THE
EXECUTION
PROTOCOL

THE EXECUTION PROTOCOL

INSIDE AMERICA'S CAPITAL PUNISHMENT INDUSTRY

Stephen Trombley

CROWN PUBLISHERS, INC.

New York

Published by Crown Publishers, Inc., 201 East 50th Street,
New York, New York 10022. Member of the Crown Publishing Group.

Random House, Inc. New York, Toronto, London, Sydney, Auckland

CROWN is a trademark of Crown Publishers, Inc.

Manufactured in the United States of America

Book design by James K. Davis

Library of Congress Cataloging-in-Publication Data

Trombley, Stephen.
  The execution protocol: inside America's capital punishment industry/by Stephen Trombley.
    p. cm.
    1. Executions and executioners—United States—Case studies. 2. Capital punishment—United States—Case studies. I. Title.
  HV8699.U5T77 1992
  364.6'6'0973—dc20   92-22805
                                                                            CIP

ISBN 0-517-59113-8

10 9 8 7 6 5 4 3 2 1

First Edition

Contents

Preface

THIS IS a story of men and machines: the story of how a team of men, sanctioned by the highest courts, sets out, deliberately, and according to a well-defined plan, to take a life.

This book, and the documentary film of the same title, are based on unprecedented access to the execution team and condemned inmates at Missouri's Potosi Correctional Center. They offer no personal judgment of the crimes committed by the seventy-nine men and two women facing execution there, or of the men who carry out those executions.

The research for this book was, to say the least, unusual. I became a tourist in another America, a netherworld where men wait for their appointment with death, and where another group of men wait to execute them.

My strange odyssey began in the dusty basement of a tiny house in Massachusetts, where the machinery of killing is made; it ended in the Midwest, where I became close to members of the Missouri execution team, spending weeks with them as they went about their business, and relaxing with them on weekends.

I spent hundreds of hours with Missouri's condemned men, all convicted of capital murder. Some are mass murderers, some are contract killers. Some had tortured their victims before killing them. Others I met on death row may not be guilty of capital murder, and in another court could have been found guilty of a lesser charge—manslaughter, or second-degree murder.

All the principal real-life characters of this book have one thing in common: They have taken human life.

Death Row U.S.A. (as of May 31, 1992)

NUMBER OF DEATH PENALTY JURISDICTIONS:
38 (36 states, U.S. government, U.S. military)

TOTAL NUMBER OF DEATH ROW INMATES:
2,588

NUMBER OF EXECUTIONS SINCE 1977:
174

STATE PERFORMING MOST EXECUTIONS:
Texas (48)

STATE WITH LARGEST NUMBER OF
PEOPLE ON DEATH ROW:
Texas (349)

NUMBER OF DEATH ROW INMATES IN MISSOURI:
81

NUMBER OF EXECUTIONS IN MISSOURI
SINCE THEY RESUMED IN 1989:
6

NUMBER OF STATES USING VARIOUS METHODS OF
EXECUTIONS (SOME STATES HAVE OPTIONS):
Lethal injection 20
Electrocution 11
Lethal gas 6
Firing squad 2
Hanging 2

PART ONE/LABOR DAY

Massachusetts

MY JOURNEY began in Ballston Spa, New York, the town in which I was raised before moving to England at the age of nineteen. When I arrived for the Labor Day weekend, the small upstate town, located at the foothills of the Adirondack Mountains, 150 miles south of the Canadian border, was enjoying Indian summer. On many of the trees that lined High Street, faded yellow ribbons continued to welcome home those who had served in Operation Desert Storm.

It was a fine weekend, a reunion with family and old friends. We barbecued in the backyard, and caught up on news and gossip. Eventually the conversation turned to the purpose of my trip, and everyone was curious about the journey I was about to set off on. My mother couldn't understand why I would want to do it. My friends, some of whom were strongly against capital punishment, had misgivings about the whole project. They felt it was a subject better left alone. So had some of the publishers and television networks I had spoken to about the project during the previous year. Their misgivings only strengthened my resolve.

The day after Labor Day broke cool and pleasant in Ballston Spa, though by the time my commuter flight landed at Boston's Logan Airport the temperature was heading for 100 and the humidity was in the eighties.

The day had barely started, and tempers were already short. Outside the arrivals terminal, executives in business suits jockeyed for advantage at the cab rank. A sour-faced Boston Brahmin turned and hissed at a woman who had lit a cigarette, "Do you *have* to?"

The back of my shirt was soaked inside my crumpled summer suit, and sweat rolled off my brow.

The Haitian cabdriver's English wasn't as good as my French, but he did know two routes to Malden, my destination. The cab was an old Pontiac station wagon. The air-conditioning had failed a couple of days before, the driver apologized. I rolled down the window and let the hot, sticky air blow on my face.

Twenty minutes later the taxi dropped me at my motel, situated at a busy intersection of U.S. Routes 1 and 99. It had a sign saying "Truckers Welcome," and the parking lot was full of eighteen-wheelers. Checking in, I could hear traffic roaring on either side of the motel, and the humid air was full of gas and diesel fumes.

I carried my bags across the parking lot to my room. Just to the left was a filthy swimming pool, separated from the highway by a rickety chain link fence. I let myself into the room, which was painted hospital green. I turned on the air conditioner. It started up with a rattle and climbed to a deafening volume, where it would stay for the next four days. I unpacked and sat down to call Fred Leuchter, the man who would start me on my journey through the world of executions.

"What's your room number?" he said. "I'll be over in a minute."

I went outside and took a seat on the plastic chair next to my front door, watching the traffic go by and preparing for my week of interviews. I had a strange, empty feeling in my gut as I wondered what lay ahead.

Half an hour later, Fred Leuchter pulled up to my front door, driving a brand-new Ford. It looked as though the execution business was booming. The man who climbed out of the car was small and wore thick glasses. He was dressed in gray trousers and a striped short-sleeved shirt with the monogram FAL printed over the pocket, which was stuffed with pens and a pack of Marlboro Lights. He blinked shortsightedly as he stuck out his hand and gave mine a firm shake.

"Hi, how you doing. Nice to meet you," he told me, in the hardest, raspiest Boston accent I'd ever heard. He looked like Alfred E. Neuman, the impish *geist* of *Mad* magazine. He was forty-eight, but didn't look his age. This was the man that ABC News had dubbed "Dr. Death."

We climbed into Fred's car, which he explained was on loan from the garage while his was being fixed. He'd had an accident, he said, looking directly at me as he talked. His driving made me nervous. The knot in my gut tightened.

While I considered how to begin an interview with someone who made a living from inventing the lethal injection machine and supplying other execution hardware, Fred chatted comfortably about the unseasonably warm weather, and told me about Malden.

The town I looked at through Fred's car window was like the mill towns I was familiar with from my childhood—a working-class community that had been built on traditional values of hard work and civic pride, but blighted by industrial decline and left out of the economic boom of the 1980s. Malden had now become part of greater Boston, a bedroom community, a relatively cheap place to buy a house and commute on the T train to an office job with a bank or insurance company.

The road to Fred's house wiggled off the end of one of Malden's main streets, over a bridge and up a small dead-end drive. Fred's blacktop driveway led right up to the front door, almost as if it were a garage, not a residence. It's an unusual two-story affair; a small clapboard rectangle with a pitched roof perched on top. The entrance was on the side of the house, rather than at the front. It had a porch with a few steps and, alongside it, a peach tree. A few small, hard peaches hung from the limbs, encouraged by the humid end of summer weather; but most of the fruit lay rotting on the ground around it.

Fred took me inside. Off the tiny living room was the kitchen, decorated in light-colored wood-effect paneling. To the left were the refrigerator, oven, and work surfaces. To the right, against the wall, was a round, varnished Colonial reproduction table with four matching chairs. There was a video recorder on the kitchen table, and on top of it a portable television. The table was covered with a jumble of stuff: videotapes, a calculator, quiz books, ashtrays full of butts, cans of diet Coke, and the *TV Guide*. Fred introduced his wife, Caroline, who was sitting at the table watching TV.

"You're from *England?*" she said, allowing me to shake her hand.

Caroline is a large lady who wears generously cut trousers, voluminous tops of man-made fibers, and big, amber-tinted glasses. She was drinking a can of diet Coke.

"Caroline's diabetic," Fred told me.

"I've got to be careful about sugar," she explained. "I drink *a lot* of diet Coke."

Caroline introduced me to Rex, the family pet. Rex is an elderly and overweight dog that looked as if it could barely walk.

"She's a girl, despite her name," Caroline told me. A black bitch of mixed parentage, Rex raised her head a fraction at the sound of her name, then settled into a wheezy snooze at the feet of her mistress.

After pouring coffee for everyone, Caroline resumed watching "The Fugitive."

Over the next week I learned that Caroline spent most of the day sitting at the kitchen table, her back to the living room, watching television. She's a die-hard fan of old black and white shows like "The Fugitive" with David Janssen, "Highway Patrol," with Broderick Crawford, and "The Saint," when he used to be Roger Moore. Her other passion, which involves using the modem-equipped computer in Fred's office, is playing general-knowledge quiz games through the night with fellow insomniacs. The computer is connected via a telephone line so that Trivial Pursuit–type games can be played simultaneously by people all over the United States.

Fred indicated that I should take a seat on the sofa. The living room was painted white, and had a suspended ceiling and a brown nylon patterned carpet. There was an overstuffed three-piece suite in brown polyester and a heavy wooden coffee table with ceramic tile inlays. An oval mirror in a gilded frame hung over the sofa, with matching wall lamps on either side. Each of the wall fittings had three pink candles in fancy glass lamps fixed to curly brass buttresses. From the top of each of the fittings protruded a number of thin branches bearing delicate gilded butterflies; while beneath each one hung a circular arrangement of artificial pink roses complete with stems and leaves. Other bric-a-brac decorated the wall behind the sofa, including a white plastic fan, its pattern reminiscent of Spanish wrought ironwork; and a fluffy miniature pink dog on a tiny glass shelf supported by an ornate brass fitting.

Fred told me that Caroline was an avid collector of Hummel figurines, some of which she had purchased on a trip to Germany. Oak and glass cabinets on either side of the room were crammed with a huge assortment of the gnomelike Teutonic ceramics. Above the electric light switch, a small statue of the Virgin Mary was recessed in a glass-covered niche in the wall. In front of the little window protecting the Virgin was a votive candle in a glass lamp, with a bunch of artificial purple lilies. At one end of the room, a grandfather clock chimed out the hour. Hanging next to the grandfather clock was a "Bless This House and All Who Enter Here" sampler.

We drank our coffee and then Fred took me into his study. It had a paper-strewn desk at one end and a computer workstation at the other. Against one wall was a bookcase, on top of which was a telephone answering machine. It was switched on, even though Fred was at home. He explained that, in his business, he received threats regularly, so he screened all of his calls before picking up the phone.

Opposite the bookcase was a little table, on which was spread out a set of architectural plans. I looked more closely and saw that it was the layout of the Nazi concentration camp at Auschwitz. I looked around the room to see what other objects were in it. Next to Fred's desk was a low filing cabinet, from which a number of thick manila files had been removed and then replaced at an angle on top of the cabinet. I looked at the labels and saw that they were autopsy reports from the coroner's office in Gainesville, Florida. Alongside them were color photographs of an unspeakably gruesome nature. They showed the heads of men whose brains had been removed, and the two halves of the head sutured messily together.

Odd bits of hardware were strewn about. In a small cardboard box was a weird object, a metal cap like a yarmulke with a wire grid inside, onto which was sewn, with very thick thread, a sponge. It had a metal fixture protruding from the top of it.

"Is that a head electrode?" I asked, hesitantly.

"Yes," said Fred. "It's from South Carolina's old electric chair. It's pretty much the same as the ones I've made for Tennessee and Indiana."

I looked on Fred's desk. There was a Mystic Valley Gun Club paperweight.

"Are you a marksman?" I asked, wondering how Fred's severe myopia could make that possible.

"Yes," Fred told me. "I used to be president of my local gun club. I'm an instructor for target and combat shooting."

There was a jumble of papers on Fred's desk, but my eye fell on one document in particular: a grubby, dog-eared copy of the NAACP Legal Defense Fund's bimonthly report, *Death Row, U.S.A.* It was opened to the page headed "South Carolina (Electrocution)." There were forty-six names—the names of men who are scheduled to die in the electric chair. A check mark had been placed alongside the name of inmate number nine on the list, Donald Gaskins. On the front of the report, Fred had kept score of the number of executions carried out in the United States since 1973. There was a long line of crossed-out numbers, ending with the current tally: 152.

Fred went to the kitchen to get more coffee, then began to tell me how he had got into the execution business. He explained that his father, Fred senior, had been employed as a driver for the Massachusetts prison system, eventually becoming transport supervisor. On weekends and during the school vacations, Fred would accompany his dad while he drove equipment—including, on one occasion, the state's electric chair—and inmates between the various Massachusetts prisons. As a child, Fred found the world of prisons fascinating, and he told me an anecdote about his early experience of them.

"When I was a kid," he told me, "I used to go with my father to the prisons here in Massachusetts. There was another kid, a prison worker's son, who sat in the electric chair. Eleven years later, he was killed in the same chair. He was involved in a murder. Anyway, the legend came about that if you sat in the chair, you'd die in it. Well, I sat in that chair. And I didn't get electrocuted in it later. I sat in the electric chair, and now I *make* electric chairs." He laughed, his eyes sparking with delight.

Fred offered to show me a photograph of the electric chair he designed for Tennessee. It was in an album of family snaps, as if his machines were also his children. One showed Fred in his backyard, standing proudly next to the Tennessee chair. Beneath it, like a footnote to his story about the Massachusetts chair, was a photo of Fred's own son sitting in the chair, smiling for the camera on a sunny day.

Fred has no formal training in engineering. At school, he was more interested in carpentry than electronics, and when he went to college, he studied history. His first job after graduation was with North East Aerial Photos, where he learned to assemble aerial photographic systems from World War II vintage equipment. Fred learned quickly and was promoted to technical director. The job taught him good practical engineering skills, and he developed a kind of genius—albeit more the genius of combination than the genius of invention.

As an inventor, Fred holds numerous patents, though he complains that former employers or their clients own the rights to his more lucrative inventions. Among them is one which could be considered a lifesaving device, the first electronic sextant. Fred also designed and built, on a subcontract for General Electric, the first low-level, color stereo helicopter mapping system. It is a quick way of producing accurate maps and was first used by the U.S. Air Force in Vietnam. It is still in use today. But patents are something of a sore point with Fred. "I've had a number of major companies infringe on my patents," he told me, half-bitter, half-resigned. "In the United States, a patent is only a license to sue, and if you ain't got the money, you can't sue."

In the early 1980s, Fred came to the conclusion that he would be more successful working for himself than for other people. He combined the practical knowledge of prisons he had gained as a child with his engineering experience and became America's first and foremost supplier of execution hardware. His products include electric chairs, gas chambers, gallows, and lethal injection machines. He offers design, construction, installation, staff training, and maintenance.

The execution business got off to a slow start. There were no executions in the United States between 1972, when the Supreme Court declared capital punishment unconstitutional, and 1976, when it was reinstated. The first American to be executed after 1976 was Gary Gilmore, who was put to death by firing squad in Utah on January 17, 1977. The next execution did not take place until two and a half years later, when Florida sent John Spenkelink to the electric chair on May 25, 1979. Then, on October 22 of the same year, Nevada put Jesse Bishop to death.

After the Gilmore execution, there was not, as some had expected, an avalanche of state-directed killings. It started slowly. No one was put to death in 1980. There was one execution in 1981; there were two in 1982 and five in 1983. (None of this compared with the numbers of executions

America had witnessed in the 1930s and 1940s. In 1935 alone, there were 195; and the total number of executions between 1930 and 1949 was 2,951 —an average of 148 per year.) In 1984, however, the number jumped to twenty-one. Executions became a business opportunity for someone with the right knowledge and the stomach for the job.

Fred did what any small businessman does when starting out on a new venture. He sized up the market. There were thirty-eight jurisdictions with capital punishment (thirty-six states plus the U.S. military and the U.S. federal government). There were more than two thousand people on death row. Thirteen of his potential clients used electrocution as a method of execution. During the 1980s, some of the thirteen would change over to lethal injection. Seven states had the gas chamber, three prescribed hanging, and two sent their condemned to the firing squad. Fred researched each method to discover what happened to the condemned and what equipment and procedures were necessary to carry out the execution successfully.

As we sat in his living room sipping coffee, Fred gave me a crash course in execution technology.

Death by firing squad, he said, is caused by massive damage to the heart, central nervous system, or other vital organs, or by a combination of these effects with hemorrhage. He told me that probably the quickest way to execute a human being with a gun is to fire a single bullet from a pistol at point-blank range into the head. That is the procedure in China, and it usually guarantees instantaneous death. In Idaho and Utah, the law specifies a five-man rifle squad.

Execution by shooting has a long history in America. The first recorded execution by this means was in 1608, when George Kendall, one of the original councillors for the colony of Virginia, was put to death. For centuries, the military favored execution by shooting, and it was also the choice of many Native American tribes, once they had obtained guns from European settlers. Idaho had carried out one execution by firing squad in the 1950s; Utah's last, before Gary Gilmore, had been in the 1960s.

A first glance at the market told Fred there wasn't a fortune to be made out of firing squad executions, since they don't require much in the way of equipment—apart from guns, a blindfold, a chair, some sandbags to stop the bullets, a target to pin to the condemned man's chest, and a slit screen to conceal the gunmen.

Looking at the information he'd gathered on execution by shooting, Fred concluded that it was a painful way to die.

"There's no way of knowing for sure if someone hurts," Fred told me. And then he pointed his hand at me, as if it held a pistol, and said: "But if I shoot you, I *know* you hurt."

Fred also concluded that it was a messy procedure, both physically and ethically.

I asked Fred why he found firing squad executions messy in an "ethical" sense. He explained that the tradition in firing squads is to issue a blank round to one of the gunmen. The idea is that, since one of the rounds did not kill the victim, no one of the five-man squad need ever know that he was responsible for the death of another human being.

"And that's *ridiculous*," Fred practically screamed. "Anyone who's ever fired a gun knows if he's firing a blank, because he won't get any recoil!"

The problem is that some members of firing squads have been known to aim away from the condemned man's heart, leaving others to fire the fatal shot. This happened in Utah on September 10, 1951, in the execution of Elisio Mares, who had been a popular inmate with prison staff. During his execution, all five marksmen aimed away from the target over Mares's heart and shot him on the right-hand side of his chest. The firing squad and witnesses watched in horror as Mares bled slowly to death. When Gary Gilmore was shot to death in Utah in 1977, all four bullets pierced his heart. However, heart death was not immediate. The doctor had to check twice before pronouncing him dead, two minutes after the firing squad had let go its lethal volley.

Fred explored hanging, and he is one of the few experts on the subject. Prior to British refinements of hanging procedure in the nineteenth century, the punishment consisted of looping a rope around the condemned man's neck and dropping him from a height so that the rope tightened, causing a slow death—cases of up to ten minutes have been reported—by asphyxiation. Before unconsciousness intervenes, the strangled hanging victim's face turns purple as he struggles for air. His eyes bulge, his tongue hangs out, and he loses control of his sphincter. Fred studied a British government report of 1888 which detailed a method of hanging designed to cause instant death through dislocation of the vertebrae; and he studied subsequent inquiries and autopsies in which the ratio of rope length to victim weight had been miscalculated, resulting in decapitation. Fred is the author of the most modern hanging manual, prepared for the state of Delaware, which specifies precise rope length to body weight ratios to ensure instant death without decapitation.

While hanging may be viewed as an anachronism, an uncivilized hangover from the days of the Wild West, four states used it as a method of execution when Fred started his market research: Delaware, Montana, Oklahoma, and Washington. Since that time, Oklahoma and Washington have converted to lethal injection. In Montana, the condemned are given a choice of lethal injection or hanging. In Delaware, inmates convicted prior to June 13, 1986, are hanged; lethal injection is the method of execution for those convicted after that date. Fred pushed hard in all four hanging states, and he secured a gallows and lethal injection machine sale to Delaware.

When Fred set out to research the execution market, seven states executed capital offenders in the gas chamber: Arizona, California, Colorado, Maryland, Mississippi, Missouri, and North Carolina. Three of them looked like real business opportunities. California had executed 292 people between the introduction of the gas chamber in 1933 and 1969; North Carolina ran a close second with 263; followed by Mississippi with 156.

The gas chamber was invented in 1924 by D. A. Turner, a major in the U.S. Army Medical Corps. Turner began by studying the effects of gas warfare during World War I. The lethal gas in those shells went under a variety of names, including prussic acid, cyanide gas, hydrogen cyanide, or hydrocyanic gas, but the effect was always the same. Breathing in cyanide gas paralyzes the heart and lungs. The victim becomes giddy. Panic gives way to severe headache, followed by chest pains. Respiration becomes impossible, so that the victim struggles vainly for breath, eyes popping, tongue hanging thick and swollen from a drooling mouth. His face turns purple. Turner's idea, in creating the gas chamber, was to find a more civilized alternative to the electric chair.

Most gas chambers are octagonal in shape and are made of steel, with glass panels held in place by airtight seals. All except Missouri's, which was constructed by inmates, were manufactured by Eaton Metal Products of Salt Lake City. The condemned man is strapped into a metal chair with a perforated seat. A long stethoscope is taped to his chest and passed through the chamber so that a physician on the other side can pronounce death. A bowl is placed under the chair, and over this, suspended on a hook which the executioner controls by means of a lever, is a gauze bag containing one pound of cyanide, or a number of cyanide tablets. The executioner also controls a tube through which sulfuric acid is introduced into the bowl. Once the bowl is filled with acid, the cyanide is dropped into it, causing a chemical reaction which slowly releases the poisonous gas.

Before the much-publicized execution of Robert Harris in California in 1992, the last American gas execution had taken place in Missouri in 1989, when Leo Edwards was put to death. In 1987, Mississippi also executed Edward Earl Johnson and Connie Ray Evans. After Mississippi's 1983 execution of Jimmy Lee Gray, several witnesses reported that he had convulsions for eight minutes; that he gasped eleven times during that period; and that he repeatedly struck his head on a pole behind him while struggling in the gas chamber. Anxious prison officials at Parchman Farm finally ordered the witnesses to leave the observation area. As they left, Gray was still banging his head against the pole. One of the witnesses demanded to know if Gray was dead. Warden Eddie Lucas replied confidently: "No question."

A similar scene occurred during a 1976 gas execution in California. Howard Brodie, a journalist who had witnessed three executions, was present when California put Aaron Mitchell to death in its two-seater gas chamber. He reported that Mitchell was dragged struggling and screaming into the death chamber, where Warden Lawrence Wilson read the death warrant and gave the signal to release the deadly gas. Brodie told how when "the gas hit him his head immediately fell to his chest. Then his head came up and he looked directly into the window I was standing next to. For nearly seven minutes, he sat up that way, with his chest heaving, saliva bubbling between his lips. He tucked his thumbs into his fist and, finally, his head fell down again." The prison records show that it took twelve minutes for Mitchell's heart to stop beating.

Incidents like these make Fred Leuchter uncomfortable with gas chambers.

"They're dangerous," he told me. "They're dangerous to the people who have to use them, and they're dangerous for the witnesses. They ought to take all of them and cut them in half with a chain saw and get rid of them."

In the late 1970s and early 1980s, lethal injection was the coming method. But when Fred began in the execution industry, it was difficult to see how anyone could make money with it. All that was apparently required was a supply of lethal drugs, syringes, and an IV (intravenous) line. Electrocution, on the other hand, was still popular. And because electrocutions were regularly going wrong—gruesomely wrong—they represented a prime business opportunity. Fred believed he could step in and put things right.

Since the 1980s, botched electrocutions have made sensational headlines. In Virginia's execution of Albert Clozza by electrocution on July 24, 1991, faulty electrodes and improperly applied voltage led to a slow and agonizing death. Steam pressure in Clozza's head caused his eyeballs to pop so that blood ran down his chest from the sockets. He died after no fewer than four jolts of electricity had been applied. Florida State Prison, on May 4, 1990, was the setting for what was perhaps the most gruesome execution in American history. Flames, smoke, and sparks shot six inches out of the head of Jessie Tafero as three 2,000-volt shocks were administered. Because the amperage was incorrect, Tafero's flesh cooked on his bones before he died. Indiana, October 16, 1985: The state's seventy-two-year-old electric chair required five jolts of electricity and seventeen minutes to execute William Vandiver. Georgia, December 12, 1984: Alpha Otis Stephens received a two-minute jolt of electricity and appeared to slump in the electric chair. In the six minutes that doctors waited for his body to cool so they could check his heartbeat, Stephens took twenty-three breaths, according to eyewitness reports. Two doctors checked Stephens and found he was still alive. He died after a second jolt was applied.

Lethal injection, meant to be the neat and modern execution method, was also plagued with problems, or "execution glitches," as they are referred to in the business. Most of the problems have occurred in Texas, which has executed more people than any other U.S. jurisdiction since 1976—forty-eight at time of going to press—despite the fact that executions were not resumed there until 1982. In May 1992, it took forty-seven minutes for the execution team to insert an IV line into Billy Wayne White, a former drug user. White actually tried to help the executioners locate a vein. It took nine minutes for him to die. In May 1989, an incorrect mix of lethal drugs caused Stephen McCoy to choke and heave throughout his execution. That terrible death chamber scene was preceded in December 1988 by another, in which the IV line carrying a lethal injection into the arm of Raymond Landry sprang a leak, spraying technicians and witnesses with the fatal drugs. The tube had to be reinserted while Landry was half-dead. It took twenty-four minutes for him to die. Three years before that, in March 1985, Stephen Morin lay on a gurney for more than forty minutes while technicians in the Texas prison failed repeatedly to insert the IV needle into his veins.

What gave Fred the conviction to start up in the execution business was the belief that all of the execution methods used in the United States were subject to glitches. He believed that, through modern hardware and rigorous training, executions would become glitch-free and professional.

* * *

Fred Leuchter's approach to the execution industry was simple. He realized that the technology required to kill another human being deliberately, legally, already existed and only needed updating. The real problem wasn't hardware, it was people. Killing another human being, Fred realized, was one of the more difficult things a state employee had to do; and it was especially difficult when things went wrong. Fred reasoned that, when things went wrong, the condemned man suffered. And when that happened, it was difficult for the execution team, difficult for the witnesses, and difficult for the politicians who had to defend a botched execution in which the state was seen to have blood on its hands and egg on its face.

By the time executions resumed in the late 1970s, a new generation of prison wardens had inherited a collection of electric chairs, gas chambers, and gallows which looked more like museum pieces than instruments of modern justice. Few wardens knew how they worked, or even *if* they worked. Most of the electric chairs had been built by inmates around the turn of the century and were based on designs dating back to 1890. The gas chambers were old and leaky and posed as much of a threat to the executioner and witnesses as they did to the condemned. Fred Leuchter came along and said, 'I can make this work for you.' The wardens were thinking, before they even knew Fred's name, 'We need you, or someone like you.' Understanding the customer's needs was going to be the key to Fred's success in the execution industry.

The next task was to develop a thorough understanding of methodology and equipment. Fred decided to study the history of his new profession. He went to the library and dug up scholarly papers, discovering through his research that the story of the electric chair had been one of chance, personal rivalry, and commercial greed, and was a little-known but fascinating footnote in the careers of Thomas Edison and George Westinghouse.

The electric chair was invented because hanging had had its day. Hanging, on the authority either of the sheriff or the lynch mob, had been a common feature of American life during the westward expansion. The noose came to symbolize the outrage of the community in response to violent crime. In the days of the Wild West, no one seriously argued that hanging was a deterrent to crime. It simply ensured that the man who was hanged would no longer commit crimes. It was the means by which the community took vengeance, and it provided a feeling of comfort and reassurance during violent times that something was being done.

By the end of the nineteenth century, New York State authorities came to believe that hanging was a method of capital punishment at odds with the modern, sophisticated, and civilized society they judged themselves to be. Faced with a number of impending executions, they cast about for a method more in keeping with their view of themselves. In 1886, Governor David Hill set up a commission to find a form of execution "more humane than hanging."

Combing through back numbers of obscure technical publications like *Medical Instrumentation* and *IEEE Spectrum,* Fred came across articles by Professor Theodore Bernstein which told the story of how Governor Hill's three-man commission included a dentist, Dr. Alfred P. Southwick, who had heard about the accidental death by electrocution of a man in Buffalo, New York, in 1881. The victim, Samuel Smith, while under the influence of drink, put his hands across the terminals of a direct current generator that had recently been installed by the city. Eyewitness reports said he apparently died instantaneously and painlessly. Southwick's colleagues on the New York commission were busy studying European methods of execution, including the guillotine and garotte. Both these methods were as unsatisfactory as hanging. While the guillotine might be quick and sure, it mutilated the body in a way that was unacceptable to the American public. The garotte simply guaranteed the worst that could happen with hanging: slow strangulation rather than sudden death. Southwick reasoned that electricity could do the job neatly and cleanly, and so began electrocution experiments on animals.

Electricity was just the thing Governor Hill's commission was looking for. The invisible and imperfectly understood form of energy was quintessentially modern (electricity was then so new that Edison had only discovered the electric light bulb a few years earlier, in 1879). It had the advantage of being clean, and was relatively cheap. Southwick's experiments on animals convinced Governor Hill that hanging should be abolished as the means of execution in New York State, and on June 4, 1888, he signed into law a bill which prescribed death by electrocution for capital crimes committed after January 1, 1889.

During the 1880s, a controversy of epic proportions was raging between Edison and his rival George Westinghouse, each of whom had harnessed electrical power in different forms and was competing to make his system the standard. Edison argued for direct current; Westinghouse was the champion of alternating current. Each man reckoned that whoever won the battle would reap the richest payday in the history of science.

On March 29 of that year, William Kemmler, by coincidence a resident of Buffalo, New York, murdered his lover Tillie Ziegler with a hatchet. He was the first man to be sentenced to death by electrocution, and the date was set for June 24, 1889, at New York's Auburn State Prison. The state now had two urgent decisions to make. Would it use Edison's direct current system, or Westinghouse's alternating current? And what hardware would be required to carry out the death sentence? The modern execution industry was born on the horns of this dilemma.

Kemmler's impending execution also gave birth to one of the classic appeals in capital punishment law. The flamboyant lawyer and former congressman Bourke Cockran took on Kemmler's case and immediately lodged an appeal against the sentence as a cruel and unusual punishment in violation of the Eighth and Fourteenth amendments to the U.S. Constitution. The state was caught off guard and had no alternative but to issue a stay of execution.

Undeterred by Kemmler's appeal, New York decided to build three electric chairs, which were installed in prisons at Auburn, Sing Sing, and Clinton. The $8,000 contract went to an "electrician" by the name of

Harold Brown, who favored alternating current. Thomas Edison, an opponent of capital punishment, believed that his rival George Westinghouse's alternating current would do the job more satisfactorily than his own direct current and snidely promoted the idea that alternating current was more "dangerous." Westinghouse fumed. If his alternating current were used for executions, the Westinghouse image could be tainted, and public opinion might take against alternating current.

Meanwhile, Kemmler's lawyer was calling in a now familiar—but novel at the time—cast of expert witnesses to try and save his client's neck. The state found doctors who argued that electrocution was instantaneous and painless, while the defense called doctors who said no one could be sure. Kemmler's lawyer also tried to discredit Brown by showing that he lacked any formal scientific education and alleging that he was an agent of Edison's, paid not only by the state to build the electric chair but also by Edison solely to besmirch the name of Westinghouse.

However, Brown eventually got his contract to supply New York with three Westinghouse generators capable of producing more than 2,000 volts, along with exciters, rheostats, Cardew voltmeters, ammeters, Wheatstone bridges, switches, electrodes, bell signals, waterproof insulating wire, and insulators. The electric chairs he fashioned were made of oak and contained two electrodes: one for the head, and one for the lower back.

But when Brown tried to buy the generators from Westinghouse, the company refused to supply them. Undeterred, he obtained them from a secondhand dealer in Boston, increasing his profit margin substantially.

On October 9, 1889, the Cayuga County Court denied Kemmler's appeal. Cockran made further desperate attempts on Kemmler's behalf, but to no avail. The execution was set for the morning of August 6, 1890.

The electric chair used in Kemmler's execution was, in most ways, fairly similar to those in use today. The event excited a great deal of medical interest, and of the twenty-five witnesses who watched Kemmler killed by electricity, fourteen were doctors. The executioners were electricians. Later, the man who actually threw the switch, Edwin Davis, was named the official New York State executioner. Davis went on to execute 240 people before his retirement in 1914, when he was replaced by his assistant, Robert G. Elliott.

Two New York State physicians were officially in charge of the execution, both of them specialists in mental illness: Dr. E. C. Spitzka and Dr. Carlos F. MacDonald, chairman of the New York State Lunacy Commission. MacDonald later described what happened on the fateful day.

"Before Kemmler was brought into the room the warden asked the physicians how long the contact should be maintained. [I] replied, 'Twenty seconds,' but subsequently assented to ten seconds in deference to the opinion of another that a considerably less period of time would suffice—an opinion which doubtlessly would have sustained had the electro-motive pressure [voltage] been sufficiently great.

"Unfortunately, in this instance, the voltmeter, ammeter, switchboard, etc., were not located in the execution room; hence, none of the official witnesses could know precisely how much the electro-motive pressure and current strength were at the time of making and during the continuance of the first contact. *Nor has the voltage or amperage in this instance, to the writer's knowledge, ever been officially determined.* But reasoning from the known lethal effect of an electro-motive pressure of 1600 volts and upward, as shown by subsequent executions and by deaths which have occurred from accidental contact with live electric wires . . . solid ground is afforded for the conclusion that no human being can survive the passage through his body of an alternating current of more than 1500 volts for a period of even twenty seconds, the contact being perfect."

Kemmler's execution in the electric chair being the first, no one had thought to establish the protocols that now exist—the death sentence protocols that ritualize every moment of the deathwatch and execution process from the time the governor signs a death warrant to the time a body is removed from the death chamber. The execution protocol arose as a necessary device to keep order in the prison around the time of an execution, to keep the execution party's mind off the grisliness of their task over a period as long as ten days, and to control the condemned man's fear by making him believe he was a part of a ritual that was being conducted in a competent way by trained people, including doctors and clergymen.

Because there was no protocol for Kemmler's execution, the event was an oddly casual affair. After the witnesses had gathered in the death chamber, and were seated on chairs in a semicircle around the electric chair, Warden Charles Durston led Kemmler into the death chamber, where the curious doctors, reporters, and law enforcement officers were waiting.

Kemmler's entrance was theatrical. A short man with an attractive face and a neatly trimmed black beard, Kemmler was dressed in his Sunday best, and he appeared to enjoy being the center of so much attention. In the absence of any protocol, Warden Durston, uncertain as to what he should do next (and apparently reluctant to dispatch Kemmler to his death without some form of ceremony), offered the condemned man a seat in front of the electric chair.

"Gentlemen, this is William Kemmler," he announced.

Kemmler nodded at the warden, as if he had been introduced to give an after-dinner speech, and made a short statement. "The newspapers have been saying a lot of things about me which were not so. I wish you all good luck in this world. I believe I am going to a good place."

The warden nodded back at Kemmler and said, "Now we'll get ready, William. Let me take your coat."

Kemmler declined any assistance and placed his coat across the back of the chair he was sitting on. He started to remove his waistcoat, but the warden told him that would be unnecessary, as it had been slit up the back to accommodate the spine electrode. However, Kemmler's shirt was then cut at the back, baring the flesh at the base of his spine.

A deputy sheriff, Joe Veiling, guided Kemmler to the chair to strap him in. Veiling and Kemmler had built up a rapport during the days before the execution. The condemned man's only sign of fear had been a comment to Veiling earlier that morning: "Joe, I want you to stick by me through this thing. Don't let them experiment on me more than they ought to."

As the reluctant deputy sheriff started to strap him into the electric chair, Kemmler quipped, "Don't get excited, Joe. I want you to make a good job of this."

Veiling stepped away and Warden Durston came forward to place the head electrode on Kemmler. The witnesses could see that while Kemmler was neatly dressed and groomed, the hair at the crown of his head had been shaved haphazardly to facilitate the electrical contact. After the head electrode had been applied, Kemmler moved his head from side to side and said, "I guess you'd better make that a little tighter, Mr. Durston." The warden complied, and then attached the spine electrode. He placed a black mask over Kemmler's face and said, "Good-bye, William."

"Good-bye," Kemmler replied.

Durston knocked twice on the door of the room adjacent to the death chamber, and Edwin Davis threw the switch.

A reporter from the New York *World* described what followed. "Suddenly the breast heaved. There was a straining at the straps which bound him. . . . The man was alive. Warden, physicians, everybody, lost their wits. There was a startled cry for the current to be turned on again. Signals, only half understood, were given to those in the next room at the switchboard. When they knew what happened, they were prompt to act, and the switch-handle could be heard as it was pulled back and forth, breaking the deadly current into jets."

The first electrocution, like many others which followed, was botched.

Dr. Southwick reported that "When the electrical contact was broken . . . superficial discolorations . . . were observed on the exposed portions of the face. The body remained limp and motionless for approximately half a minute, when there occurred a series of slightly spasmodic movements of the chest. . . . There were no evidences of a return of consciousness or of sensory function, but in view of the possibility that life was not wholly extinct, beyond resuscitation, and in order to take no risk of such a contingency, the current was ordered to be reapplied, which was done within about two minutes from the time the first contact was broken. . . . The second closure of the circuit was inadvertently maintained for about seventy seconds, when a small volume of vapor, and subsequently of smoke, was seen to issue from the point of application of the spinal electrode due . . . to scorching of the edge of the sponge with which the electrode was faced, and from which the moisture had been evaporated. . . .

"A careful examination of the body was now made. . . . The radial pulse and heart's action had ceased. . . . In other words, William Kemmler was dead, and the intent and purpose of the law to effect sudden and painless death in the execution of criminals had been successfully carried out."

Dr. Southwick, the deadly dentist who has gone down in the history books as the father of electrocution, called Kemmler's execution "the grandest success of the age." While Dr. MacDonald and Warden Durston were well pleased with the results—after all, Kemmler had been put to death, and fairly rapidly at that—some witnesses and at least two participants thought the first execution by electricity to have been bungled. Dr.

MacDonald's colleague, Dr. Spitzka, was disgusted by the historic event. He told reporters, "The execution was not a failure, for the man is dead. But," he added, "today's performance has satisfied me that the electrical system of execution can in no way be regarded as a step in civilization. The guillotine is better than the gallows, the gallows is better than electrical execution."

SITTING IN Fred Leuchter's living room on the first day of my interview with him, I could hear commuter trains rumbling past as he explained the history of executions, and his loathing for execution glitches. He told me his motto is "Capital punishment, not capital torture." And he said: "As someone who believes in capital punishment but does not believe in torture, I sleep well knowing that as a result of what I do, fewer people are tortured. I'm very uncomfortable when the state does something that causes pain or traumatic damage to the individual being executed." The purpose of his business, he said, is to ensure "a dignified and professional execution."

Fred lit a cigarette and explained: "It's not up to me to determine whether or not the person gets executed. It's up to me only to see that the person gets executed properly—if I'm asked. And that's all I do. And I'll be more than happy to set up the execution and do everything but throw the switch for them. I'm a proponent of executions. But I think it's a disgrace that somebody would torture somebody to death in my name, or any other citizen's name."

In October 1990, the *New York Times* published an editorial on Fred and his lethal injection machine under the headline "Dr. Death and His Wonderful Machine." "With capital punishment in vogue," it pointedly argued, "Fred Leuchter should be the man of the hour. He's a readily available source of technical support for states seeking new or improved execution machinery. When Missouri needed a lethal injection machine, he was not only the low bidder, but the only bidder. Mr. Leuchter, after all, only designs death machines: others create their market."

Once Fred had identified the market and made some initial, successful forays into it, he decided he would be better off setting up in business with a partner. He found a man called Norbert Lynch, an unfortunate name for someone whose business included the design and installation of gallows. Fred's choice of partner was to prove ill-fated. Norbie Lynch describes himself as a "self-employed business entrepreneur." Before he teamed up with Fred, forty-eight-year-old Lynch had previously owned a car dealership, from which he sold car insurance on the side. He lost that job when questions were raised about the financing of insurance policies he arranged for two girlfriends. After the car business, he got involved with Peabody Trading Company, a Boston commodities outfit. In 1983, the Commodities Futures Trading Commission raided Peabody and closed it down. They took away Lynch's license and barred him from selling commodities for life.

That life sentence made Lynch available to become a partner in Fred's first execution hardware company, American Engineering, Inc. American Engineering used an office address at 265 Main Street in Boston, but most of its activities were based in the "engineering facilities" at 108 Bunker Hill Street, in a drafty basement in a run-down part of Charlestown. It was here that Fred perfected the electric chair and invented his lethal injection machine. To come were the headiest days of the execution industry for Fred and Norbie.

In some ways, Fred and Norbie were well matched. Both are garrulous, chain-smoking, ebullient men able to talk the hind leg off a donkey. They were a Mutt and Jeff duo, a pattern from which lesser stereotypes are cut. If Fred is Alfred E. Neuman, Big Norbie is Archie Bunker.

The basement in Charlestown was a buzzing hive of frantic activity. Letters were dispatched to prison wardens, designs were worked out and refined, and equipment was assembled on the spot. There was a boyish enthusiasm for the business, and a sense of fun. Tacked to the wall over a giant spool of electrical cable was a pistol target with a photograph of Colonel Qaddafi pinned over the bull's-eye. Norbie got into the spirit of Fred's "Capital punishment, not capital torture" slogan and would explain American Engineering's repeated failure to sell a lethal injection machine to Texas by bawling at a *Boston Globe* reporter, "In Texas, people could beat the person to death with a shovel and no one would care. I hope the Civil Liberties Union goes after them." Norbie always maintained that he was anti–capital punishment but justified his involvement in American Engineering by insisting that "Our society has determined that it is the ultimate penalty a man can place on another man. These deaths are going to occur anyway. And I think it's wrong to carry out executions under antiquated methods."

While Fred's commitment to American Engineering was full-time, Norbie's restless entrepreneurial spirit could never be satisfied by having his fingers in just one pie. He became a not-so-silent partner in a sexually explicit lesbian magazine called *Eidos,* whose answering machine would chirp, "Hello, thanks for calling *Eidos,* where we say, 'Sex is here to stay'!" When *Eidos* started printing poetry, Norbie's enthusiasm for the project waned. "It was supposed to be erotica for all women," he said dejectedly, "but the articles have gotten a little spacey."

In 1987, Norbie left American Engineering after Fred discovered a large sum of money missing from the company's bank account. With Norbie gone, the business continued as Fred A. Leuchter Associates, Inc.

American Engineering had always been a low-tech, no-frills operation. The pitches that Fred sent out to prospective clients were form letters that had been prepared on a word processor. They had a sans serif typeface and justified margins, and were printed on American Engineering letterhead; but the date, the address of the potential client, and the salutation were typed on an old typewriter, in a different typeface.

A typical sales letter is one addressed to Superintendent Glen Parks of the Virginia Department of Corrections, dated August 20, 1985. "Dear Glen," it begins, "American Engineering, Inc. is a consulting engineering and hardware fabricating firm located in Boston, Massachusetts. In the past, it has been engaged in the design and fabrication of execution devices for state governments enforcing capital punishment. Entry into the market was determined by a requirement to standardize hardware and procedures, reduce costs and eliminate problems and complications inherent in execution. Most of the equipment in use today is a quarter of a century old, or older, and although operating, is either sub-standard, imprecise or problematical from a medical standpoint. Our aim is to offer hardware and personal support in all phases of the problem, not limited to, but including, technical assistance in the field. We are prepared to address any problems you might pose, and research any problems you might have, not only via letter or telephone but by actual physical inspection, certification, repair, maintenance and set-up of your hardware and systems for use prior to, and during, any execution. We are familiar with most systems and procedures and are prepared to discuss any problems or reservations you might have.

"Specifically, we can supply any hardware, design, modifications or complete systems needed, and further, back-up said systems and hardware with support. We can test and certify your system and equipment prior to its use and be present during its use to ensure proper function. We have a successful track record in the field and a complete, computerized lethal injection system in place in the New Jersey State Prison in Trenton.

"Enclosed is a description of our Modular Electrocution System, the only state of the art system available today. This system will minimize your problems and ensure trouble free electrocutions. It has been designed utilizing the best medical and engineering expertise available and has been thoroughly considered from a human factors, legal and public standpoint to minimize error and guarantee ease in operation.

"Further, after installation of the system, we can supply support by testing and certifying the system as operational prior to each use, eliminating the human apprehension caused by infrequent use of the system. In this case, your people need only connect the subject to the system and the executioners perform their mechanical function.

"I will be in touch with you in the near future in the hope that we may assist you in your needs."

Fred signed the letter, "Fred A. Leuchter, Jr., Chief Engineer."

Fred does not claim that his design for the electric chair is 100 percent original. He is generous in his acknowledgment of the achievements of others and says that his design "goes back to the good electrocution systems developed on the East Coast of the United States at the beginning of this century: New York, New Jersey, Connecticut, Massachusetts. Some of the other chairs you get, out in the Midwest, for instance, were put together by inmates and an electrician, and they don't work properly." He said with a shake of his head, "Most of the good electrocution systems are sitting unused in museums."

In the early days of electrocution, there was little stigma attached to working as an engineer in the execution industry. Fred recalled how General Electric and Westinghouse were both involved in supplying components to prisons. "But they would stop at the point where you connect the components to the system," said Fred. "They'd supply a transformer and deliver it to the floor in front of the chair." The components were high quality, but in many cases they were assembled by a prison electrician of limited experience, whose chief role was everyday maintenance, such as ensuring that all the light bulbs worked.

Looking at old photographs of New York and Massachusetts electric chairs spread out on his desk, Fred said: "This is where it all started." Pointing at the electrodes, he observed: "They're probably just pieces of copper that have been bent and molded, form-fitted to the chair, with a wire soldered on. They're not capable of carrying the sustained current that ours are because we've used naval bronze. But it's the right design, it works well. It's just that in 1900 they didn't have the technological capability that I have now. I also have the opportunity of standing back and looking at a hundred years of screwups, which doesn't necessarily make me a genius. It just means that I have a very distinct advantage."

Fred told me some stories of botched electrocutions he had read about in his researches. He said that learning from the errors of the past had helped him perfect the electric chair. He began with the abortive electrocution in 1946 of Willie Francis, a seventeen-year-old black youth. Louisiana's traveling executioner threw the switch, and the transformer blew up. Francis went momentarily unconscious, but lived. He later described how his mouth tasted like cold peanut butter, and how he had seen little blue and pink speckles. What had happened, Fred explained, was that the voltage had dropped low enough to cause unconsciousness, but not to kill. Fred told me that maintaining the correct voltage was fundamental to a successful electrocution.

I asked what had happened to Francis after the failed execution, and Fred told me that he had appealed against his death sentence on the grounds that he'd already been "executed" once.

"Then what happened?" I asked.

"Well, the Supreme Court determined that he hadn't been executed. Execution means death. So they strapped him in a year later and finished the job. Only the second time they did it with new equipment, and they did it right."

Fred then told me about a botched electrocution in New York in 1893. When the executioner threw the switch on William Taylor, his legs stiffened, tearing away the front of the chair. A guard placed a box under the unfortunate man's feet, and a second jolt of electricity was applied. This time, the generator burned out. An hour passed while the chair was connected to the city power supply. The two jolts of electricity had caused terrible third-degree burns to Taylor's head and spine, and he died before a third jolt could be applied.

"There have been some very uncomfortable and painful things," Fred observed, "and these people were crying and screaming while this was going on. So it's unfortunate, but that does happen."

Fred explained that the problems executioners faced in the past were not simply mechanical, they were also human. "In the old days, being an executioner was an art. But I don't know what their art was, because most of them didn't know what they were doing anyway, and they were botching these things right and left. But it was an *art*," he said contemptuously, stretching the "a" in his rasping Boston accent until the word died in his throat. "They didn't tell anybody who they were. They'd come in and they'd put a hood on them and they'd spit out instructions to everybody, and everybody followed their instructions to the letter. They probably wouldn't if they realized the damn fool didn't know what he was talking about in the first place. And they conducted the execution. Some twenty percent of them were humane, and probably sixty percent of them were inhumane and nobody knew it."

The terrible history of the electric chair bothers Fred. When he talks about botched executions, his face screws up, the pitch of his voice rises, and the veins stand out on his neck. It's that exasperation verging on anger that gives impetus to Fred's "Capital punishment, not capital torture" slogan. When his anger is vented, Fred calms down and speaks in a low voice, his palms extended upward in an appeal to mercy and common sense. "Look, until I became involved, I didn't realize that there were so many problems. The average person doesn't. The average person thinks the equipment in the death house in his state is state-of-the-art. If they knew some of the things that went on, if they knew some of the horror stories . . ."

Fred's first commission, even before American Engineering was formed, was to repair an electric chair which had been damaged in a riot. The next job came via a call from a prison warden who needed a device to hold his electric chair's head electrode in place. The vast majority of botched electrocutions Fred had studied were due to defective electrodes. If the electrical circuit attached to the condemned man is imperfect, his body's natural resistance combines with poor conduction to lower the voltage of the current passing through his body, thereby causing pain. It is then necessary for the executioner to increase the current beyond what should be necessary, giving appalling results. "If you overload an individual's body with current," Fred told me, "more than six amps—you'll cook the meat on his body. It's like meat on an overcooked chicken. If you grab the arm, the flesh will fall right off in your hands. That doesn't mean he felt anything. It simply means that it's cosmetically not the thing to do. Presumably the state will return the remains to the person's family for burial. Returning someone who had been cooked would be in poor taste." The key to successful electrocution, he determined, is to establish "good circuit continuity at the electrode contacts to help reduce flesh burning."

Fred's second commission resulted in a head electrode assembly that, at a cost of $1,400, ensures "good circuit continuity." The helmet, the strange yarmulke-like object I'd noticed earlier, is made of soft, dark brown leather. "This is a *used* helmet," he said, handing it to me. I turned it over in my hands. It felt strange to be holding the thing.

"It's used?" I asked.

"Yup."

"How many times?" It felt silly asking the question. What difference could the answer make?

"I don't know. Dozens."

Dozens of times, the thing in my hands had been strapped onto the head of a condemned man, and 2,000 volts had been pumped through it, frying his brain, searing the flesh of his shaved head like a piece of meat on a hot grill.

"I wish I could take credit for the design," Fred offered with genuine modesty, unaware of the discomfort I was feeling, "but this was based on the medical research that was done in the latter part of the nineteenth century." He took it from me and held it up in one hand as though it were a delicate, living organism, while he pointed out its principal features with the other. Typical of Fred, he described it from the inside out, from the functional parts inside to the outer shell that holds it all together. "It consists of an inner helmet of copper screening and sponge, and an outer helmet of leather," he explained.

The copper screening was a mesh made of ordinary copper wire, such as one might use in a household electrical repair. The sponge was actually a number of pieces of ordinary sea sponge, but their irregular shape and dirty color were made ominous by the use to which they had been put. The cotton thread that held the patchwork of sponge to the screen acquired a sinister quality from its very naturalness, and from the unavoidable irregularity of the stitching which held the sponge to the mesh. The random patterns of sponge and stitching had an oddly messy, perversely natural quality which was unsettling.

"The screening is connected to the electrode," Fred demonstrated, pointing to a little bronze spike on top of the helmet. "The electrode is unscrewed, the wire is put through, and then it's tightened up again." As simple as that, and a vast improvement on the cobbled-together devices of the past, such as old football helmets converted to the deadly purpose.

While he is pleased with the results executioners have had with the design, Fred is constantly revising the helmet in small ways.

"I made several improvements on this," he said proudly. "In addition to making it larger, I use a piece of artificial sponge which I can get as a one-piece sponge. Using real sea sponge, you can never get a piece big enough, and you end up with a patchwork."

Perhaps the most thoughtful detail of his latest helmet design is the four snap fastenings to which may be attached a removable denim "face curtain." (A feature that Warden Mike Dutton of the River Bend Maximum Security Institution in Nashville, Tennessee, particularly likes is the fact that the helmet has no back or front. "In an execution," Fred told me, "it's impossible to put it on the wrong way. And you see this?" he said, holding up the denim face curtain. "No matter which way you put the helmet on, you've still got the three fasteners right there to attach the face curtain.") This small detail makes the helmet foolproof and reduces nervousness and awkwardness for everyone.

FRED'S GRANDFATHER was born in Maine, but he came down to Massachusetts to work as a machinist. Fred's design methods owe as much to the art of skilled engineering such as his grandfather did, as they do to fancy theories. Fred freely admits that most of his work is done with schoolboy math and science, supplemented by good research and the use of skilled consultants to help with various aspects of design and construction.

Fred's ability to design efficient execution hardware isn't based on any extraordinary engineering ability per se. The engineering knowledge required to build Fred's state-of-the-art electric chair is fairly commonplace. What makes Fred successful at what he does is the way he poses the problem; the essence of his electric chair design lies in what questions he asked himself, and how he asked them.

Fred's method is to turn a problem or a received assumption on its head and see how it looks from that angle. For instance, the problem in redesigning the electric chair was to think of the "comfort and dignity of the executee and the executioner" as well as to consider the engineering and medical aspects; and, where the latter was concerned, Fred came up against a problem: doctors. "The problem is they're afraid of the issue," Fred complained. "They don't really want to get involved. They freeze up."

In explaining the problem to me, Fred shouted: "Doctors save lives." He fixed me with a look that said, Figure that one out. The electric chair is, after all, the progeny of a medical mind. From the very start, doctors have been involved in electrocutions, despite the fact that the Hippocratic oath (and American Medical Association proscriptions) make their participation in executions at any level a dubious business. "Even when they have to participate," Fred mused, "even when they have to supervise, they're not operating at full capacity, because they have to think backwards. *They have to think about destroying a life rather than saving it.* They're trained to think the opposite way. It's like the difference between an engineer and a repairman. An engineer can't repair a television as fast as the repairman because the engineer thinks backwards. The engineer thinks about how it works. He'll fix it two hours after the TV repairman fixed it. But the TV repairman don't know how it works. All he knows is, he checks the voltages till he finds the problem. Two different ways of thinking. And that's the same thing here. To execute, you've got to think in one direction, to save lives, you're doing the other."

Most of the design work goes on in Fred's head. When it's time to put it on paper, he makes scale drawings with a ruler, which he gives to a draftsman who turns out the production drawings. Fred acknowledges that his draftsman and his machinist are important members of the design team. Both have made significant contributions in suggesting more economical ways to build particular components of his execution systems.

The introduction to the specification manual for Fred A. Leuchter Associates' Modular Electrocution System puts the electric chair problem in a nutshell: "The design of an electrocution system involves the consideration of a few, but very significant, requirements. Voltage, current, connections, duration and number of current applications (jolts)." At the heart of Fred's electric chair are three electrodes: one for the head, two for the ankles. "If you use one leg electrode," Fred cautioned, "and that's what most of the states do, you only half electrocute the body. You don't guarantee death. And that's why half the states have to electrocute the guy five times instead of using two jolts."

Fred's electric chair manual is an unusual document in that it never discusses the use of the apparatus in the abstract; it assumes, on every page, that a human being is strapped in, and that another human being is operating the controls. Under the heading "Requirements," Fred writes: "First, the system should contain three (3) electrodes. The head should be fitted with a tightly fitting cap containing an electrode with a saline moistened sponge. It is through this electrode that the current is introduced. Second, each ankle should be tightly fitted with an electrode, causing the current to divide and guaranteeing passage through the complete trunk of the subject's body. Use of one (1) ankle electrode (instead of two [2]) will almost always ensure a longer and more difficult electrocution. These two (2) ankle electrodes are the return path of the current. Contact should be enhanced by using saline salve or a sponge moistened with a saline solution at each of the ankle connections. It is of the utmost importance that good circuit continuity, with a minimum amount of resistance, be maintained at the electrode contacts. Further, a minimum of 2000 volts ac must be maintained, after voltage drop, to guarantee permanent disruption of the autonomic nervous system. Voltages lower than 2000 volts ac, at saturation, cannot guarantee heart death and are, thus, not adequate for electrocution, in that they may cause unnecessary trauma to the subject prior to death. Failure to adhere to these basic requirements could result in pain to the subject and failure to achieve heart death, leaving a brain dead subject in the chair."

Fred's reading of the medical literature on electrocution and his historical research led him to conclude that, "During electrocution there two (2) factors that must be considered: the conscious and the autonomic nervous systems. Voltages in excess of 1500 volts ac are generally sufficient to destroy the conscious nervous system, that which controls pain and understanding. Generally, unconsciousness occurs in 4.16 milliseconds, which is $\frac{1}{240}$ part of a second. This is twenty-four (24) times as fast as the subject's conscious nervous system can record pain. The autonomic nervous system is a little more difficult, however, and generally requires in excess of 2000 volts ac to seize the pacemaker in the subject's heart. Generally, we compute the voltage at 2000 volts ac plus 20%. After the voltage is applied and the subject's body saturates, the voltage has dropped about 10% (depending upon the resistance of the electrode contacts and that of the subject body) and this should be taken into consideration, as well. Current should be kept under six (6) amperes to minimize body damage (cooking)."

Fred has calculated that the correct voltage for electrocuting human beings is 2,640 volts AC. He arrived at this figure by assuming that an average man weighing 154 pounds (or 70 kilos) requires 2,000 volts AC to seize the heart. Fred increases that voltage by 20 percent to accommodate subjects with greater resistance, giving a subtotal of 2,400 volts AC. He then adds a further 10 percent to compensate for the voltage drop at saturation. This total of 2,600 volts at five amperes is ideal, Fred believes, because it will not cause "unsatisfactory trauma to the subject prior to death." The secret of his success, Fred told me, is that "I control the current and let the voltage do its thing."

Fred trains the prison wardens who carry out executions to administer two 2,600-volt jolts of one-minute duration, with a ten-second interval between them. In most cases where Fred's equipment is used, the condemned will be dead after the first jolt of electricity. But Fred recommends a second jolt because, "on occasion, the subject's heart will *spasm* instead of seizing, during the first application of current. This spasm is due to excessive chemical buildup (acetylcholine and sympathin) at the nerve junctions and the ten (10) second wait generally allows for dissipation of the chemicals. The second jolt will generally eliminate this problem."

"What basically happens," Fred told me, "is that the first jolt causes an adrenaline riot." While this should make the victim go into shock, the adrenaline keeps the heart beating. Allowing ten seconds for the adrenaline to dissipate ensures that the second jolt stops the heart. "Basically," said Fred, "it's a matter of speed. If all goes well, it should take just 4.16 milliseconds to lose consciousness in an electric chair."

Fred Leuchter's modular electric chair—the most advanced ever built —is made of oak. It doesn't have four legs. Instead, the back is a stout wooden frame which sits flush against the floor; the arms and seat extend from this frame, and at the front, a wooden support descends from the seat to the floor, giving it a three-legged appearance. The chair is much larger than traditional ones still in use; Fred designed it that way because today's inmates are, on average, much larger than those the electric chair was originally built to accommodate at the end of the last century. The back and arms are adjustable, and Fred thoughtfully provides a padded backrest to make the condemned man's final moments more comfortable.

Fred didn't have an example of his latest electric chair to show me, but I later went to see one at Tennessee's death row in Nashville. The warden there had sent the old one up to Boston for Fred to rebuild. Apart from the fear of it being unreliable, the warden pointed out that it was too small to accommodate most of the men on death row. Fred used some of the original oak from Tennessee's "Old Sparky" (which was made from the state's old gallows. The rest of the oak is stacked in a corner of Fred's basement). The chair I saw in Tennessee was fixed in the center of the floor of the death chamber and was cordoned off on all four sides by blue velvet ropes fixed to brass posts, as if it were an object in a museum. On the back of the Tennessee chair is a discreet brass plaque with Fred's name and address on it.

The seat is made of Plexiglas, and it is perforated so that when the victim loses control of his bowels and bladder, liquid waste will pass through the chair. It is collected by a removable drip pan positioned under the seat. This feature makes the execution team's task of removing the dead inmate from the chair less unpleasant and presents a more hygienic image to witnesses.

All electric chairs in the United States, apart from Fred's, have heavy leather straps to restrain the inmate. These can be awkward for the execution party to fasten, particularly if the inmate offers resistance. They also cause pain and discomfort to the inmate (autopsies of those who have died in the electric chair regularly show facial bruising and even laceration from the straps). When the execution is over, the execution team's job of unstrapping the dead man from the chair is often repugnant, as they have to tug and push at the body. There is always suppuration from the third-degree burns on the head and leg, and in some cases the "cooked" flesh comes away from the body when touched, Fred told me. He added in a low voice, "We teach them to handle the body in such a way that they don't make a mess."

Fred's solution to this problem was to introduce a "nonincremental restraint system"—basically, a seat belt made of aircraft nylon with a single, quick-release fastening. The harness comes down across both shoulders and up across both thighs and is clasped at the inmate's chest. This makes it easy for the executioners to position the man in the chair prior to the execution. Once he is in the harness, they have only to secure the nylon restraints at the wrists and ankles. It also makes it easier to dispose of the body after an execution. "Since everything is quick release," said Fred, "you don't have to fool with the body. It was particularly distasteful to fool with the head. The head, of course, has just one strap you loosen, and you lift the helmet off. With the quick release, you don't have to play with a strap that's got blood and materials on it. The chair has been designed with a backrest, which is adjustable. The minute you hit the release and open it, the individual slumps forward and hangs in the straps, which makes it much easier to take him out, put him in a body bag, and get him to the gurney. I can make the process as palatable as possible. It's always going to be a distasteful operation. We have to worry about the humanity of the people who have to deal with the execution."

Another unique feature of the Leuchter electric chair is integral ankle electrodes. Turned of solid brass and fabricated onto the leg stock, they are designed for simple connection to a #6 conductor, as is the helmet.

The control console of the Leuchter chair is a metal box standing around four and a half feet high and two feet across. Finished in blue enamel, with a sloping control panel at the front, it looks like a cartoon object: Across the front of the panel is printed, in large, white lettering, ELECTRIC CHAIR CONTROL. The executioners stand in front of this blue box, inside of which are the timing circuitry, computer-controlled switching circuitry, and controls. It has two key switches for circuit control (one for each executioner) and a key-controlled fail-safe switch for high-voltage output.

Fred's *Electric Chair Catalogue* also lists an option that states can purchase for testing their equipment: the Fred A. Leuchter Associates, Inc., Modular Power Supply Test Unit. "Essentially," said Fred, "it's a bank of resistors that thinks there's a person in the chair." The test unit "replaces the electric chair in the system during testing and simulates the load of the chair occupied by an executee." A human "load" is replicated by "an especially fabricated, harmonically balanced, twenty-component, high-wattage resistor package which is cooled by a quadrafan assembly having an area of some 255 square inches and an aggregate airflow of some 2320 cfm [cubic feet per minute]."

In addition to the hardware he designs, Fred offers various customer services, including "equipment certification," "certified training," and "execution support." In his catalogue, Fred states that execution team training "consists of a one day combination lecture/seminar at your facility with actual hands-on training with your equipment. This training to include all aspects of your mode of execution, including, but not limited to, the medical, technical and practical problems and procedures required for a competent execution. Additionally, there will be a discussion of the theory, design, maintenance and operation of your equipment. Resultant to this training program, Certificates will be issued to all those attending Certifying them as Execution Technicians in your mode of execution. Training and Certification is available in any of the following disciplines: Lethal Injection Technician, Electrocution Technician, Lethal Gas Technician, Hanging Technician. Training and Certification minimizes legal problems in the event of a problem during an execution. Further, it guarantees the Executee a dignified and professional execution."

The most personalized service Fred offers is an "execution support" contract. "Under the terms of this contract Fred A. Leuchter Associates, Inc. will assume the full responsibility for the technical aspects of your execution. The State need only supply the executioner and, in the event of Lethal Injection, an I.V. Technician. Fred A. Leuchter Associates, Inc. will Test and Certify all equipment as Ready, set up all equipment, supply all consumables needed for the execution (except electricity) and ensure a competent execution which will maintain the dignity of the executee, as well as, the dignity of those responsible for the execution. This requires one engineer and one technician. An Execution Support contract guarantees a smooth and competent execution for the executee and minimizes legal problems in the event of a failure during the execution."

Despite this guarantee, and the others Fred offers, his catalogue contains a disclaimer at the end of it: "Fred A. Leuchter Associates, Inc. assumes no liability for the actual or intended use of its devices or services."

I asked Fred about the cost of his various execution systems. The cheapest is the modular lethal injection system at $30,000. His preferred method of execution, the electric chair, sells for $35,000. A gallows, because it is an unusual and infrequently requested product, sells for $85,000. The most expensive execution product is a Fred Leuchter gas chamber, costing more than $200,000. Fred had created another product designed for states which either have no execution facilities in their new prisons or have not carried out an execution for many years. The Leuchter "Execution Trailer" provides a mobile execution facility including a lethal injection machine, a steel holding cell for the inmate, and separate areas for the witnesses, chaplain, prison workers, and medical personnel, at a cost of $100,000.

Of all Fred's execution products, the electric chair presents the state with the cheapest consumables bill at the end of the day. Only thirty-one cents' worth of electricity is required to electrocute someone in a Leuchter chair. The chemicals for lethal injection cost between $600 and $700, while the cyanide required for a gas chamber execution costs around $250.

I was anxious to know how profitable Fred's business had been. He told me, "The state shouldn't be over a barrel to bring in somebody that's going to haul them over the coals and charge them a small fortune for executing somebody. Executions are not something people should be making money hand over fist on. I don't make any bones about it. I don't get rich with what I do. I make a decent living. I have a twenty percent markup on my equipment, and I think that's more than fair. And I think anybody that would try to price the equipment would come back and think I was making less. I have people who when they find out what my prices are they say, 'That's all?' "

E ACH DAY during my post–Labor Day visit, I lunched with Fred and Caroline at a local Italian restaurant.

"Have I seen you on TV?" the waitress shrieked at Fred on our first visit.

Fred nodded modestly. She had, in a report on ABC's "Prime Time Live," demonstrating the gallows he'd built for Delaware. The program shows Fred putting the noose around a bag of sand of the same weight as a man, and pulling the trapdoor with a stern look on his face.

The waitress put down the menus and glasses of ice water, and hurried off.

"I think she's new here," Fred told me.

Caroline squeezed into the booth. "I *know* what I'm going to have without looking at the menu," she declared. "I have the same thing every time," she confided to me in a low voice. "It's not very adventurous, but I just love it. I'm having the veal parm with angel hair pasta."

Despite being tempted by Caroline's recommendation, I went for sausages and angel hair pasta.

"Can I have steak tips that haven't been marinated?" Fred asked the waitress.

"Sure."

"You're sure they won't be marinated?" Fred asked.

"Sure."

"I've got an ulcer," Fred explained to me. "I can't eat things that are marinated."

Fred and Caroline both drank coffee with their lunch. I ordered a glass of wine.

Over lunch, Fred made small talk and offered anecdotes about his business. "Do you remember when we took the chair down to Tennessee?" he said, looking at Caroline.

He told me the story. "We drove it down. I had it in the back of a U-Haul van. Anyway, we stopped at a Ramada Inn somewhere along the way, and there was a sign that said no trucks or vans could park in the parking lot. So, we checked in, and I said to the lady behind the desk that I needed to keep an eye on the van, and I'd like to park just under the window of our room so I could see it. She said it wasn't allowed. So I told her what was in the van. She looked at me and said that her daughter had been raped a few weeks ago, and so she made an exception, and let me park the van under my window."

Fred told me more about the Tennessee chair. "The wood goes back to their original gallows. After they took the gallows down, they made their first electric chair with the oak. Then, they sent me the old chair, and I used some of the wood in the one I made for them. The problem is, we couldn't match the new oak with the old oak. The other oak had darkened so much that we had to end up putting epoxy paint on it. Of course, it'll last forever, but it's not quite as sexy looking as natural wood. But they're keeping their tradition alive and well in Tennessee."

While we were eating, I asked Fred whether he thought any of the execution methods, as carried out using his equipment, were painful to the person being executed.

"There's no way for sure of knowing whether anything hurts," he said, suggesting, *Here's the bottom line.*

He went on: "We certainly try to be human beings. And everything we know indicates that electrocution is painless if you do it right. Everything we know indicates that hanging is painful for one brief instant. Gas is not painful, but it has a tendency to be difficult, because the individual tends to hold his breath. We also know that lethal injection is not painful. We can pretty much determine what's painful emotionally or painful physically. There are probably two areas of pain. Looking at the ceiling while stretched out on a gurney waiting for a lethal injection is painful emotionally."

"Do you think about what goes through a person's mind when they're taken in to be executed?" I asked.

Fred lit a cigarette and ordered more coffee. "Tradition shows us that there is very little objection. Most of these people go like lambs to the slaughter. The bottom line is, if you're going to be executed in an hour, or ten minutes, you know you're going to be executed. And if you think you've got a shot, you're going to fight. The problem is, most people know they haven't got a shot. I would think most people would be sick. I think I would be sick to my stomach. I don't know about you, but I think if I was waiting to be executed, I'd want an Alka-Seltzer." He raised his hands in despair and bellowed: "*So give the guy an Alka-Seltzer!* But they don't." He thought again. "I'd probably want a shot of something. But they don't do that. You're not supposed to have alcohol in the prison, so they can't give it to the guy. *Come on . . .*" Fred groaned rhetorically.

"What about you?" I asked Fred. "If you were going to be executed, and you had a choice of method, which would it be?"

Fred didn't hesitate. "I would prefer to be electrocuted as opposed to lethal injection."

"Why?"

"Because I'd rather deal with three minutes than deal with five. With the firing squad, the man is strapped into a chair and he's wearing a target over his heart. The problem is that the average police officer in the United States is a poor shot. Corrections officers are a step below them. So, if you have another alternative, don't let them shoot you. And shooting is painful. Even the best way to do it, it's going to hurt. With electrocution, I think it's just a cessation of feeling."

The waitress brought the coffee. Her eyes widened at the conversation we were having, and she scurried away.

I asked Fred whether he had ever witnessed an execution.

"No. It's not necessary for what I do. If I do see one as part of my job . . . it's not something I'm sitting on the edge of my chair waiting for. It's distasteful. It may go with the territory, but it's still distasteful."

"How do you think you'd react?"

"There's going to be a loss of the clinical detachment. That I don't look forward to. My resolution would grow even more if I had to witness it. I've been lucky. I didn't have to watch them burn Tafero to death."

JESSIE TAFERO's execution was probably the most gruesome in U.S. history. It led to a move to stop executions in Florida when Fred became involved as an expert witness against the state. It was a decision which was to have disastrous consequences for Fred A. Leuchter Associates, Inc.

Tafero was convicted of the 1976 shooting deaths of Florida highway patrol trooper Phillip Black and Donald Irwin, an Ontario police officer and friend of Black's who was visiting Florida. Tafero was executed at Florida State Prison on May 4, 1990, the 219th person to die in the Florida chair since capital punishment began there in 1924.

The Florida press is no stranger to sensationalism, but the headlines which appeared the day after Tafero's execution were no exaggeration: "Florida Execution Becomes Gruesome Display" (*St. Petersburg Times*); "Tafero Meets Grisly Fate in Chair" (the *Gainesville Sun*); "Smoke, Flames Erupt as Killer is Executed" (the *Orlando Sentinel*); "3 Jolts Used to Execute Killer: Flames and Smoke Spew from Face Mask as Policeman's Slayer Sits in the Chair" (the *Miami Herald*).

Tafero's execution was the third that staff writer Bruce Ritchie had covered for the *Florida Times-Union*. He wrote, "I don't know if I want to watch another."

Ritchie reported: "Tafero's body did not just stiffen upright when the electricity was applied at 7:06 A.M., it seemed to reel backward. Smoke rose from the inmate's head, not his leg. Within seconds, small sparks or flames appeared from the right side of the shroud that hid his face. The electrical current ended quickly—quicker than usual, it seemed—and the flame disappeared. 'Had one minute passed already?' I thought to myself. I looked at the clock, but it seemed that less than 30 seconds had elapsed. I looked to [prison superintendent Tom] Barton to see what he would do. Barton did nothing except stare at Tafero, then past him. He appeared to be glaring in consternation in the direction of Ronald Thornton, prison maintenance chief. Thornton was wearing rubber electrician's gloves. He had applied the skullcap to Tafero's head. Then I looked to Lt. Don Davis, who had remained on the telephone to the Governor's Office. Davis was speaking into the receiver. Then he said something to Barton that I couldn't hear. There was the humming again, and Tafero's body reeled backward again. The clock on the wall showed 7:08 A.M. This time, 3-inch flames shot from the left side of the facial shroud, and there was more smoke. Quickly, the current ended, perhaps in about 20 seconds this time. Again the body slowly came to rest. After the pause, there was the heartbeat again. Another deep inhale and then an exhale. Another inhale and an exhale. Tafero's left hand was clenched into a fist except for the little finger, which was straight. But the hand had the same ashen color I had seen in the two inmates whose executions I had witnessed. I looked to Barton and saw a face that had lost its tightness and seemed to sag. Duty and frustration seemed replaced by pain and uncertainty, but he gazed straight ahead. Barton said something to Thornton, and Thornton spoke back. Then Barton paused, and he swallowed. Davis spoke again into the telephone, listened, and then turned to Barton and said something. Barton turned and nodded to the executioner in the booth behind him. There was the hum again, and the body reeled again. Five-inch flames quickly burned from the left side of the shroud, and smaller ones burned to the right. It was 7:10 A.M. The hum was gone again, perhaps in 30 seconds. But the body did not relax this time. The little finger on the left hand was now part of the fist. There was no breathing or visible heartbeat. After a pause, one prison doctor, then another, checked for the inmate's pulse and heartbeat. At 7:13 A.M., Frank Kilgo, the prison's chief health officer, spoke in Barton's direction. Then Davis walked across the room, lifted a microphone which was wired to the witness booth, and said, 'The sentence of Jessie Tafero has been carried out at 7:13 A.M.' "

The Department of Corrections nominated Bob McMaster to act as spokesman in the aftermath of the Tafero execution. He told reporters, "The execution was carried out. That's what is the important priority." In response to *Gainesville Sun* reporter Cynthia Barnett's question as to why Tafero continued to breathe after the first and second jolts of electricity, McMaster said, "In the doctor's opinion, Mr. Tafero was dead within a second or two. In his opinion, there can be involuntary respiration." Barnett reported that "McMaster would not say afterward why Tafero had to be jolted with electricity three times if doctors believed he had died within seconds." She also reported that "Superintendent Barton said he did not believe an investigation was necessary, and he would not say whether he thought what took place in the death chamber Tuesday morning was unusual. 'I won't discuss my feelings with you under any circumstances,' he said. 'We got the wrong type sponge in the headpiece and we went into manual, that's it—we'll just try to get the right, proper equipment next time.' "

In the aftermath of the Tafero execution, the secretary of the Florida Department of Corrections, Richard Dugger, sent David Brierton, a former superintendent of Florida State Prison, to "review the circumstances of the execution." In his report to Secretary Dugger on May 8, 1990, Brierton wrote that "Two problems emerged as central to this set of circumstances: 1) What could have caused the flame and smoke? 2) What effect did it have on the inmate being executed?"

The report infuriated Fred Leuchter, who told me: "The Department of Corrections committed incest by investigating itself and then determined that Jessie Tafero didn't hurt. And I think that Dugger has no concept at all about how the equipment works except for pushing the button. He's not even qualified to make a determination of whether or not it hurt."

Brierton's report is based on sworn affidavits from the execution team led by Superintendent Tom Barton. Most of the affidavits are brief, tight-lipped statements which are short on information and long on self-congratulation. The affidavit of Rankin L. Brown, a regional director for the Department of Corrections, is less than two hundred words long and concludes with the information: "It should be noted that during these unusual circumstances, Superintendent Barton and his staff remained calm and exhibited the highest degree of professionalism. All are to be commended for their performance during this highly stressful period." C. G. Strickland, superintendent of facilities in Region II of the Department of Corrections, stated that "Superintendent Barton and his staff should be commended."

A significant feature of the affidavits sworn by prison staff and officials on May 7 is the variation in accounts given of the nature of the flames which erupted from Tafero's head. Superintendent Tom Barton saw flames "approximately two and one-half to three and one-half inches high," and so did other prison personnel. But Gary McLain, the deputy inspector general of the Florida Department of Corrections, saw twelve-inch flames. He also saw Tafero breathing after the application of the first and second jolts of electricity. And he noticed that the head electrode appeared not to be tightly fastened to Tafero's head. "As the electric current was flowing," McLain swore in a terse and carefully worded statement, "a blue-orange flame appeared from both sides of the mask. It extended approximately twelve inches on both sides. When the power stopped, the flames disappeared. I observed what appeared to be deep breaths taken by Tafero and, after a few seconds, another charge was given. When the power was started again, the flames reappeared. I observed movement by the right index finger of Tafero and, after the power stopped, the flames disappeared. Once again, I observed what appeared to be a couple of deep breaths from Tafero. The power was administered the third time and, once again, the appearance of the flames. When the power ended, so did the flames. A cloud of smoke filled the upper space of the chamber after each power surge. The head attachment appeared to be leaning slightly to the inmate's left. The two medical staff checked for pulse and at 7:13 A.M., Tafero was pronounced dead. We were ordered to depart the Execution Witness Room."

The affidavit of Al Martin, the assistant maintenance superintendent, gives an unusual firsthand account of conducting an execution as a routine part of prison life. "On May 4, 1990 at approximately 7:02 A.M. while working the Death Chamber, proceeding with the execution as scheduled, I received an indication from Mr. Barton to close my electric breaker. I then told the executioner to close his electric breaker. When the executioner completed the circuit, I noticed unusual fire and smoke coming from the inmate's headpiece. After several seconds, I received an indication to open the electrical breaker to stop the electrical flow. At this time, I noticed the body move as if to be gasping for air. After several seconds, I received the indication to close the breaker the second time, which I did. Again, I noticed the unusual fire and smoke coming from the headpiece. After several seconds, I received an indication to stop the electricity. After several seconds, I received the third indication to close the breaker and, again, the fire and smoke came from the headpiece. After several seconds, I received the indication to stop the electrical flow. The inmate was pronounced dead and, after the visitors left the area, I realized we were using the new sponge I installed in the headpiece and it was not conducting electricity as the old ones had in the past. This new sponge was installed because the older ones were breaking at the lead joint and the string was deteriorating. The sponge was purchased from one of the local stores because of its size to be able to cover the wire mesh.''

It would appear that prison officials had decided to blame the sponge, since Martin (who had once asked his former assistant, Robin Adair, how to wire up a 110-volt light in his house) swore that *after the execution, while the witnesses were leaving,* he noticed that the new sponge wasn't conducting electricity.

The sponge was nominated as the cause of the malfunction. But what of the second question that Brierton's inquiry set itself: "What effect did it have on the inmate being executed?" Dr. Frank Kilgo, Florida State Prison's medical executive director, was a veteran of six executions and dozens of death warrants that received last-minute stays. His affidavit offers a rare insight into execution protocol in Florida, a state that is notoriously secretive about its capital-punishment procedures. "With each warrant that has entered the final week," Kilgo says, "there has been a preparatory walkthrough within twenty-four (24) hours of the scheduled execution. Such walkthroughs are serious and decorously directed exercises attended by critical attention to every detail encompassed. Each exercise is routinely critiqued at conclusion and repeated, as may be necessary, until optimum performance by all involved is effected. In the Death Chamber, only the electrocutioner [*sic*], the current and the actual condemned are missing. On May 3, 1990 at 3:30 p.m., as scheduled, a step-by-step walkthrough was conducted in preparation for the following morning's proceedings. From inception to completion, not one flaw was recognized."

However, when the switch was thrown on Jessie Tafero, Kilgo noticed that the procedure had gone wrong from the start. "The accompanying first sounds were different. The current was interrupted and spasmodic respiratory sounds were audible. A second application of current was directed and again produced unfamiliar sounds. Electrical arc light issued from the headplate region and smoke was produced. The current was interrupted and spasmodic respiratory sounds produced oral and nasal fluid gurgling. A third current application followed with further arc phenomena and smoke. Upon current cessation, the chamber was silent." Though he offers no reasons for his conclusion, Kilgo says, "It is my considered opinion that with the initial surge of the electrical energy applied, conscious mental awareness and all sensate appreciation is interdicted instantaneously." It is a cannily worded statement, for Dr. Kilgo does not say that Tafero lost consciousness and felt no pain; he is stating that, in general, people who are executed by electrocution lose consciousness rapidly.

Dr. Kilgo concludes his medical opinion with a paean to the execution team which is faintly reminiscent of *The Charge of the Light Brigade*: "It is further my opinion that a persevering group of Correctional public servants attended publically [*sic*] delegated responsibility with uncommon professional demeanor in the face of unexpected and unexperienced circumstances of adversity. There was understandable human consternation, but there was no collapse. There was understandable human perplexity, but there was no panic. What was necessary was done. What was intended was accomplished." In a brief acknowledgment of the fact that Tafero's execution was unusual, Kilgo concludes his affidavit: "Under given circumstances that surfaced, the results were far less than aesthetically attractive. But with rare serene exceptions, after forty-odd years of experience, it is held that most deaths are without aesthetic attractiveness, regardless of causation."

Brierton wrote in his report to Dugger that "The next step was to review those variables which were present at the actual execution but not intrinsic to the circuitry itself. The most obvious was the sponges used during the execution." The finger is pointed at Al Martin, the assistant maintenance supervisor. Brierton writes: "Upon examination, it becomes quite clear that the newly acquired sponge is synthetic and not the natural 'elephant ear' variety that has been historically used. Mr. Martin freely admits in the interview that at the time he (Martin) elected to change the sponge after a conversation with his supervisor but no thought was given to acquiring a natural sponge. Mr. Martin went to a local store in Starke and purchased a sponge which proved to be of synthetic composition."

Having deduced that the sponge was at fault, Brierton tested the hypothesis by subjecting a piece of the sponge used in the head electrode during the Tafero execution to a test. "It was important to demonstrate whether the newly acquired sponge would produce the amount of smoke that was present on May 4, so a piece of sponge was cut from the headpiece insert which had been used during the execution. This piece was subjected to 120 volts of heat [*sic*] by placing it in a common household toaster. It took only five seconds to begin smoking and produced a noxious odor which became more intense as the sponge burned. Although the sponge was only in the toaster for ten seconds, it produced a large amount of smoke and reduced in size by approximately two-thirds. *It is reasonable to conclude that* [sic] *problem was due to human error by replacing the natural sponge with a synthetic sponge*" (Brierton's italics).

As for the effect of the bungled execution on Jessie Tafero, Brierton concludes that "Dr. Kilgo has given an affidavit which indicates that, in his professional opinion, 'what appeared to be spasmodic respiratory activity leaves no connotation that life existed.' "

On the day that Brierton's report arrived, Dugger wrote to Governor Bob Martinez that, "Essentially, this execution was procedurally and mechanically routine but flawed by an inadvertent human error that served to create an atypical event." He noted that "involuntary muscle movement stimulated by the electrical current was reported by some observers as signs of life," and that "these unfortunate circumstances, coupled with the natural anxiety of some witnesses, resulted in rather bizarre visual accounts of the execution." In conclusion, Dugger told the governor that, if anything, Tafero took *less* time to die than most other inmates who had met their fate in the Florida chair: "The autopsy report and the attending physician's account reflect instant death as normally occurs under more routine circumstances experienced in past executions. This is substantiated by the first application of current recorded as beginning at 7:06 A.M. and pronouncement of death at 7:13 A.M., a seven-minute total time frame. This is actually less time than has been taken in most previous executions. I and the Florida State Prison staff deeply regret the concern and anxiety arising from this incident, but the process of legal execution in Florida should not be abated by this error that is readily identifiable and now corrected."

*   *   *

When Fred Leuchter talks about the Tafero execution, he uses it as a case in point to explain the reason why he is in the execution business: "The reason I became involved in execution hardware is to eliminate pain and suffering all around, for all concerned. These inmates have the *right* to be executed with competent equipment."

In pursuit of this goal, Fred has not only supplied states with hardware he guarantees will result in a "competent execution," he has also acted as an expert witness for condemned inmates who appeal against their death sentence on the grounds that the state's execution equipment is likely to malfunction, resulting in a cruel and unusual punishment. Throughout the 1980s, Fred's rate for acting as an expert witness was five hundred dollars a day plus expenses.

In June 1990, Fred was approached by Florida's Office of Capital Collateral to assist in the appeal of Judy Buenoano, one of forty women on death row in America. Buenoano was scheduled to die in the electric chair on June 21. She filed an emergency motion in the Ninth Circuit Court to vacate judgment and seek a stay of execution. Part of her claim was that the Tafero debacle proved that *any* execution in Florida using its current equipment would be unconstitutional, violating the Eighth and Fourteenth amendments. Buenoano wanted Fred to supply expert testimony that the Florida electric chair did not function properly, and that the Florida authorities were incompetent to conduct an execution.

From the time that Fred Leuchter founded American Engineering, Inc., Florida had been high on its list of potential clients. After Texas and

California, Florida ranks third in the death row league table, with more than three hundred people currently awaiting execution. Only Texas has executed more people than Florida. Since 1977, the electric chair at Raiford Prison, near Starke, has been used twenty-seven times. It wasn't only the frequency with which the Florida chair was used that made Fred think of it as a prime target for a contract: It was the number of times it had malfunctioned.

At the end of 1986, Fred was contacted by Thomas Barton, superintendent of Florida State Prison, and Robin Adair, who worked at the prison as electrical supervisor during 1986–87. In an affidavit sworn on June 13, 1990, in connection with the defense of Judy Buenoano, Fred said that "Mr. Adair told me that the leg electrode they were using in the electric chair in Florida had proved defective on their last execution and that the condition of the head electrode was questionable. He asked me to submit a bid for a new leg electrode and headpiece for the electric chair house at Florida State Prison."

On December 11, 1986, Robin Adair asked Fred to quote for a new leg stock and helmet for Florida's electric chair. On December 12, Fred submitted a quotation of $3,429. This including a leg stock at $2,200, a helmet at $1,200, plus $29 shipping charges. Fred also sent a letter in which he "explained to Mr. Adair that in my expertise I did not believe that a single leg electrode was capable of properly conducting the electricity during an execution, and that the system I had designed included two leg electrodes. The system in place at Florida State Prison simply was not functioning properly."

In his affidavit of June 13, 1990, Fred Leuchter continued the narrative of events in Florida. "Mr. Adair responded that my price quote was too high, and that he and Mr. Barton wanted me to fabricate a leg electrode from an old army boot and a copper strip. At this juncture it became apparent to me that the Department of Corrections was not competent to design electric chair components and no one there seemed to fully apprehend the principles involved. Explaining that an electrode fabricated from an old army boot was inadequate for a competent execution I declined further participation in these efforts." Fred reported that "Mr. Adair later told me that he had fabricated his own army boot electrode and that it had worked on the next executee."

Robin Adair also prepared an affidavit for the Buenoano appeal. He explained that his duties "encompassed all electrical systems and the maintenance of those systems within the prison, including the electrical generating and transmission devices associated with the electric chair." His affidavit came as a shock to the secretive Florida authorities, as it revealed a number of peculiar execution practices. "During my employment at Florida State Prison," Adair wrote, "I participated in numerous 'walkthroughs,' tests of the electric chair which were conducted in anticipation of imminent executions. As a result, I became intimately familiar with both the procedural aspects and the electrical hardware utilized in executions at Florida State Prison. In addition, I am also familiar with the electrical training and education of numerous employees of Florida State Prison who are currently involved in the maintenance and operation of the electric chair, including Mr. Al Martin, the current Assistant Maintenance Supervisor."

Adair stated: "Much to my disbelief, I found that the prison did not have —nor have they ever employed to my knowledge—a licensed electrician at the prison. I soon found out that I, by virtue of my completion of basic and advanced electrical courses and prior on the job experience, along with several of the prisoner helpers, were the only individuals at Florida State Prison with any comprehension of electrical principals [*sic*], wiring and circuitry."

Adair criticized prison maintenance staff for their lack of expertise in electrical engineering. "It was my experience during my employment that Mr. Martin was completely ignorant of the most rudimentary principles of electricity and secured his position as head of the power plant at the prison through political patronage within the Department of Corrections. Mr. Martin's incompetence with respect to the principles of electricity were amply demonstrated on several occasions. I distinctly recall Mr. Martin bringing me a common 110 volt outdoor light explaining that he had tried to install the light in his home but could not make the light work and asked me to explain how he should go about wiring it. I simply could not believe that this man, who could not even wire a 110 volt light, was in charge of the electrical generating plant at Florida State Prison."

Perhaps the strangest revelation in Robin Adair's affidavit is a description of how Florida tests its electric chair prior to an execution. "The chair is tested prior to an execution by filling a tub with saline solution and placing the wires with lugs crimped on into the tub and administering current. The saline solution is supposed to simulate the resistance of the prisoner's body; it is the amount of salt added to the water during the test which determines the resistance. Based on the resistance encountered in the bucket, the control panel is then adjusted by two dials which control the amount of voltage and amperage so that during the execution 2400 volts at eight amps is administered to the prisoner." The problem with the salt-water test, Adair explained, is that unless you can accurately measure the degree of salinity in the water, you have no way of knowing how much resistance it has created. The whole point of determining the amount of resistance is so that the voltage and current can be calibrated.

Adair described how "the first time that Mr. Martin attempted to conduct a saline solution test he tripped out one of the two main breaker boxes in the death chamber by creating a short circuit. Mr. Martin and Maintenance Supervisor Mr. Ron Thornton then looked to me and said we had to fix the chair immediately as the chair was not working. After contacting the only individual who had been trained by the chair's manufacturer, who was not working at Florida State Prison, and who has since retired, I reset the breaker, threw out the water Martin had used, got new water, put in the salt and conducted the test without any problems."

Adair complained of "the prison's unwillingness to make any expenditure of funds to obtain professionally made components for the electric chair or to conduct more than limited maintenance and inspection on the chair." He told how "Mr. Leuchter advised me in 1986 that two leg electrodes should be utilized to obtain a uniform passage of current through the body. I informed Maintenance Supervisor Mr. Ron Thornton and the Assistant Maintenance Supervisor of the shortcomings in using only one electrode and also provided them with the price quotes and diagrams for purchasing these components manufactured by Mr. Leuchter. I was later told that the prison was unwilling to pay that amount to purchase professionally constructed components specifically designed for electrocutions and was instructed by my superior officer to fabricate an electrode from materials available at the prison. Accordingly, I obtained a boot and by cutting off the lower portion of the boot and then using aluminum rivets, riveted lead, copper, shim stock, and copper screen (some of these materials were designed to be used as roofing materials) to the interior of the boot, and finally adding a stainless steel bolt from a hardware store to attach the leg electrode to, I fabricated the homemade leg electrode currently being used in executions at Florida State Prison. I should add that I did not use the original electrode provided by the manufacturer of the chair as a model for the design I was instructed to build, but rather copied another homemade electrode that had previously been made at the prison. I simply could not understand why the prison was not willing to make any expenditure to see that human beings were properly executed."

After showing me the affidavit, Fred told me that Robin Adair had been "uncomfortable with what he had wrought."

"What happened to him?" I asked.

"He left the department and went to work on the outside. He subsequently testified against the Department of Corrections, and at the trial I found out something that I was totally unaware of; that the reason why the Department of Corrections and the prison didn't buy the electrodes was because they decided to spend the two or three thousand dollars that it would have cost for the helmet and the leg stock on painting and remodeling the warden's personal house. That's true, that was testimony that was given by the electrician. He's now no longer the warden, he's the secretary of the Department of Corrections. Richard Dugger."

Fred was angered by what he saw as the penny-pinching ways of the Florida authorities. And he was astonished at their use of the "saltwater test." One of the things he had learned from his research into the history of execution technology is that, in the early part of the 1890s, Thomas Edison came up with an idea to improve the electric chair. Rather than place electrodes on the head and leg of the condemned man, Edison had him strapped into a chair with his hands plunged into vats of salt water on either side of the chair. The current was then passed through the salt water and the inmate's body. The Edison procedure was tried on Charles McElvaine on February 8, 1892, in New York's Sing Sing prison, with horrible results. "McElvaine's torture to death in New York is abundant proof that you can't use salt water," Fred told me. "That's documented."

The problem wasn't that the Florida electric chair didn't *work*. It works well enough, in the sense that no one comes out of it alive. Fred's point was that while Florida may have the right, under state law and the Constitution of the United States, to execute people, they don't have the right to torture them to death. In searching for evidence that electrocution is painful when improperly administered, Fred began to study autopsy reports of inmates executed in Florida.

"Some states do not routinely perform autopsies on executed inmates," Fred explained. "But Florida does. And you ought to see the autopsies that I get from Florida. 'Most probable cause of death is electrocution,' " he spat in disgust. "I mean, *most probable?* Give me a break. They open him up, they look at the brain, they take all the organs out and put 'em in a bag. Why cut the guy open for nothing, unless there's a problem?"

Fred was genuinely angry. When he calmed down, he told me: "If it's determined that we want a watchdog capability, then maybe we should autopsy everybody and look for the necessary things that indicated there was pain."

"How would you know if there was pain?" I asked. "When the only person you could ask is dead?"

Fred got up and walked over to the low filing cabinet next to his desk. He pulled out a number of manila files and stacked them on the coffee table.

"I hope you have a strong stomach," he said. He began to deal out a pile of glossy, stomach-churning photographs showing close-ups of the heads and legs of men who had died in Florida's electric chair: Ted Bundy, Daniel Thomas, David Funchess, Ronald Straight, Beauford White, Willie Darden, Jeffrey Daugherty, Aubrey Adams.

"When you conduct a competent electrocution," Fred reminded me, "there should be minimal trauma to the body."

Each of the head photographs that I shuffled through showed one obvious trauma: In each case, the coroner had cut the top of the head open from side to side to remove the brain, and then had sewn the two halves back together in a haphazard way. I tried to ignore that and focus on what Fred was pointing out to me: the area of burnt flesh on the top of the head, caused by defective electrodes and incorrect voltage and current.

I studied the photograph of Ted Bundy's head in conjunction with the coroner's report. The "burn ring," as the coroner called it—a third-degree burn caused by the head electrode—had cross-sectional diameters of 6.5 inches by 5.5 inches. It virtually covered the entire head. The burn was so severe that the flesh had been cooked away to reveal the bone of the skull. The burn on Bundy's right leg, where Robin Adair's boot electrode had been strapped on, measured 7 inches by 8 inches.

The other photos were more or less the same. I read through the neatly typed three-page reports which detailed the size and weight of the executed men's organs, and I looked at the line drawings of their bodies on which were marked the burns as well as bruises from the strap which holds the head electrode in place. It seemed an ultimate invasion of privacy. The documents had a macabre fascination. They gave almost no clue to the person they referred to; they were mainly concerned with the results of the actions of others. The only indication of the executed man as a living, acting being was to be gleaned from the comprehensive toxological studies attached to each autopsy, in which the dead man's body was tested for the presence of illegal drugs. Daniel Thomas went to the chair with .032 gm/dl alcohol in his blood; Ronald Straight's urine showed he was using the amphetamine orphenadrine; Willie Darden had smoked marijuana before his execution.

I put the reports down and ask Fred how they could be read in such a way as to determine whether or not the execution was painful.

He responds with a question. "What's the thing that happens in all forms of execution—hanging, electrocution, lethal injection?"

"You lose . . ."

"The man's bowels open," Fred says for me, nodding at me, glad that I'm following his line of thought.

The grandfather clock seems to tick very loudly in the oppressive, humid air of the small room. The ashtray in front of us has butts from two packs of cigarettes. Caroline is sitting at the kitchen table, and I can hear the muted voice of the presenter on the Weather Channel, discussing the continuing warm weather.

"Okay," Fred continues. "If the bowels don't open immediately, that means the executee is trying to control his bowels. He's still alive. And he's hurting."

I nod in understanding.

"Look at Ted Bundy's autopsy and tell me how much urine he had in his bladder."

I search through the pages and find the information near the end, sandwiched between reports on "renal vessels" and "prostate." I read out, "Urinary bladder contains twelve ounces of straw-colored urine."

"Either an execution is good, or it's bad," Fred tells me. "There's no in-between."

Fred lights another Marlboro Light and pushes his lighter in front of my old-fashioned Marlboro regular.

"According to all reports," he continues, "Ted Bundy's execution was flawless. But there's no way that anybody's ever going to convince me that Bundy didn't hurt."

"The urine proves that?"

"It doesn't one hundred percent guarantee that there was pain, but there's no other explanation for it. And it would tell us that we should look for problems with the equipment. I think that every one of these people that are executed, that is a key thing that they should look for. There's nothing else that it could mean. And if the bladder's full—and you don't have to autopsy them to do this. You could catheterize them. I'm not advocating that you mutilate people's bodies, and I think that the state of Florida does it as a matter of course and they do it to everybody, whether they want it or not; I think, basically, just for the sake of autopsying people. And there's a lot of that done. But the consideration here is that it may have come back to bite Florida in the ass. It did come back to bite Florida in the ass in the terms of the photos that were taken and the description of the burning."

But the executions of Jessie Tafero or Ted Bundy hadn't really come back to bite Florida in the ass. In the case of Ted Bundy, his crimes had so outraged America—including other people on death row, many of whom have said to me, "If anyone deserved to fry, he did"—that no one was going to take notice of an argument that electrocution hurt, because a very large number of people would simply have responded, *Good.*

If anyone ended up getting bitten in the ass by the Tafero execution, it was Fred Leuchter. By testifying against Florida in the Buenoano appeal, he invited the wrath of other capital punishment states, which would eventually cancel their contracts with him.

A month before the Buenoano appeal came to court, Fred appeared on ABC's "Prime Time Live," criticizing the Florida authorities. He was shown photographs of the sponge which the Florida Department of Corrections had determined was the cause of Tafero's botched execution, and he challenged their conclusion: "The burning that we have on sponge number two, at least as far as I'm able to tell from the photographs, is consistent with the type of burning that we would get from a broken or defective electrode and that would indicate that it was not the sponge. There's a good possibility that this will happen again in the future. Maybe not on the next one, but on a subsequent execution."

The Florida Office of Capital Collateral, which was conducting the Buenoano appeal, wrote to Florida State Prison superintendent Barton asking to examine the electric chair. On May 21, 1990, Barton wrote: "This request is denied. This writer stands by the report released by the Department of Corrections and will not entertain further requests of this nature." Undeterred, Buenoano's lawyers sought to challenge the Tafero report and built their argument from the available evidence: journalists' eyewitness reports, prison employees' affidavits, and expert testimony from Fred and other witnesses. These included public defender Susan Cary and forensic expert Dr. Robert Kirschner, the deputy chief medical examiner of Cook County in Illinois.

The Department of Corrections report accepted Dr. Kilgo's statement that "in most procedural physical assessment, the areas of dermal and right calf burns were of no greater extent or intensity than that observed in prior experiences. There was no evidence of flame charring of any portion of the head." However, Susan Cary, who was with Tafero up until seven hours before his execution, later examined his body at Chestnut's Funeral Home in Gainesville. She found evidence which contradicted Dr. Kilgo's assessment. In her affidavit, Cary said: "I have seen the bodies of three other inmates executed by officials at Florida State Prison. I saw them at approximately the same length of time after they were executed as I saw Mr. Tafero's body. None of the other bodies I saw before had the severe burning and scorching and damage to the head as did Mr. Tafero's." The burning of Tafero's head was so severe, Cary noted, that "the autopsy incision line was stitched but the skin was approximately ¾ inch apart in a large area. I asked the funeral director if he would be closing that wound during his final preparation of the body for burial and he told me that he could not because the skin was so badly burned that the thread would just tear through it and it would not stretch to its original shape. Mr. Chestnut has prepared the bodies of several persons executed in Florida and he said that the deceased's skin had never been so burned that he had been unable to close the autopsy incision."

Dr. Kirschner, who has a special expertise in the documentation of torture and human rights abuses, reviewed the available evidence and concluded, "within a reasonable degree of medical and scientific certainty," that "Mr. Tafero was not dead until the third application of electricity." He also stated that "It is not possible to say that Mr. Tafero was 'unconscious' after the first and second applications of electricity. Furthermore, it is medically and scientifically irresponsible to reach and articulate such a conclusion based on the observed reactions of Mr. Tafero during the execution. Indeed, it is not unlikely that he was conscious after the first, or first and second, applications of current."

Dr. Kirschner believed that "Mr. Tafero did not receive the prescribed lethal dose of two thousand (2000) volts of electricity that was reportedly applied," and that "the failure to administer the requisite voltage combined with the other physiological reactions noted by observers of the execution raises the substantial possibility that Mr. Tafero experienced conscious pain and suffering during the execution." He criticized Secretary Dugger's letter to Governor Martinez, in which Dugger claimed "the autopsy report and attending physician's account reflect instant death." Kirschner wrote, "I find no such statement in either the autopsy report or the affidavit of the attending physician, Dr. Kilgo. The autopsy cannot possibly determine how rapidly unconsciousness or death occurred in this case."

Dr. Kirschner's view was based partly on Fred's analysis of what had happened: that flames which erupted from Tafero's head were proof that a defective head electrode created a high resistance connection. Not only was Tafero set alight, but because of the resistance created by a defective electrode, the current that was repeatedly passed through his body dropped to as low as 90 or 100 volts—insufficient to cause death, but enough to cause unnecessary pain.

On June 20, 1990, Buenoano's petition to the Florida Supreme Court was denied by four to three, in a judgment which concluded that "death by electrocution is not cruel and unusual punishment, and one malfunction is not sufficient to justify a judicial inquiry into the Department of Corrections' competence."

Two judges dissented in the strongest terms. Judge Barkett wrote that "Judy Buenoano has made a simple constitutional claim: The electric chair is not working properly." Yet the decision in this "simple" matter was for him historic in that, as he wrote, "To my knowledge this is the first time any court has ever held that it is the executive branch that decides, without question or appeal, a constitutional claim of cruel or unusual punishment. Interpreting the Constitution is a *judicial function*." In Barkett's view, the Department of Corrections had usurped the role of the court.

Barkett concluded his dissenting remarks with a scathing condemnation of the majority opinion: "Although relief is foreclosed to Buenoano, according to the majority, she can die taking comfort in knowing that her death may contribute to some other person's relief if her execution, and perhaps countless others, prove to be as horrible as Tafero's. Only then, according to the majority, will there have been a sufficient number of malfunctions to justify a judicial inquiry. This is a bizarre twist to death penalty jurisprudence. It is even more bizarre when one considers the pragmatic implications here. The state conceded at oral argument that it has spent more time and money disputing Buenoano's claims in court than it would have spent simply by replacing the alleged malfunctioning electrode. The humane thing to do, not to mention the more economical and efficient thing to do, would have been simply to replace the electrode that Buenoano's experts say malfunctioned. That would have caused no delay in the administration of the penalty, contrary to the delay caused by litigating this simple claim. I guess this is too easy a solution."

Judge Kogan concurred with Judge Barkett, and added some remarks of his own. He was particularly critical of the "toaster test" that the authorities performed on the artificial sponge used in the Tafero execution. Pointing out the obvious scientific fact that voltage is a measure of electromotive force and that temperature is a measure of heat, and that "electricity and heat are not the same thing," he also made an appeal to common sense on the grounds that the sponge used to execute Tafero was soaked in a saline solution, whereas the sponge placed in the toaster was dry. Further, he questioned whether the sponge used in the toaster test was actually a piece of the sponge used to execute Tafero. "In fact," Kogan wrote, "DOC [Department of Corrections] presents this Court with a paradox. DOC asks us to believe that *120 volts* caused the sponge to shrink by two-thirds in a mere ten seconds, but that three separate *2,000-volt* surges over a six- to seven-minute period had two inconsistent results: (1) The sponge in the skull cap burst into profuse flames that literally danced around the head of Tafero during all three jolts of electricity; and yet (2) the sponge remained sufficiently intact that a piece could be removed for testing. Indeed, the fact that the sponge reduced its volume by two-thirds after being placed in the kitchen toaster for ten seconds indicates not only that the sponge survived the electrical jolts, but that portions of it had not even *melted* to any significant extent. Otherwise, the sponge already would have been reduced in size *prior to* being placed in the kitchen toaster. Thus, I find it difficult to believe that the sponge was the only, or even the primary, reason for the flames that burst from Tafero's head on May 4. The state's own version of the facts is illogical and contrary to scientific principles.''

Having studied photographs of Tafero's body, and having considered Fred Leuchter's testimony, Judge Kogan found that Buenoano's arguments "make scientific sense." He wrote, "Under Buenoano's theory the flames that arose around Tafero's head were not produced primarily by the sponge, but by Tafero's own body tissue being superheated by an inefficient flow of electricity through his body." Kogan took as evidence of this the fact that "most of Tafero's eyebrows and eyelashes had been burned away, curled or singed by the flames, especially on the side of the head showing the most serious charring."

The evidence Kogan considered—especially that of Fred Leuchter and Robin Adair—led him to the conclusion that "this Court thus is faced with a ghastly possibility: A homemade electrode fashioned out of a used Army boot, spare parts, and roofing material may sometimes result in flames, smoke, and extensive charring of flesh during an execution. If the facts as alleged by Buenoano are true, even more serious malfunctions may occur in the future."

Kogan felt that the court should have at least ordered an evidentiary hearing "to determine whether there was *any reasonable possibility* that the flames that occurred during Tafero's execution were the fault of a faulty electrode or electrodes," and should have stayed Buenoano's execution "until the state overhauls the electric chair in a manner consistent with standards generally accepted in other states and by qualified experts."

The first Buenoano appeal left Fred feeling bitter. The state had declined to spend the money necessary to update their chair. They had spent more money contesting Buenoano's appeal than they would have spent on his proposed modification of the electric chair. The court had denied Buenoano's petition, much of which was based on Fred's diagnosis of a faulty electrode rather than the use of the wrong sponge. Fred had failed to secure a contract, and other executions were likely to be botched. After describing to me the state of the equipment in Florida, and relating the story of the first Buenoano appeal in which he was involved, Fred exclaimed in disgust: "I mean, the next step would be to uncap the condemned person's head and screw wires to it!"

Part of the problem, Fred suggested, was the difference in attitudes between northern and southern states. He tried to put it as diplomatically as he could, using Florida State Prison as an example. "The people who work there are all related or friends. They're family—cousins, brothers, sisters, uncles, nephews, whatever. They get very resentful when an outsider comes in and tells them what to do. They even gave the governor a hard time. They're clannish. Probably what they should do is they should fire everybody and start all over again. Or move the death penalty out of there and put it in a newer facility. I'm not knocking the people who work there, I'm sure they're all good people. The problem is that they don't want outsiders coming in telling them how to do it."

In a second appeal on June 20–21, 1990, Fred testified for Buenoano in the U.S. District Court in the Middle District of Florida. Buenoano succeeded in her petition for a stay of execution, and she continues to wait on death row.

But the success of the second Buenoano appeal had disastrous consequences for Fred A. Leuchter Associates. The problem stemmed from apparent conflicts of interest that arose from his acting as an expert witness for states as well as defendants. Essentially, what was at issue was the credibility of Fred's "Capital punishment, not capital torture" slogan. Is it a deeply held belief, or a sales line?

Fred explained to me: "I feel that I'm in the courtroom representing the people of the state and representing humanity." His critics felt that he was in the courtroom representing his business interests.

The first glimmer of a problem is found in Fred's affidavit of June 13, 1990, for Judy Buenoano. Fred had failed to inform Jerome Nickerson of the Florida Office of Capital Collateral that he had previously quoted for repairs to the Florida electric chair. The fact that this was viewed as a potential source of problems is reflected in an unusual paragraph in the affidavit: "When I spoke to Mr. Nickerson previously I did not inform him that I had been contacted in the past by representatives of the Florida State Prison. . . . I regret not providing this information previously."

It was to prove a costly mistake for Fred A. Leuchter Associates, Inc. The following month, on July 20, 1990, Alabama assistant attorney general Ed Carnes wrote a memorandum addressed to "All Capital Punishment States" on the subject of " 'Execution Technology Expert' Fred Leuchter." The purpose of the memo was to suggest that, because he has a degree in history rather than engineering, Fred Leuchter is not qualified as an expert in execution technology, and to alert other capital punishment states that Fred may testify *for* them one day and *against* them the next. (It is customary for expert witnesses to supply their services to prosecutors and defenders.) The Carnes memo makes much of Fred's lack of an engineering degree or "medical training," but it falsely states that he "had never installed an electric chair or other execution system that had actually been used."

At the time of the Carnes memo, Fred was under contract to provide Alabama with a new electric chair. Alabama had been the venue for two botched executions. In their first execution since 1965, Alabama had to use three 1900-volt jolts to kill John Evans on April 22, 1983. The leg electrode burned through and fell off after the first jolt, so that the execution team had to perform a makeshift repair while Evans was still alive in the chair. Flames and smoke erupted from Evans's head and leg, and the execution took fourteen minutes. Then, on July 14, 1989, because the execution team had confused the connections of the electric chair and a bank of resistors, the execution of Horace Dunkins took nineteen minutes.

On July 15, 1989, the day after the Dunkins execution, the Alabama authorities contacted Fred. He consulted with Holman State Prison warden Charlie Jones and with Billy Johnson, director of the Engineering and Administrative Division of the Alabama Department of Corrections. He gave them advice as to how the problem could be resolved. Ten months later, on May 31, 1990, the state accepted Fred's bid to design and build a new electric chair.

Shortly after approving Fred's bid for a new electric chair, the state set an execution date for Wallace Thomas: July 13, 1990. As soon as the date was set, Charlie Bodiford, the administrative service officer, called Fred on behalf of Warden Jones to ask if the new electric chair could be ready in time for the Thomas execution. Fred replied that it could not. On June 8, he submitted a proposal for supervising the Thomas execution using the old electric chair. He would service the chair and make sure that the electrodes were functioning properly. Fred says that "while the warden, Commissioner Thigpen and the department were very enthusiastic about my proposal, it was not approved by someone in the state finance department."

In July, Carnes reported in his memo, "Leuchter called my office in connection with an attempt by the attorney for an Alabama death row inmate, Wallace Norrell Thomas, to raise a claim involving Alabama's electric chair. The claim stemmed from a problem that had occurred two executions back (the execution personnel had plugged the cables into our electric chair in such a way that it received no electricity the first time the switch was thrown). The problem had been permanently fixed, but Thomas' attorney raised a claim concerning the reliability and efficacy of our electric chair system, anyway. Leuchter told us that he was under contract with the Alabama Department of Corrections to install a completely new electrocution system; that there was nothing fundamentally wrong with the old system except that it was old; and that he did not anticipate there would be any problem with the scheduled execution of Thomas in the old chair. He said he had told Thomas' attorney all that, and he volunteered to give us an affidavit saying all that. We got the affidavit from Leuchter (we paid $450.00 for his time)."

On July 2, 1990, Fred had received a phone call from Thomas's attorney, Bryan Stevenson, having been recommended by Florida's Office of Capital Collateral. In an affidavit of July 4, Fred wrote: "Mr. Stevenson said he was calling me because he wanted to raise a claim for Mr. Thomas involving Alabama's existing electric chair, and he wanted to see if I would testify in support of that claim. Mr. Stevenson told me that he believed that I was the only person he could talk with on the subject because of my knowledge both of Alabama's existing electrocution equipment and of the electrocution equipment that was being built for Alabama. I told Mr. Stevenson that

I had an existing contractual relationship with the Alabama Department of Corrections to build a new system, but I would be glad to answer any of his questions. I did answer all of the questions Mr. Stevenson asked me."

Carnes's office submitted the Leuchter affidavit, along with one from a "highly qualified electrical and biomedical engineer," to the Federal District Court. There was an evidentiary hearing on July 10, and the court denied Thomas a stay of execution. This was affirmed by the Eleventh Circuit Court the next day, and on July 12 the U.S. Supreme Court denied certiorari.

What Carnes's memo implied up to this point is that while Fred Leuchter believed the Alabama electric chair to be old and possibly faulty, he would support the state in its execution of Wallace Thomas, secure in the knowledge that he had a contract to supply a new chair (which would take three months to build and deliver).

But, Carnes continued, "At approximately 6:30 or 7:00 P.M. on July 12, 1990, less than six hours before the scheduled execution, Thomas' attorney filed in the Alabama Supreme Court a motion for stay of execution. The sole ground of that motion was that Leuchter had that day contacted Thomas' attorney and told him that Leuchter had just learned: his contract to supply Alabama with a new electric chair was being re-bid; he felt he had been used; and, on second thought, Alabama's existing chair was old and unreliable and might not work in the scheduled execution." Carnes wrote that Fred's second affidavit "makes it clear that he contacted Thomas' attorney after he had tried unsuccessfully to contact the federal judge who had denied Thomas' petition upon consideration of evidence which included Leuchter's first affidavit. Fortunately," Carnes wrote, "the Alabama Supreme Court denied the last-minute motion, and Thomas was executed on schedule a few minutes past midnight on July 13, 1990."

On July 12, 1990, Fred had sworn an affidavit in which he put his version of the story on the record: "In the last 48 hours, I have been notified that the Finance Department is not honoring my contract arrangement and that I will in all likelihood not be building or designing a new chair for the State of Alabama. While any change of mind concerning plans for a new electric chair in Alabama could have been revealed to me several weeks ago by the Finance Department, the State did not disclose this to me until this week. I find the State's action reprehensible and I feel that I have been used in relation to the Wallace Norrell Thomas case. I am deeply disturbed that my representations in the *Thomas* case may have influenced the outcome of the *Thomas* litigation when what the State had represented to me previously about their intentions about Alabama's electric chair appear to be no longer true. I have attempted today, July 12, 1990, to contact the federal court to inform the Court of my views concerning this matter. It is my opinion that a court should stay the execution of Mr. Thomas until a full inquiry has been made into this matter. Today, July 12, I made an unsolicited phone call to counsel for the petitioner, Wallace Norrell Thomas, and informed him of what had happened. I have not spoken to Mr. Stevenson before today or since he first called me some two weeks ago and I informed him that I could not assist him."

Carnes also cites as evidence of Fred's dangerousness to states the testimony he gave on behalf of Ricky Boggs, who was executed in Virginia on July 19, 1990. On the day before his execution, Boggs filed a federal habeas petition claiming that Virginia's electric chair might be faulty (as the gruesome execution of Albert Clozza one year later, on July 24, 1991, would prove). Boggs's petition was supported by an affidavit from Fred Leuchter which stated that there could be a malfunction which would leave "a living, brain-dead vegetable sitting in the electric chair, the state having no means to complete the execution." Carnes cited the court's opinion that Boggs had "not proffered credible evidence," and noted that, in spite of Fred's efforts, "Boggs was executed on schedule."

The Carnes memo shows another part of the execution industry at work. Angered by Fred's attempt to stop an execution in his own state (and by Fred's efforts in Florida and Virginia in the same thirty-day period), Carnes offered practical advice to attorneys general in other capital punishment states: "If Leuchter has consulted with your corrections people and has offered to replace their execution system or some component of it and has been turned down, you had better prepare to meet his affidavit or testimony before your next execution. Even if he has not consulted with your corrections people, Leuchter may still appear against you. The fact that he was contacted by the other side for use in three states during the same month indicates how fast word about his availability has spread among the anti–death penalty people.

"The best way to prepare to rebut Leuchter's testimony that your execution system is too old, is unreliable, or is defective or outmoded in design, is to prepare in advance to present expert testimony. If yours is an electric chair system, have a bona fide electrical engineer inspect your entire system and thoroughly test it, and if he makes any suggestions, follow them. There are different subspecialties of electrical engineers, and the best one to check out the functioning and reliability of an electric chair system is a power engineer who knows high voltage equipment. Another type of electrical engineer who is very useful is a biomedical engineer, which is an electrical engineer who specializes in application of electricity to the human body (as in design of devices to administer low current to treat spinal injuries, in design of pacemakers, and so forth). In our Alabama proceedings, we used a very good biomedical engineer who was also qualified and accepted as an expert in the functioning of electrical equipment. His name is Dr. Michael Morse, and he is in the process of moving from Auburn University in Alabama to San Diego, California."

Unsure of how states with lethal injection might counter Fred's expert witness for the defense, Carnes suggested: "If your method of execution is lethal injection, I do not know how Leuchter will be used against you, if he will be, nor do I know how you can prepare for it. What Virginia did in their case, and what might work regardless of the execution method, is to obtain in advance affidavits establishing that their system has been successfully used and has never failed." (Carnes neglected to say what should be done where the system has been used, and has repeatedly failed—in Texas, for instance. He also neglected to mention that in Missouri, where the Leuchter lethal injection machine has been used on six occasions, no failure has ever occurred.) Carnes gives other attorneys general the names and phone numbers of contacts in Florida, Virginia, and Alabama, should they wish to discuss how best to rebut Fred's arguments. The memo ends, "Let us know if Leuchter shows up in your state."

Fred took the memo from me and dropped it onto the coffee table. "It's a conspiracy," he said. "They're trying to put me out of business."

*   *   *

Later that afternoon (September 4, 1991), Fred got a call from a journalist in South Carolina, where Donald "Peewee" Gaskins was scheduled to die in the electric chair in two days' time. Gaskins had been convicted of a total of eleven murders, and was linked to others. He had received a death sentence for one of the murders, which was subsequently commuted to life and added onto the eight consecutive life sentences he had already received. The eleventh killing, for which he was to be executed, was a murder for hire inside the prison. In 1982, Gaskins (who was white) planted a bomb in the radio of a black inmate, a convicted murderer named Rudolph Tyner. The bomb had been given to Gaskins by the son of Tyner's victims. The pending execution was seen as controversial, because it would be the first time since 1944 that a white man would be put to death in the United States for the murder of a black man.

When Fred picked up the phone, I could see his penciled notation alongside Gaskins's name on the NAACP list of death row inmates that was on the left-hand side of his desk. The journalist was phoning because he had received a briefing from corrections officials on the planned execution procedure, and he wanted Fred's opinion. Fred motioned for me to listen in on his half of the conversation, and he repeated what the journalist was saying because he thought it would be of interest to me. I heard Fred say that South Carolina planned to give Gaskins 2,000 volts for five seconds, followed by an eight-second jolt of 1,000 volts, *followed by* a two-minute application of 250 volts.

The reporter wanted to know if Fred foresaw any problem with this.

The news brought out the veins on Fred's neck. "The problem they could have," Fred told him, "is that the first jolts could cause brain death, turning Mr. Gaskins into a vegetable. And then the lower voltage may *undo* what the higher voltages have done. The two hundred fifty volts might have the effect of fibrillating his heart. It could restart his heart, leaving him alive in the chair."

Fred patiently explained his views on correct voltage, amperage, and duration of current to the reporter and told him to phone back anytime if he had further questions.

He put down the phone and frowned. "I don't get it," he told me. "I was talking to the engineer down there yesterday, and he told me that they were going to start with twenty-four hundred volts." He shook his head. "I guess southern blood is thicker than Yankee water."

The day after the execution, CNN carried a seconds-long item mentioning that Gaskins had tried to commit suicide. The *New York Times* carried a front-page story headed "White Dies for Killing Black, for the First

Time in Decades." It told how, during the week before his execution, Gaskins had swallowed a razor blade and then coughed it back up when his guards weren't looking. A few hours before he was to be escorted to the chair, he slashed his wrists. The doctor at Broad River Correctional Institution put twenty stitches in his wrists, saving his life so that he could not cheat the executioner.

When I left Fred's house that afternoon, he joked: "You already know as much as I do about this business. If they bring back capital punishment in England, you could go into business for yourself."

IF HISTORY remembers Fred Leuchter for anything, it will probably be as the inventor of the lethal injection machine by which executions are now carried out in five states. He invented the machine in response to New Jersey's passing of a lethal injection bill to replace death by electrocution. It was first used in Missouri, in the execution of George "Tiny" Mercer on January 6, 1989.

Just as the electric chair was invented as a modern and "humane" replacement for hanging, so lethal injection emerged, a hundred years later, as the "humane" execution method of the late twentieth century. Lethal injection has become popular not so much because it works *better* than other methods of execution, all of which leave the condemned person equally dead; it has become popular because it is, first and foremost, a medical procedure. It has the appearance of being more "scientific" than shooting, hanging, gassing, or electrocution. It is clinical. The equipment includes intravenous lines, prescription drugs, a hospital gurney, medical technicians, doctors, and an execution protocol in which the condemned person is sedated prior to being executed. With lethal injection, there is no obvious damage to the inmate. The theory is that the inmate simply "goes to sleep."

New York governor Hill's commission of 1886 considered lethal injection along with other forms of execution but decided that electrocution was the more humane alternative. Lethal injection was next considered in the United Kingdom, in the 1949–1953 Royal Commission Inquiry on Capital Punishment, which explored alternatives to hanging. The Royal Commission had established three criteria that any method of execution must satisfy: humanity, certainty, and decency. At first, it appeared to the Royal Commission that lethal injection would meet these criteria and would be a suitable alternative to hanging. However, evidence from physicians and anesthetists dissuaded them, and hanging was retained until its abolition in 1965.

Medical witnesses objected to lethal injection on a number of grounds. An important question was, who would administer the lethal dose? The British Medical Association made it clear that their members would be prohibited from so doing. Another difficulty arose with the procedure itself. Lay members of the inquiry learned that there are two sorts of injections: intramuscular and intravenous. For lethal injection purposes, an intravenous injection is necessary to ensure unconsciousness, followed by death, in a short space of time. Intramuscular injections would be undesirable because they are extremely painful, and because the lethal drugs would take minutes rather than seconds to take effect. Doctors explained that giving an intravenous injection is a skilled procedure, and one that requires constant practice to maintain. Successful intravenous injections require the full cooperation of the subject, which cannot always be guaranteed during an execution. And, a percentage of the population suffers from venous abnormalities which make it extremely difficult to administer an intravenous injection. (In the case of American prison inmates today, a significant proportion of whom are former drug users, the administration of an intravenous injection is frequently difficult.) Then there was the problem of which drugs to use, and what would constitute a lethal dose. This was not a question to which doctors had ever been asked to turn their minds, and therefore they had no answers. And, finally, the British Medical Association issued a statement that "No medical practitioner should be asked to take part in bringing about the death of a convicted murderer. The Association would be most strongly opposed to any proposal to introduce, in place of judicial hanging, a method of execution which would require the services of a medical practitioner, either in carrying out the actual process of killing or in instructing others in the technique of the process." While the Royal Commission could not advocate lethal injection on this occasion, its report recommended, "unanimously and emphatically, that the question should be periodically examined, especially in the light of progress made in the science of anaesthetics, with a view to a change of system being proposed to Parliament as soon as it can be shown that there are no longer any grounds for the doubts that now deter us from recommending it."

In Britain, support for the death penalty dwindled in the period after the Royal Commission. Executions had been running at an average of fourteen per year in the decade before the inquiry published its report; and in the ten years prior to abolition in 1965, hangings had declined to an average of three per year. There was no periodic review of lethal injection, and there the matter has rested.

In 1977, Oklahoma was the first state to adopt lethal injection as a means of execution. Other states followed in quick succession, and the first person to be executed by lethal injection was Charles Brooks, on December 7, 1982, in Huntsville Prison, Texas. He was the sixth person to be executed after the reinstatement of capital punishment in 1976.

Texas, with its method of manual lethal injection, has executed more people than any other state since 1976. Executions are carried out in the maximum security prison at Huntsville. While Texas might have abandoned its electric chair in favor of lethal injection in pursuit of a more modern and "humane" means of execution, the procedure has been plagued by glitches and botched executions, attracting more attention than any other state, with the possible exception of Florida.

Fred Leuchter is familiar with the Texas procedure and knows Huntsville's warden, Jack Pursley, personally. He told me: "Texas has done more than forty lethal injections, and about eighty percent of these executions have had one problem or another. In the final analysis, it looks disgusting." The condemned men routinely choke, cough, spasm, and writhe as they die.

Fred described how many condemned men are lifelong drug users, whose damaged vascular systems make it difficult to carry out an execution by lethal injection. He told me how, contrary to what many people might think, lethal injection is not a simple matter of injecting a single lethal dose into the inmate's arm. Three separate drugs are required, and the procedure is fraught with difficulty if attempted manually. He complained that doctors are not allowed to be involved in executions. "But even if they were," he says, "it is very difficult to introduce these three substances by hand in the correct order and at the correct pressure. That's why I invented my machine, which is based on the most up-to-date pharmacological research."

Fred told me the story of how he came to invent the lethal injection machine. He began with an account of events in Texas. "I know Warden Jack Pursley down in Texas. He's done the most lethal injections. He did the first three or four before I had designed and built the machine." For Pursley, the nation's busiest executioner, his task has been fraught with difficulty from the beginning. The most notorious problems have occurred in the executions of Stephen Morin (March 13, 1985, when he waited more than forty minutes on the gurney while technicians repeatedly failed to insert the IV line into his veins); Raymond Landry (December 13, 1988, when the IV line carrying the lethal drugs burst, spraying the execution team with the fatal chemicals; a new IV line had to be inserted while Landry was half-dead, and he took twenty-four minutes to die); Stephen McCoy (May 24, 1989, when an incorrect mix of drugs caused him to choke and heave throughout the procedure); and Billy Wayne White (May 23, 1992, when it took forty-seven minutes to find a vein, even after White tried to assist the executioners in locating a suitable one).

But Fred is deeply sympathetic to Warden Pursley's predicament as an executioner. "Every time he does one, he tries to persuade the state of Texas to buy him a machine. And they keep patting him on the head and saying, 'You're doing a good job, Jack, don't worry about it.' They don't want to put out the money for the machine. But the problem is that it's taking its toll on Jack Pursley. He's the one that has to operate the syringes. He's doing it by hand. It's all manual. They have six syringes. There are three chemicals in the process—sodium pentothal, Pavulon [pancuronium bromide], and potassium chloride. The syringes tie into an IV line and there is a redundant set. The redundant set goes into a bucket. The purpose of the thing is so the witnesses don't know which one's operating it. Jack knows, because Jack's the one that has to do it." Fred sighed. "He's had more problems. He's had hematomas; he's gone through veins putting the needle in."

Fred stared hard at the floor and then looked at me. "Doctors, as you know, will not participate. It's so bad that the state doctor down there *watched* Jack Pursley at the first execution. Jack mixed the chemicals. *And the doctors won't help.* Occasionally you find a doctor or a medical technician who'll do that. To show you how bad it is, the first execution that Jack Pursley did, he took all the chemicals and mixed them together and put them in one syringe. The doctor stood there watching him. Some forty minutes later, after they got everything set up, they go in there and he's pushing the syringe and the syringe won't work. He's got *white sludge. Everything precipitated.* You can't mix the three chemicals together. The doctor was standing there shaking his head and he said, 'I could have told you that.' "

Fred exploded with exasperation. "You know, give him a break! You've got a man who doesn't know anything about medical procedures, and here he's doing something—he's totally out of his element—and the doctor is going to allow him to torture the inmate!

"Poor Jack Pursley," Fred said softly. "In ten years, he's aged about thirty. It's really taken its toll on Jack. Jack is a good law enforcement official, and if the governor told him to march into the mouth of hell, he'd march into the mouth of hell. That's his job. And I think he decided that when he took it. But it doesn't mean he likes it, and it doesn't mean he's comfortable with it. He every so often asks for a machine, and every so often they give him his pat on the head and say, 'Nice Jack, nice Jack, go back and do it again.' He's doing a yeoman's job without the equipment and they probably won't buy it while he's alive. Because the next guy they get is probably going to say, 'I ain't going to do it.' "

In addressing the problem of how to conduct a lethal injection, Fred looked to veterinarian science, and at the "euthanasia kits" used to put down animals. If it worked on animals, Fred saw no reason why it shouldn't work on human beings.

"Like any engineer that's going to design something," Fred told me, "you don't want to reinvent the wheel. So you go and find out what the last guy did. Sodium pentobarbital is excellent for destroying the respiratory system. What I would have done is recommend sodium pentobarbital, and I would have recommended potassium chloride. The doctors in New Jersey were in agreement with me. Those were the same chemicals that they would have used."

But as New Jersey's lethal injection statute took shape, doctors progressively distanced themselves from it. Ultimately, the statute forbade the participation of doctors in the actual execution, although they were allowed to give a pre-execution sedative. It called for the commissioner of the Department of Corrections to "designate persons who are qualified to administer injections and who are familiar with medical procedures, other than licensed physicians," to assist in the execution. The law also stipulated that "the procedures and equipment . . . shall be designed to ensure that the identity of the person actually inflicting the lethal substance is unknown even to the person himself." The New Jersey law pretty much described the machine that Fred would go on to invent.

"By the time New Jersey called me in," Fred told me, "the doctors had made a decision that they didn't want to touch lethal injection. They were afraid of it, because Texas had just done three botches. They witnessed the botches. And the chief doctor in New Jersey said, 'I don't think I can do it any better. There's got to be a way to do it, there must be a machine.' They checked the medical catalogues, and there's no machine. *We got to get a machine.* They found out I was building execution equipment, so they contacted me."

Fred had no track record in lethal injection technology; but then, neither did anyone else. "I got the job in New Jersey," Fred told me, "only because I built the electric chair helmet for South Carolina. The first meeting we were at we had a deputy commissioner who was totally disinterested in the meeting. He was looking at the walls, the floor, the ceiling, and I expected him to snore any minute. The doctors—there's quite a repartee going back and forth between the doctors and myself and the warden. Finally," Fred related with a smile, "the commissioner's like this." Fred slumped over in his chair, as if asleep. "One of the doctors turned around and he says, 'Commissioner, Fred was the one that made the helmet for South Carolina.' He looks at me and he says, 'You made the helmet? The one that they just used?' I says, 'Yes.' He said, 'Okay.' He turned around to the doctor and he said, 'I don't care what it costs, give Fred the contract. He builds the equipment.' That's it. Meeting over.''

Fred had a number of problems to solve. What drugs should be used, and in what combinations and quantities? What kind of machine would be right for administering the lethal injection into the condemned person? "I had to come up with a universal dosage that would work with everybody," Fred explained.

As he did before redesigning the electric chair, Fred took himself off to the library—this time, a medical library—to research the effects of barbiturates and other drugs on the human system. He discovered that "there's absolutely no documentation on lethal dosages. I had to go back to the original Pentothal literatures. What I was working with was a paper written by the two doctors that developed Pentothal back in 1947, I think it was. There was more information on pancuronium bromide, but again, nothing relative to lethal dose. Pancuronium bromide is a muscle relaxant. It's used primarily for heart operations where they paralyze a portion of the heart muscles so they can suture it. And you can see right off the bat where there would be no lethal dosage information. They didn't even do any lethal tests on animals. There were some numbers, but they were not good numbers because they hadn't done it from a lethal dosage point of view. They just wanted to determine whether it was lethal. Pancuronium bromide is in effect a synthetic curare. It's the same chemical that the natives in South America use in their blowguns. As far as I know, it has no other medical use. And potassium chloride, that's been around for years and used for various heart conditions.

"So," Fred continued, "there's no lethal dosage information for human beings. But I have information on rabbits and pigs. What I did is, I took the pig, because it's got the closest system to the human being, and I ran the numbers. I gave these numbers to the state of New Jersey. The doctors duplicated my efforts and they were in agreement. The dosage amounts were passed to Texas, and it eliminated eighty percent of their problems. Before, they were just pumping as much as they could get into the syringe. And the executees were coughing and spasming. When New Jersey communicated the proper dosages, Texas tried them. They worked better. They still had coughing and choking and spasming, but not as much. The problem was that they needed an antihistamine. I said to the doctors in

New Jersey—and I'm not a physiologist and I'm not a doctor, so I'm coming in from left field here with these suggestions—I said, 'Why don't we use an antihistamine to drop the coughing and spasming?' And I said that I would recommend using Benadryl. The doctor in New Jersey looked at me and he started to laugh. He said, 'Doctors all over the country are watching this happen, and they said there was no way to do it, and you've just solved the problem! Why did you think of it?' I said, 'Everybody with allergies takes antihistamine.' He said, 'We're supposed to know that!' You should have seen the expression on the doctor's face. He said, 'Damn, why didn't we think of that? We're paid to do it!' "

"The lethal dosages were based on running the pig numbers?" I asked.

"Correct."

"So your prescription for lethal dosages is based on numbers rather than actual tests?"

Fred shook his head and lowered his voice. "In an undisclosed location, one pig was executed."

I made a note of this and tried to keep a straight face. We're talking about killing human beings, but being secretive about "executing" a pig. Fred admitted that he was worried about an adverse reaction from the NSPCA if word got out.

"So," I asked, "what are the dosages?"

"The dose is twenty percent larger than would be necessary for the average person. Possibly if you had a seventy-pound child, or a seventy-pound woman, you could have a problem with that. It's not likely that's going to happen, and the people that are doing the execution have enough savvy to cut back on the dosage a little. It's not likely that you're going to execute somebody that weighs less than ninety pounds, though."

Thinking back to the problem that Tennessee had with its old electric chair, that it was too narrow to accommodate the average inmate, I asked: "What about very large people?"

"Fifteen to seventeen cc's will put anybody away," Fred reassured me. "Even if the dosage is not enough to do it in one minute, it will do it in ten minutes. Within four minutes you're going to get brain damage, so that will work with just about anybody."

The basic design requirement of Fred's lethal injection machine is that it should kill quickly and efficiently, and in a way that causes the least pain and distress to the condemned person, the executioners, and the witnesses. Fred concluded that the way to achieve this is to give the condemned person a pre-injection of 10 cc of antihistamine half an hour prior to the execution. This ensures that choking, coughing, and spasming will be reduced to a minimum. He recommends that the inmate also be sedated with a pre-injection of 8 cc of 2 percent sodium pentothal five minutes prior to bringing him into the death chamber. Fred argues that this helps to calm the inmate; it also makes him docile and less resistant to his fate. Forty-five minutes before the start of the execution, the condemned person is attached to an IV line delivering saline solution, which allows the lethal drugs to pass more easily into his veins.

Once the execution has commenced, three drugs are administered. The machine introduces 15 cc of 2 percent sodium pentothal over ten seconds, followed by a one-minute wait. This causes unconsciousness. The machine then injects 15 cc of pancuronium bromide, followed by a one-minute wait. Finally, 15 cc of potassium chloride is injected, and death should follow within two minutes.

The problem in designing the machine was how to introduce the relatively large volume of drugs into the condemned inmate in a regular flow. The answer is a delivery module, mounted on a wall in the execution chamber, which holds eight syringes—two complete sets of the three lethal doses, along with two purge syringes filled with saline solution. It is essentially a manifold with eight inlets and one outlet. Each of the syringes containing the lethal drugs is fitted beneath a weighted piston. When activated from the control panel, the pistons depress the syringes in the timed sequence described above.

The control module is typically placed on a wheeled trolley on the other side of the wall on which the delivery module is mounted. It is a 2 feet by 1.5 feet box which is operated by the two executioners. It has two complete sets of controls. They are marked, military-style, Station 1 and Station 2. Each station is armed by turning a key at the bottom of the panel. When it is time for the execution to commence, each of the executioners presses a button. A computer in the machine chooses which executioner has activated the sequence, and the choice is then automatically erased from memory. A series of lights on the panel indicates three stages of the execution procedure: Armed (red), Start (yellow), and Finish (green). The executioners use these lights to monitor the three injections during the execution process.

In order to avoid execution glitches caused by power or system failure, Fred added a number of fail-safe devices in the machine. It is powered by a 12-volt battery which can be recharged from a 110-volt line in fourteen hours, making it independent of the prison power supply. If multiple executions are required, the battery can power the machine six times at fifteen-minute intervals before it needs to be recharged.

In the event of a timing system failure, Fred incorporated an electrical override which can be used to activate any or all of the three pistons. Both executioners operate the electrical override, and the on-board computer has already chosen, during makeready, which of the executioners has actually activated the system. When using the electrical override, assistants in the execution control room must time the administration of each drug with a stopwatch and give the order to commence the next stage.

In the event of total electrical failure, or failure of the prime system, the delivery module has a mechanical system comprising three sets of double pull knobs, which manually activate the pistons that drive the syringes.

Fred described the machine to me using two poster-size color photographs he had dry-mounted for exhibition purposes. He would bring them —along with posters and specifications for his electric chair—to prison wardens' conventions, where he would tout for business alongside manufacturers of nightsticks, firearms, and other security products. After he explained the machine, he asked if I'd like to see the control module he had supplied to Delaware.

"Of course," I said.

Fred led me into the kitchen, past Caroline, and into a corner where a door led down to the basement. He switched on the light, and I followed him down the steep cellar stairs.

On a shelf along the wall were boxes of Bisquick, Quaker Oats, and other staples. At the bottom of the stairs, off to one side, were cases of diet Pepsi and cans of Hawaiian Punch, along with enough paper bags full of canned goods to withstand a siege. Electrical cables ran in crazy patterns across the ceiling, and given Fred's profession, the cobwebs that hung everywhere gave the place an eerie feel.

At the back of the cellar was a giant pile of electrical junk. Empty packaging for computers and VCRs was strewn about. Fred pointed out the new gas furnace he'd installed and led me to the end of the cellar, where the Delaware lethal injection machine sat gathering dust on his workbench.

The area around the bench was cluttered with tools and electronic paraphernalia. Next to the control module were a soldering iron and voltmeter, and one end of the bench had a vise. The area was lit by a single naked bulb suspended from the ceiling.

"Here it is," said Fred, peering at me through his thick glasses in the gloomy cellar.

I walked up to it and read the control panel, standing where the executioners would when they pressed the buttons that pumped the lethal dose.

Fred explained its operation again, reminding me that this was only half a machine; the delivery module was down at the prison in Delaware. As he described its functions, I couldn't help focusing my attention on the key —like a car ignition key—that was protruding from system control at Station 1. A key ring was hanging from it, and I picked it up for a better look in the poor light. It was made of black rubber and cut in the shape of an electric chair. On the front, the image of an electric chair, complete with harnesses and restraint fastenings casually positioned across the seat, was etched in white. I turned it over. On the back was printed "Fred A. Leuchter Associates, Inc., Execution Equipment and Support," along with his address and phone number.

Fred observed me toying with the unusual promotional device. "Oh," he said with a smile. "I give those out at wardens' conventions." He said he also had pens, and he'd give me one later.

"You see this?" he said, pointing to a small stack of wood in a filthy corner next to the workbench. "That's oak left over from the Tennessee chair."

I went over to it and poked with the toe of my boot. It was covered in cobwebs, and a spider emerged, then scurried for cover in the shadows.

When Tennessee took the power of hanging convicted murderers and rapists away from the county sheriffs and handed it over to the state authorities in 1909, they built a gallows from this wood. Then, in 1916, they switched over to electrocution, tore down the gallows, and used the wood to make their first electric chair. Execution records in Tennessee are incomplete, but scholars have documented that at least 134 men had been hung or fried on the pile of wood in the corner of Fred's cellar. Part of the "living tradition" Fred had told me about in the restaurant the day before.

"So," I asked, "why is the Delaware control module in your cellar?"

He told me that the Delaware authorities had been concerned that the machine was not in good working order and had required a service. Fred had looked at it and found that the delivery module and the control module had been stored in damp conditions and were corroded.

Fred explained that Delaware had issued a purchase order to repair the machine (and their gallows, which had fallen into disrepair). They had shipped the control module back to Fred in Malden, but he was having difficulty getting paid after the furor raised by the Carnes memo.

"The Department of Corrections is up against the traditional rock and a hard place because they had been given strict orders not to deal with me," Fred explained.

It seemed as though recently Fred's business had suffered one setback after another, and I began to suspect that some of them might be self-induced.

Fred then claimed that, since Delaware wouldn't pay him for the repairs to the control module, ownership had reverted to him, and he planned to sell it.

"Who to?" I asked. I wondered, Who would want to buy half of a lethal injection machine?

"I was hoping for a well-heeled collector," Fred told me.

He could see me looking skeptical.

He shrugged and explained: "The machine has never been used, but the machine is a bona fide piece of equipment, and I would supply it with certification that it was in fact a machine that was removed from the state of Delaware correction facility at Smyrna. I was asking ten thousand dollars. Ten thousand dollars is probably a reasonable price for someone to pay."

I wondered how Fred would go about selling the thing, and he showed me. He'd taken out an ad in a Boston weekly called the *Want Advertiser*. It calls itself "The Honor System Magazine" because it's free to advertise in, and you pay the magazine only after you've made a sale. He showed me the ad. On either side of the notice for his lethal injection machine were ads for items as diverse as Beatles bubble gum cards and Budweiser steins. Fred's ad said: "EXECUTION DEVICE Control module for lethal injection machine. Being sold for non-payment. $10,000." At the end of the ad was Fred's phone number.

Two days after the ad came out, the *Boston Herald* ran a story headlined "Controversial Inventor Places Ad Aiming to Sell Execution Device." The story has a photograph of Fred sitting between his electric chair and lethal injection posters, grinning widely and looking much younger than forty-seven years old. "I knew this was going to be a problem," a spokesperson for the *Want Advertiser* was reported as saying. "We are a family publication and this is not something we really want in the book."

Fred told me he'd received more than a hundred calls in the days after the ad appeared. "Most of them were hang-ups, or nasty or obscene calls," he said. "Thirteen or fourteen of them were threats.

"It's all part of the campaign to persecute me," said Fred.

T

HE STORY of why Fred Leuchter believes he is "persecuted" goes deeper than the Carnes memo and its allegations that Fred threatens to turn expert witness against states that don't use his services.

In April 1988, Fred appeared in a Toronto court as an expert witness for the defense in the case of Ernst Zundel. In 1985, Zundel was tried for publishing a pamphlet entitled *Did Six Million Really Die?*, in which he argued that the Holocaust was a fiction (his previous works include *The Hitler We Loved and Why*). Zundel was found guilty of spreading false information and was sentenced to fifteen months in prison.

Zundel appealed against his conviction and secured a retrial. In preparing for his new trial, Zundel had the support of extreme right-wing historians from Europe and North America. The most active of these was David Irving, the British writer who has been one of the leaders of the worldwide revisionist movement. Irving had long maintained that a study of executions by lethal gas in the United States would help to "prove" that the Nazi gas chambers never existed. He argued that American prisons are the only place where cyanide gas has been used to kill human beings deliberately; and that American prison wardens who have carried out gas executions could be important sources of evidence which could disprove the Holocaust "myth."

In January 1988, David Irving flew to Toronto to help Zundel prepare his defense. He suggested to Zundel's lawyers that they write to an American prison warden who had carried out gas executions and persuade him to go to Toronto and testify. They chose Bill Armontrout, who was warden of Missouri State Penitentiary in Jefferson City. Bill Armontrout replied to Barbara Kulaszka on January 13, 1988. He explained that he himself had "considerable knowledge in that area." However, he suggested that, in his opinion, the Zundel defense should contact Fred Leuchter in Massachusetts. He described Fred as "an engineer specializing in gas chambers and executions." He explained that Fred was well versed in all of the execution technologies and, as far as he knew, the only American specialist working in this area.

In January 1988, Fred received a telephone call from the French Holocaust revisionist Robert Faurisson asking if he would agree to act as a witness for Zundel. Fred agreed.

The Zundel defense lost no time. On February 3–4, 1988, David Irving was in Malden, Massachusetts, having conversations with Fred. Fred outlined his experience in the execution industry and explained that he had carried out a study of the Missouri gas chamber for Bill Armontrout, and had proposed a redesign of it. Irving was impressed with Fred's qualifications and returned to Toronto to advise Zundel that Fred could be his star witness.

In Irving's mind, Fred's expert testimony could "prove," once and for all, that the Holocaust never happened. He thought he was on the verge of making history.

Zundel proposed that Fred should visit three "alleged" Nazi gas chambers in the concentration camps at Auschwitz, Birkenau, and Majdanek. His job would be to make a forensic determination of whether or not they had ever contained gas chambers which had been used to kill human beings.

On February 24, 1988, Fred set off on an eight-day mission to Poland, along with his draftsman, Howard Miller; his wife, Caroline; a Polish interpreter, Theodore Rudolph; and a video cameraman, Jurgen Neumann. Neumann's video shows Fred and Howard Miller at work in the Nazi death camps. Fred, wearing a fur hat and carrying a small hammer, takes samples of the floors, walls, and ceilings of gas chambers and crematoria, while Howard Miller bags and tags them. In the amateur-looking video, Fred addresses the camera directly from time to time, giving his opinion of what he is observing forty-three years after the end of World War II. He states that where there is clear evidence of cyanide gas (Zyklon-B), this was used to delouse the clothing and blankets of concentration camp victims.

Upon his return to the United States, Fred sent samples of brick and "gasket material" to Alpha Analytical Laboratories in Ashland, Massachusetts, for analysis. During March 1988, he wrote up the results of his trip to Poland, producing a document which David Irving's Focal Point Publications issued as *The Leuchter Report* (the full title Fred gave it is *An Engineering Report on the Alleged Execution Gas Chambers at Auschwitz, Birkenau, and Majdanek*). In the report, Fred finds insufficient evidence of levels of cyanide gas to suggest that large numbers of people were put to death. He judges that because the gas chambers do not meet the technical specifications of the ones used in American prisons, they were not, in fact, gas chambers.

The report also claims that the crematoria could not process the number of bodies that were "allegedly" fed into them at the height of the Nazis' Final Solution. The report, which Fred finished on April 5, 1988, concludes: "After reviewing all of the material and inspecting all of the sites at Auschwitz, Birkenau and Majdanek your author finds the evidence overwhelming. There were no execution gas chambers at any of these locations. It is the best engineering opinion of this author that the alleged gas chambers at the inspected sites *could not have then been, or now be, utilized or seriously considered to function as execution gas chambers.*"

Fred's report had cost Zundel more than $30,000. He and Irving had staked a lot on Fred. On a personal level, Zundel was hoping to reverse the first court's verdict of guilt; and, in the larger arena, both men were excited because they felt on the verge of a revisionist victory, in which they would "prove" that the Holocaust was a Zionist hoax.

During the third week of April 1988, Toronto was the setting for a meeting between an odd network of people from the American execution industry and Holocaust revisionists. On April 19, Missouri State Penitentiary warden Bill Armontrout took the stand as an expert witness for Zundel and answered questions about the procedures used in executions by lethal gas. He was followed on April 20–21 by Fred Leuchter. At the beginning of the trial, Judge Ronald Thomas had taken judicial notice of the Holocaust: Zundel, not the Holocaust, was on trial. As a result, Fred's report was not admitted in evidence, and he had to summarize it from the witness box. In court, the prosecution made much of the fact that Fred had no formal engineering or medical training.

The jury found Zundel guilty, and he was sent to prison for nine months.

In the months following their testimonies at the second trial of Ernst Zundel, Fred Leuchter and Bill Armontrout worked closely on the plan for refurbishing Missouri's gas chamber, as it became increasingly clear that executions would resume there. At the last minute, the Missouri legislature passed a lethal injection bill, and Armontrout recommended that the state purchase one of Fred's lethal injection machines.

The paths of Fred and Bill Armontrout crossed again on ABC's "Prime Time Live" capital punishment program of May 10, 1990, in which both men appeared. The *Village Voice* was critical of the program, calling Fred "the executioner's best friend" and taking ABC to task for not mentioning that Fred has no engineering degree, and that *The Leuchter Report* had made him "a star of the anti-Semitic far right's crusade against what they call 'the Holocaust hoax.' " It also revealed that the report had since been published in the United States by the white supremacist group Aryan Nation, and by the Institute for Historical Research, the American branch of a French organization run by the far-right historian Robert Faurisson.

A *Village Voice* report of May 22, 1990, also revealed that in February 1989, Fred was the featured speaker at the ninth annual conference of the Institute for Historical Research, and that the meeting was much publicized by the anti-Semitic group Liberty Lobby. It also reported that David Duke's National Association for the Advancement of White People featured *The Leuchter Report* on its mail-order list of racist publications.

Other journalists, and Jewish groups such as the Anti-Defamation League of B'nai B'rith, began to focus on *The Leuchter Report*. The

Boston Globe called it "the backbone of the revisionist movement." Fred told the *Globe:* "I am not an anti-Semite. I am not a revisionist and I have no use for Nazis. The report is a scientific document. I am not saying that atrocities did not occur, only that there were no gas chambers."

Fred's attempt publicly to distance himself from Nazi sympathizers did not convince Ross Vicksell of the Organization of New England Revisionists. He told the *Globe:* "Mr. Leuchter says he is not a revisionist, but that does not square with his actions. He is a big star in the movement."

Fred's report attracted the attention of Nazi hunters Beate and Serge Klarsfeld, as well as a group based in Latham, New York, called Holocaust Survivors and Friends in Pursuit of Justice, headed by Shelly Shapiro. Shapiro's group sought legal advice and brought an action against Leuchter, based on an obscure and untested statute, for practicing as an engineer without a license. (Under Massachusetts law, it is not necessary to be licensed to practice all types of engineering—only those which involve issues of public safety, such as building engineering.) The purpose of the lawsuit was to discredit Fred as an expert, and so discourage readers from taking his report seriously.

On October 23, 1990, Fred was charged in the Middlesex County District Court in Malden with the fraudulent practice of engineering. A packed courtroom listened as Fred faced the charge with his head bowed, and the judge set a pretrial hearing for December 11. Fred faced a maximum sentence of three months in prison and a $500 fine. Given Fred's occupation, the prospect of spending any time in prison was a particularly bleak one.

Revisionist support for Fred came quickly. The October number of the far-right *IHR Newsletter* ran the headline: "Alien Terrorists Target Leuchter." The report alleged that Fred was being hounded and harassed by the Klarsfelds and U.S. Jewish groups that had mounted an ambitious campaign "to destroy Leuchter professionally and economically."

On December 11, 1990, the day of Fred's pretrial hearing and the start of Hanukkah, Malden residents were greeted by an unusual sight. More than two hundred protesters, including Holocaust survivors and supporters, had gathered to protest against *The Leuchter Report*. Some carried placards saying "Leuchter = Nazi." Student protesters from New York City and Boston chanted, "Six million died." Separated by police, a small group of Leuchter supporters gathered on the other side of the street.

State, Metro, and local police had been called out to control the crowd, and Fred and Caroline had difficulty reaching the courthouse, since all approaches to it were sealed off by police roadblocks. Mounted police were on duty in the event of a disturbance.

Under constant police guard, Fred and Caroline were escorted into the courthouse, where there were almost as many police as observers. When the case was called, police and court officers formed a line facing the public, separating them from Fred, the judge, and other court officials.

The Malden lawyer who normally handles Fred's legal work refused to defend him in court. Fred was assigned a court-appointed attorney, Anthony Santoro, who found the work equally unappealing. (He told Leuchter, "I have to practice in Malden.") At the pretrial hearing in front of Judge James Killam III, Fred moved to dismiss Santoro in favor of Houston lawyer Kirk Lyons. Lyons had gained national attention in 1988 when he successfully defended Louis R. Beam, Jr., the former grand dragon of the Texas Knights of the Ku Klux Klan, who had been charged with sedition. Lyons heads a group called the Patriot Defenders Foundation, which offers legal representation to right-wing activists and white supremacists. He claims his organization is modeled on the NAACP's Legal Defense Fund, one of whose functions is to represent death row inmates at appeal.

After the hearing, Fred gave an outdoor press conference at which he reiterated the main point of his defense: that he was being unfairly harassed for having written a scientific report, the conclusions of which some people found offensive. While protesters chanted outside the courthouse, Fred told reporters: "I stand fully behind my report. Because certain groups did not like my findings, these groups and individuals have formed an international cabal to destroy the report. Unable to do this, since the report and the truths contained therein speak for themselves, this international gang of free-speech busters determined to destroy me personally and economically. . . . Through a program of threats to innocent people, lies, slander, and libel about myself and my equipment, they have set out to destroy my civil rights and the civil rights of every American alive today. . . . This witch-hunt must and will stop. I give fair warning to all those who are part of this international cabal, to all those who have unjustly attacked me and violated my civil rights—to the Klarsfelds, Shapiros, and Kahns of this world, Fred Leuchter is coming for you!" After sounding his warning, Fred concluded: "I'm sure Columbus, Galileo, and Copernicus caused emotional harm to those who promoted the flat earth theory, but that did not stop the earth from being a sphere."

After the pretrial hearing, extreme right-wing support for Fred accelerated. The December 30, 1990, issue of a Toronto-based publication called *Power* featured the logo of a white fist over a Star of David and the slogan, "Smash Zionist Terror!" The issue carried a two-page article by Ernst Zundel in support of Fred and his report. At the bottom of the front page is printed the message, "Help us . . . fight! We need you—you need us." At the top of the page is a photograph of Fred in a three-piece suit during his trip to Poland, and a message from him to readers of *Power*. "To my supporters: Because of the recession and uncertainty caused by the Gulf crisis, the donations are coming in much more slowly! Please send your support so that we can continue our work. Many Thanks." Zundel wrote that *The Leuchter Report* was gaining influence worldwide, having been translated into German, French, Portuguese, Spanish, Italian, Dutch, Swedish, and Japanese. He also reported that "underground editions appeared in Polish and Russian, with wide circulation in Soviet-ruled countries."

A week later, the *IHR Newsletter* carried a front-page photograph of Fred speaking at the tenth annual conference of the Institute of Historical Research under the headline: "Fred Leuchter Fights Back: Needs Financial Help for His Courtroom Battle." In its fund-raising plea, the *IHR Newsletter* presented Fred as a persecuted hero: "Fred Leuchter hasn't been, isn't, and will not be either cowed or deterred by the Holocaust lobby's efforts to destroy him. . . . Leuchter could have backed out or backed down or backed away from the facts as he found them at Auschwitz and their terrifying, revolutionary, liberating implications. But he never did. And now he intends not merely to defend himself but to launch a counterattack against some very powerful enemies of truth and freedom (or as the down-to-earth Yankee engineer puts it, 'Now's the time to kick ass and take names!')."

At Fred's next court appearance, at 9:00 A.M. on January 22, 1991, hundreds of demonstrators turned up in freezing weather. This time, Jewish groups were joined by gay activists including the AIDS Coalition to

Unleash Power and Queer Nation. Many of the gay demonstrators displayed pink triangles like those the Nazis forced homosexuals to wear. But this time, pro-Leuchter supporters nearly equaled the opposition. Fighting broke out when a pro-Leuchter demonstrator, Friedrich Berg of Fort Wayne, New Jersey, held up an Israeli flag and attempted to set it alight. An anti-Leuchter demonstrator (whose name, ironically, is David Duke), tried to stop him, and both men were charged with assault and battery. Another Leuchter supporter, Hans Beisner of Ontario, Canada, was also charged with assault and battery after knocking over a police officer while joining in the fight.

Fred was escorted into the courthouse by three police officers. The judge allowed Kirk Lyons to act for the defense. Lyons presented a lengthy motion to dismiss the case on two grounds: that the state's case was procedurally and substantially inadequate; and that the Massachusetts engineer registration statute was vague, and not applicable to Fred. Judge Killam dismissed the motion and set a trial date of May 9.

After further motions and attempts by Kirk Lyons to have the case thrown out, Fred came to court again on June 11, 1991, in front of a new judge, Christine McEvoy. He was placed on pretrial probation after signing a consent agreement with the Massachusetts Board of Registration of Professional Engineers and Land Surveyors, in which he agreed to refrain from using the title of "engineer."

Kirk Lyons claimed a victory, telling reporters: "There is no finding nor has there been any admission of guilt." Fred vowed to seek registration as an engineer in Massachusetts and pointed out that he is not barred from calling himself an engineer in the other forty-nine states of the union.

DURING THE week after Labor Day, Fred told me he didn't hold out much hope that the state engineering board would grant him a license.

"They're frightened of me," he said. And anyway, he pointed out, there was no such category as "execution engineer."

In the aftermath of his court case, Fred found that many of his old clients were reluctant to deal with him. He wore a resigned expression when he told me: "My clients, mostly prison wardens, are political appointees. They're not civil servants. They've worked all their lives to get where they are, and what they don't want to do is upset their employers, from the governor on down. If they start using me again, the Jewish groups will start complaining, and they'll be in trouble." However, that has not stopped Fred's consulting. Nowadays, his advice is given secretly.

I asked Fred to tell me the story behind *The Leuchter Report*. He explained how Bill Armontrout had passed his name on to Ernst Zundel's defense team. "I didn't even know who Ernst Zundel was," Fred told me.

He said that when he took the job, he fully expected to find evidence of gas chambers. He told me he was surprised that he didn't.

The videotape of Fred collecting evidence tells a different story.

Fred told me that the Toronto court required him to do some homework before traveling to Poland. "I was given material to review," he said. "The court required that I review material that was produced by the alleged survivors. I had to read the material of the alleged confessions of the Nazis. I had to understand how these things supposedly worked. And then, with all this information, I went to Poland."

I asked him if he had carried out any further research prior to his Polish trip.

"Sure," he replied. "As an engineer I went and obtained available material on crematories."

I began to correct Fred on his grammar, and tell him that the plural of crematorium is crematoria or crematoriums, but thought better of it. He was in full flow.

"I studied how they were built," he explained. "Then I went and I visited three crematories. I watched bodies being burnt. I handled ashes. I ran the bone pressing machines. I actually did hands-on work with the actual hardware. I had a good working knowledge, and I could build a crematory from what I know."

I thought about Fred out on his research trip, eagerly doing his homework. Burning bodies. Crushing bones to powder. Checking out the ventilation requirements.

He was angry that the judge in the Zundel case had restricted his testimony. "I *had* to be allowed to testify on gas chambers because I've actually done hands-on work," he told me. "But since I haven't actually done hands-on work *for pay,* I couldn't testify on the crematories. I wasn't allowed to testify on my chemical analysis."

Curious about the details of Fred's "forensic" methods in Poland, I asked him if he had told the chemical lab in Massachusetts what the samples from Auschwitz and the other slave labor and extermination camps were.

"Nah," he said, straight-faced. "I told them they were to do with a case of workmen's compensation, and that they might be called to testify in court."

For Fred, the whole affair is about "scientific method" and "professionalism." "It didn't faze the lab at all," he said. "They didn't care what it was. Their responsibility began and ended with the test tube, which is good. That's the way a professional's supposed to be."

Fred started to complain that he's received no royalties from *The Leuchter Report;* that it had been pirated all over the world.

I stopped him and asked if he thought the Holocaust had happened.

He explained how the judge had taken judicial notice of the Holocaust, and told me, "I wasn't testifying on the Holocaust. I was testifying on the existence of specific gas chambers at predetermined locations."

"But," I asked, "do you believe that the Holocaust happened?"

Fred answered smoothly, switching easily from evasion to frankness: "I believed there had been a Holocaust. I believed I would find gas chambers. I told Ernst Zundel—he was positive I wouldn't find them—I told him that if I did find them, or even that these facilities had the capability of being gas chambers, I was going to report such. I was like most Americans and probably most people all over the world, they believed that it happened. I believed what I'd been taught in school. I know that the facilities that everybody points to weren't gas chambers. I think probably there was a Holocaust, but I think it depends upon how one defines 'Holocaust.' There are serious questions that have to be asked and answered about that whole period in our history, and I think that this better be done before these concentration camp survivors die, because it may be that there's going to be worthwhile information that's going to be lost forever."

I pressed him further, and Fred admitted that "thousands" of people had probably been killed in the Nazi camps.

"What about the millions of people," I asked, "who had friends, family, an address, who were absent after 1945?"

Fred explained that, during wartime, there is much destruction and loss of innocent lives.

As I was getting ready to leave, Fred told me: "I do know that the Nazis were a bunch of, quite frankly, nasty bastards."

Missouri

MY WEEK with Fred had been a crash course in execution technology, and I felt as prepared as I could be for the next leg of my journey: to meet the executioners and some of the men they would put to death.

My destination was Jefferson City, Missouri, where I had an appointment with Bill Armontrout. Since the Zundel trial, he had been promoted from warden of Missouri State Penitentiary (referred to by staff and inmates as MSP, although it had recently been renamed Jefferson City Correctional Center, or JCCC) to deputy director of the Division of Adult Institutions in Missouri's Department of Corrections.

My flight from Boston was routed through Pittsburgh and took me over the midwestern states and the Mississippi River into St. Louis. The weather was hotter and more humid than it had been back East, and I was sweat-soaked as I lugged my bags to the rental car in the underground parking lot and headed west toward Jefferson City, the state capital. I was excited at the prospect of the journey. St. Louis was the farthest west I had traveled in the United States.

Interstate 70 begins near Pittsburgh and ends, abruptly, at Salina, Utah. It follows a straight line across Missouri, from St. Louis to Kansas City. My journey would take me nearly halfway across the state, to Kingdom City, where I would pick up Route 54 south into Jefferson City.

My week with Fred had seemed longer than that. It had taken some effort on my part to adjust to a daily conversation about capital punishment as an engineering problem, and now it was good to be out on the open highway, with America spread flat on either side, and the biggest sky on earth above me.

I settled into the rhythm of the traffic, falling in behind an eighteen-wheeler heading west, cruising at a comfortable sixty-five miles per hour past St. Peters, O'Fallon, Wentzville, Wright City, New Florence, Danville, Mineola. I turned left at Kingdom City and headed down Route 54 toward the capital, one finger on the radio dial, scanning the FM band to hear what was on offer, as if the choices might provide some essential clue to mid-Missouri. There was a Christian station which featured a white evangelist who got hopelessly muddled and self-contradictory in his preaching. I listened in astonishment as he stopped the live broadcast and told the audience he was going to pray to God for inspiration to go on. He abandoned his theme and asked God to give him words with which to preach His gospel.

The approach to Jefferson City from the north is a divided highway cut through rich mineral ore. Crossing the bridge over the Missouri River into the city, I could see the dome of the capitol building, tall and proud. It was late afternoon when I arrived, and a big, orange sun was setting, casting a pleasant glow over the small city.

The hotel was host to a regional gathering of an over-sixty society. The next morning, the dining room was full to capacity with brightly dressed, gray-haired groups tucking into breakfast and chatting vigorously about last night's social event.

I ordered sausage, biscuits, and gravy and settled down to rehearse everything I'd learned from Fred about gas chambers in preparation for my conversation with Bill Armontrout.

Nearly all of them were built during the 1920s by Eaton Metal Products of Salt Lake City, and very few of them had been used since the 1960s. Crumbling seals and rotting gaskets could cause leaks that would be lethal to the executioners and the state witnesses; but, apart from that, Fred believed that they contained such inherent design flaws that, as a method of execution, they should be viewed as a last resort. They are messy, dangerous, and difficult to operate. "The cost of a gas chamber that will not leak," Fred told me, "is prohibitive."

One of the main problems with gas chambers is that they have virtually no safety mechanism built in. A gas chamber should be a sealed system operated at negative pressure. That way, says Fred, if the chamber does leak, it leaks inward, not outward. The design solution, which is expensive, is to build in a vacuum pump.

The second fault Fred identified was the absence of a means to preheat the air coming into the gas chamber. The temperature in the death house should be 80 degrees Fahrenheit, because 78.6 degrees is the condensation or sublimation temperature of the gas. "Anything below that," Fred had told me "—and normally you're bringing cool, outside air in to evacuate the chamber—it condenses all over the walls and it becomes a death trap for anybody going in."

The third safety problem Fred identified "is the fact that most of the facilities generate their gas either in a bucket under the chair or in a plumbing system under the chamber, which then gets flushed out into the normal sewer system, where it really doesn't belong." The gas remains lethal for an hour or two, depending upon how confined it is and where it is. Some states used to bury it. Over two or three days, it's completely harmless. The gas that's expelled into the air is harmless because it dissipates rapidly.

With gas executions there is a residue of prussic acid left in the chamber, on the walls, floors, and ceiling—and the on the executed person's body and clothing—that the executioners have to contend with.

My note reading was interrupted by the waitress asking if I'd like more coffee.

"Thank you," I said, pushing my cup toward her.

"Say, you're not from around here, are you?"

"No," I said.

She was a friendly and inquisitive woman, as old as the over-sixties she was serving. She had strong legs. Her calf muscles were like a sprinter's.

"Are you the one from England?" she pressed, pouring the coffee.

I said I was, and rustled my notes in front of me.

She gave me a lovely smile and said, "Have a nice day."

"You too," I said. "Good coffee."

"Why, thank you."

Probably the most dangerous part of a gas execution, Fred had told me, is removing the body from the chamber. For fifteen to twenty minutes after death is pronounced, the chamber is vented to dispel as much of the gas as possible. Then it has to be sprayed with ammonia to neutralize the remaining gas. The members of the execution team detailed to remove the body then enter the chamber. They used to wear gas masks; nowadays, they wear oxygen masks.

Fred described it. "You go in. The inmate has to be completely washed down with chlorine bleach or with ammonia. The poison exudes right out through his skin. And if you gave that body to an undertaker, *you'd kill the undertaker*. You've got to go in, you've got to completely wash the body. You've got to take all of the clothes that were on there." (At that point Fred had told me, in a little practical aside, "They should execute them in a pair of gym shorts; some of the states let them wear *a shirt and pants!*")

I finished my breakfast and the smiling, gray-haired waitress came by to ask how I'd liked it.

"Great," I told her.

She asked if I'd like more biscuits, but I told her I was full.

After they wash down the body with ammonia or bleach, the execution team removes the dead inmate's clothes, which are taken away and burned. After that, the inmate is placed in a body bag and transferred to a waiting ambulance for removal to a funeral home of the family's choice or, if no one has claimed the body, to a local facility where he's given a pauper's funeral. The gas chamber only becomes safe after every inch of it has been washed down with bleach.

"Every one of these facilities is an accident waiting to happen," Fred had told me. "And I don't think any state has the right to subject its personnel or its witnesses—whether suspectingly or unsuspectingly—to an event that could take their life. The witnesses totally don't know. And the people that work in the prisons, they know, and they're taking risks. They may opt to take that risk, but they shouldn't be asked to. The gas chamber is a major problem, and I think everyone will be better off when it's finally abolished and replaced, probably, with lethal injection."

My appointment with Bill Armontrout was at eight, and I allowed myself half an hour to find the Department of Corrections building. The headquarters was a five-minute drive out of town, tucked away on the edge of the city. It's a new building, low and functional, and I pulled in alongside a battered pickup truck in the employees' parking lot. I was early. I announced myself at reception, and sat down to wait.

Among capital punishment states, Missouri has put relatively few people to death. In the period between 1938, when the gas chamber was introduced, and 1965, when Lloyd Leo Anderson was the last person to die in "the tank," there were thirty-nine executions at Missouri State Penitentiary. After capital punishment was reinstated in 1976, the ranks of Missouri death row inmates began to swell; there are presently eighty-one people awaiting execution.

Bill Armontrout is a veteran of gas executions at Missouri State Penitentiary, and he probably has more experience with the procedure than any prison warden in the United States today. When it became clear that executions would resume in Missouri, Bill was the warden of Missouri State Penitentiary. The gas chamber there hadn't been used for twenty-three years, and he did not relish the prospect of having to try it again. He called Fred in to examine the chamber, and Fred warned that it was likely to leak. Anxious to avoid the risks associated with using the chamber in its present condition, and aware of the fact that their first execution since 1965 would be the subject of close media attention, Missouri commissioned Fred to carry out a detailed study of the execution facility and to make recommendations.

Fred's report said that the Missouri gas chamber would need to be rebuilt at a cost of around $300,000. In the end, the state saved itself a great deal of time and trouble by passing a lethal injection bill which canceled Fred's gas chamber contract, replacing it with a $30,000 order for a lethal-injection machine.

At eight o'clock sharp, Bill Armontrout's secretary came down to get me and led me upstairs, to the offices of the Division of Adult Institutions.

Bill came around from behind his desk to shake my hand. A man of average height but with an enormous stomach, his face was friendly, and I took an immediate liking to him. Silver-haired and with a widow's peak, he has skinny legs and was wearing cowboy boots. Though he's in his fifties, he still has a youthful quality. For a big man, he moves quickly and economically.

Bill pumped my hand and welcomed me in his Oklahoma drawl. He sat me down and told me a little about himself. He had been a career navy man, and then worked in a military corrections facility. He told me that his wife, who had recently died of cancer, was English. I liked his frank style. When he told me about his wife, a brief shadow of sadness fell across his face.

After a few minutes of preamble, Bill called in his executive assistant, Mark Schreiber. Mark is shorter than Bill, and younger by ten or so years, and while he is working on a Bill-size gut, he still has a way to go. In contrast to Bill's relaxed jacket and trousers, Mark wore a dark gray wool suit, despite the oppressive heat.

"How you doing?" Mark asked, eyeing me critically.

Before taking his job at the head office, Mark had been a sheriff's deputy, and then a homicide investigator inside Missouri State Penitentiary.

Bill seemed more relaxed about my visit and offered me a cup of coffee.

I explained that my main interest was in capital punishment procedure in Missouri, and that I was particularly interested in Fred's machine. But before that, I wanted to learn about the history of the gas chamber in Missouri.

I realized that gas executions were a thing of the past in Missouri; but I was unprepared for the revelation that they were not a thing of the past for Bill Armontrout. He placed his large, heavily tattooed arms in front of him on the desk and said to Mark, who was sitting on a sofa off to one side: "Didn't you go down to Mississippi with me and do one?"

Mark's face did not change expression.

"Okay," Bill told me. "We went to Mississippi and did one with gas."

Bill paused for a moment, and I worried that he might not continue the story.

"Because they didn't have anyone trained to do it?" I asked.

"Well," Bill explained, "a friend of mine was the warden down there, and this was his first one. He's a young warden. So Mark and I went down and helped him. Do a complimentary one for him, you know?"

Mark, resigned to the fact that the story was going to be told, joined in.

"Our concern was, of course, here was this old gas chamber. And there were no written procedures. We have a plan here that we revise each time. We were really concerned. There was an old major, corrections major, who was extremely sharp in his time, and he had basically drafted the procedures, and he had all the original notes out at his residence. Bill and I had to go by there and get his notes, sit down and review them, and then we came up with our own plan. We were really concerned about it, because of the venting system, because of having to seal all the seals."

Mark had steered the conversation away from one about traveling executioners to one about procedure.

I asked: "How did you test the seals?"

Bill took up the story. "We measured the seals and we measured the chamber door gasket area and had manufactured a couple of new seals for it. And then, one of the things we figured out down in Mississippi was to use Vaseline on all the windows and everything, on all the seals. Once you've got it on there—"

Mark interrupts: "You mean a *lot*."

"—really coat heavy with Vaseline all the seal areas—"

"You don't want to be sparing with it—"

Bill resumed: "Even there, even with the precautions that we took there with that thing—"

Here I heard for the first time the language that Bill employs to describe an execution. It's a *thang*. He talks of, "When we do this *thing*, when we did that *thing*."

"—even with the precautions that we took there with that thing, you've got to decontaminate the chamber and the body before you can do anything, see?"

I nodded.

Bill continued: "Well, down there, when we used the gas, and started to decontaminate the inside of the chamber by blowing it out the stack, I stepped outside. I wanted to see what you could smell out there, and I could smell the ammonia that we were using, and bleach."

Bill talked as a veteran of gas executions, but not as someone who relished his task. I couldn't help noticing the difference in attitude between Bill and Fred. While the idea of gas chambers made the veins on Fred's neck stand out, and his voice rise half an octave, talking about them made Bill's voice soften. Fred was an expert on the theory of gas chambers. Bill operated them.

I asked Bill when the Mississippi execution had taken place. He told me it was 1987.

"That would be Edward Earl Johnson," I said. The BBC had made a documentary film about him.

"Was that the kid's name?" Bill asked. "I don't remember."

Bill continued to explain the difficulties involved in removing the body after he had conducted gas executions. "One of the things that cyanide gas does, it goes in the pores of your skin. You hose the body down, see. You have to use rubber gloves, and you hose the body down to decontaminate it before you do anything."

Mark picked up on a point that Fred had made to me earlier. Fred had expressed astonishment that anyone would gas a person who was fully clothed. Mark told me: "We were also concerned because, years ago, they had like black trunks and all this type of thing that the person wore. Of course we wanted to get away from that type of thing . . ."

"And be as dignified as possible," Bill said softly.

". . . and be as dignified as possible," Mark continued. "Which is what we've done. But on the other hand, we could understand why that was necessary, because you had to worry about all that clothing when you remove the body, see?"

Bill's attitude seemed to be that it may be more difficult for the executioners to put a fully clothed man to death in the gas chamber but he was owed the dignity of dying wearing a shirt and trousers, and not just a pair of gym shorts and a stethoscope taped to his chest.

Mark added: "Today, we don't want to forget about aspects you get involved with about the environment."

"You mean releasing cyanide gas into the atmosphere, and into the drainage system?" I fought back an urge to laugh at the idea of "green" executions.

"Yes," he said.

I excused myself to pay a visit to the toilet, and when I came back, Bill was talking to a tall young man in his doorway. He introduced the man as a local FBI investigator and told him I was visiting from England to research a film and book on capital punishment. As I shook his hand, the young man looked as if someone had shone a bright light in his eyes. He looked at Bill as if to say, "See you later," and hurried off.

The FBI agent made me think of the proposed anti-crime bill that would introduce a federal death penalty for some fifty-one offenses, including major drug trafficking with no murder involved. Different versions had been passed by the Senate and the House of Representatives, and it looked as though it would come onto the statute books in the near future. I had planned to discuss it with Bill, but he brought it up before I did.

We sat back down in Bill's office and he told me: "Like I say, I was certainly happy to see them at the last minute pass that lethal injection bill for us. Now the federal system, you know they're going to the death penalty now for narcotics traffickers. Now, here's what they're faced with. The way that bill reads is that the death penalty has to be done in the method of the district where the guy was convicted. We've got five different methods in this country, of executions. So that means the federal system is going to have to set up five different things."

"Will they end up subcontracting it to the states that have the death penalty?" I asked.

"They want to," Bill said. "But nobody's going to take it. They've already asked us, and we told them no. We got enough of our own to do," he groaned. "And the legal aspects of it."

Mark joined the conversation. "You *are* responsible for that. The legal hassle, the cost."

Bill turned to the question of cost-effectiveness in executions. "The chemicals you use under our state contracts in a lethal injection are less than forty dollars. Well, the thing is, you've got a lot of people involved here, and you have to compute their time. But like Mark said, there's a horrendous amount of legal stuff you have to go through. And then not only that, but the press. The press would tear you up as a state. Here we are in the business of *killing people,* you see."

"And the federal officials that would have to come in and be involved?" Mark reminded me. "You know that aspect, the accommodations. Not that you wouldn't do the best that you could, because you always do. But it would just be unbelievable, the accommodations that you would have to provide and all of that."

"So if the states won't be an executioner for the federal government," I asked, "does that mean they'll have to build an execution complex? In Washington, say, with a gas chamber, an electric chair, a gallows, a lethal injection machine, and a firing squad?"

"They're going to have to," Bill told me. "Unless they get that bill changed and just go to one method, which would be lethal injection. And I would strongly suggest they do that. Because Gary Gilmore was the first inmate executed in this country for a long time. A friend of mine, Sam Smith, was the warden out there—of course, that was a firing squad execution. And Sam Smith had camped out on the front of the prison out there, eighty-seven days prior to the execution—it looked like camp city with all the press out there watching them, waiting to see. And it was just a mess. So now when the federals do this thing, it's going to be a mess for them."

I turned the conversation to the main purpose of my visit: to learn about how Missouri used Fred's lethal injection machine. Bill started telling me about it in a frank and confidential tone.

"The machine is so precise. We have had very little problem with it."

In contrast to Fred's staccato Yankee delivery, Bill's speech is slow and considered. His tone is such that, if one were unaware that he was talking about killing someone by lethal injection, he could be mistaken for describing a particularly well-tuned car engine.

He explained: "One of the things it does is, it does not give a bolus. There's no way a bolus can go in and bust a vein, or bust a tubing. It's a very slow injection, and precise, and I would say that in less than a minute you've got about thirty cc's into the vein. It varies depending on how we set the machine up, but we've had only one hang-up."

I had not planned to explore any problems that might have occurred with executions until much later into my research. I was taken by surprise when Bill told me, "We had a hang-up on one syringe."

I remained silent, waiting to learn what that meant.

"We had it up on the machine, and it was cocked just a little bit. We didn't realize it was cocked, because you can't see it. And as the piston dropped, it hung. Well, Mark kept watching the lighting system—there's a set of lights on there which you'll see—and I was timing the light with a stopwatch, and when it exceeded the time that I thought it should be, then we used the manual pull, and went ahead and dropped the manual on, and finished the job out. But that's the only time we've had any problem with it. The machine is exceptional as far as I'm concerned."

Bill was referring to the execution of Maurice Byrd, which had taken place three weeks prior to my visit, on August 23, 1991. Something had gone wrong with one of the pistons on the syringes, and the execution team had been obliged to use the manual backup system to complete the execution.

Mark joined in the conversation.

"It really did not affect the individual," he said, anxious that I shouldn't interpret Bill's information as evidence of a glitch.

"That's right," Bill said. "The minute we bumped the machine, just bumped the cabinet, the piston came loose and came on down."

"Like hitting the water pump on an old car with a hammer to get it started again?" I asked.

"Uh-huh," Bill agreed. "And so we learned by that. And if I had a hang-up again, I wouldn't bother with using the manual pulls. I'd bump the back end of the machine and let it go on, see? But, not knowing what we had at the time, we went ahead and used the manual pull and dropped it on in."

"The thing about it," said Mark, "is that we had done a practice. I mean, the machine was tested. It's not like, well, it worked last time, so let's just take our chances this time."

Rehearsal, I was to learn, is one of the keys to Missouri's success at carrying out incident-free executions. The routine, the Missouri Protocol, is strictly adhered to, and it is drilled into every state employee involved in the execution process, over and over again.

Going back to the night of Maurice Byrd's execution, Bill told me how careful he'd been to test the machine. "This particular time, what we do about seven o'clock on the night of the execution, we'll run the machine through three cycles. And I sit there and cycle that machine out. I let that thing run through three cycles and sit there with a stopwatch and clocking it down, you know. And just like clockwork . . ."

Bill snapped his fingers to show that the machine had run through all three cycles precisely and without a hitch.

". . . and then at ten-thirty that evening we load the machine down. Like I said, the one syringe had to be cocked just a little bit, because it's very precise. The machine's very precise. And it had to be—it could have been even the syringe—or the plunger on the syringe."

"It could have been a flaw with the syringe that you didn't see," Mark added.

But not Fred's machine.

"You just don't know," Bill told me. "The minute the piston dropped, it started, and of course I started my time with it, and when I hit the one-minute mark on my stopwatch, I knew it should go, you know, it should give me the signal that it's through. It did not, so we went right to the manual pull, and—"

"Finished the thing," Mark concluded, having had enough of problems.

"—finished the thing," Bill repeated, anxious for me to understand that there was nothing wrong with Fred's machine, and nothing wrong with the Missouri Protocol. "And when we got into where we get to the cabinet from the front side and bumped that cabinet—reached up to unlatch it"— Bill snapped his fingers—"it went ahead."

I asked about how the dual executioner controls actually functioned when it was necessary to engage the manual pulls.

Bill was comfortable with this technical talk, and readily answered my question. "You have two manual pulls, and one is a dummy pull. Both have got the same size spring on them, so the person pulling doesn't feel anything different."

Mark added: "It's a matter of it being set up that way to the advantage of the individuals that are actually pushing the buttons or whatever, because there's just a very small—*very small*—group of people that have all been trained, and are all there together. No one else is there, so we all know who that small group of people is, and it doesn't make any difference to us."

So much for Fred's view on the psychological importance of the dual control, I thought, and the need for the executioner to feel that he wasn't actually responsible for the killing. In Missouri, everyone takes responsibility.

Bill turned the conversation to Fred, for whom he has the highest regard. Fred's contribution was not simply providing a machine that works; he also trained the Missouri execution team, the select corps of men including Bill and Mark in Jefferson City and Paul Delo, Don Roper, Gary Sutterfield, and Greg Wilson at Potosi Correctional Center.

During the previous week, Fred had told me how he trained the Missouri executioners: a combination of classroom teaching and "actual hands-on use of the equipment." He tells his students: "The human body is designed not to be destroyed. The minute you stop the heart, it has a mechanism for restarting the heart. And heart death is the key in all executions. So we have to design a system that, after it destroys the brain, it destroys the heart. It's crucial to electrocution, to lethal injection, even hanging. They all do the same thing. It results in brain death, and then heart cessation. So anyone who deals with these things is trained in all of the aspects, including the medical. And it makes them better people. It makes them more comfortable with their job."

Bill Armontrout leaned back in his chair and told me: "When we purchased the machine from Fred, the training was part of the purchasing package, and then Fred has graciously come out here several times, you know. He wanted to see the machine proved out, and so he came out and watched us go through an execution to see how we were doing things, and to make sure that machine was workable, you know? And, of course, it's proved very effective for us."

In the execution industry, effectiveness has never necessarily been measured by a quick, neat, or clean kill. State officials in Florida and Texas seem little concerned with evidence that inmates suffer when execution equipment fails to function properly. In Missouri, the state has decided that it *does* matter.

Missouri's determination to carry out capital punishment as quickly and painlessly as possible derives, as far as Bill Armontrout is concerned, from a "humane" desire to ensure that the inmate's suffering is reduced to a minimum. There are also other reasons behind Missouri's modern capital punishment procedures, and these have to do with reducing stress on state employees and promoting an acceptable public image of Missouri in the media.

Bill Armontrout is particularly adept at handling the press, as is the other key member of the execution team, Potosi superintendent Paul Delo. Both men confront questions head-on. Both understand that the task they are charged with is performed in the name of the people, and that state government must be accountable to those who elect it. One of the first things that Bill did when Missouri switched to lethal injection was to help develop a media policy.

The media policy is as much a part of the Missouri Protocol as are the execution procedure itself and the security arrangements which surround an execution. It's a precise and detailed three-page document which begins, "Every effort shall be made by the staff of the Missouri Department of Corrections to accommodate representatives of the news media prior to and during a scheduled execution." The department makes a videotape and photographs of the death chamber available to news organizations and provides superior press facilities at Potosi Correctional Center on execution night.

"We can all look at the press in various aspects," Mark told me. "And a lot of times we'd like to avoid them. But they're not going to go away. The key is knowing how we can handle the press in an effective way that will be to our benefit. It's been very effective for us."

At the first Missouri execution by lethal injection, the Missouri State Penitentiary and the Department of Corrections were under siege from television and newspaper reporters. Bill recalls: "The first one we did, we had twenty some of the—I call them 'Star Wars' TV trucks, you know, the big combat-size ones that got the telescoping satellites to them—we had twenty some of those for our first one. And now that we're getting into this thing, maybe we'll have one or two, and that'll be it anymore, you know."

In the aftermath of the Byrd execution, the Department of Corrections was working on the twelfth revision of the Missouri Protocol. The early versions had been written by Bill and Mark, with Paul Delo contributing to the later ones. I was allowed to read the eleventh revision, and to take extensive notes.

In Missouri, death warrants are usually issued around ten days prior to a scheduled execution date. The protocol says that the condemned person should be taken to the deathwatch, or holding, cell forty-eight hours prior to the execution—except in instances where other factors suggest an immediate isolation of the inmate. These are essentially security worries regarding the inmate's safety. Is he a suicide risk? Is there a danger that another inmate may attempt to cheat the executioner by murdering the condemned man?

The forty-eight-hour rule is only a guideline, and in reality, it is the minimum time a condemned man would spend in the deathwatch cell.

"That varies," Bill told me. "Just like this last one," he said, referring to Maurice Byrd. "This last one had professed that he would take his own life. Now, the minute that we get word that the date has been set by the court, from that date on, we can grab the guy that day and set the death-watch from that day on, you see. When they set the date, it's usually within a week or two. And we've had them set the date like, the court would meet today and say tomorrow. So we grab the guy as quick as possible, depending on the fellow's mental state. Now, another thing that attaches here is peer pressure. Other inmates on death row trying to get the guy to commit suicide rather than have the state do it." Bill referred to Peewee Gaskins's suicide bid in South Carolina the previous week. "That's the kind of thing you have to watch for."

During the deathwatch, there is an officer in the holding cell with the condemned person twenty-four hours a day. The deathwatch officer keeps a log of visitors and events throughout the period. In Missouri, condemned inmates on deathwatch have free canteen privileges, including soft drinks, snacks, and cigarettes. There is a television and VCR in the cell, and most inmates spend their time watching films on video. They are also allowed to make collect phone calls with the prior approval of the operations officer, who keeps a log of outgoing and incoming calls.

Visiting hours are from 6:00 A.M. to 10:00 P.M. (6:00 P.M. on execution night). Two visitors are allowed at any time, and this is followed religiously. "You run into some real security risks if you don't do it that way," says Mark.

When he was discussing this part of the protocol with me, Bill said: "We're not too concerned about hours here, either. We don't restrict visits to one hour or whatever. Like, on the last day, they can sit there with their family or whoever, all day if they want to, until it's about six o'clock at night. Then, at six o'clock at night, we've got things that we need to do. So we make the visitors leave."

The prison doctor is notified forty-eight hours in advance, and the protocol states that the inmate is given a physical examination twenty-four hours prior to being executed. During the time he is on deathwatch, the inmate may receive visits from up to two ministers or religious advisers.

On the day of the execution, media contact with the prison is suspended from 6:00 P.M. (or sooner if deemed necessary) until the post-execution press conference. A sophisticated security operation, involving nearly 150 prison officers, state highway patrol, sheriff's deputies, and local police forces, is mounted. With the Mercer execution in 1989, the Department of Corrections took extra precautions. The area around Missouri State Penitentiary was closed off, there were snipers on rooftops, extra security was assigned to the state capitol and the governor's mansion, and the river police patrolled the Missouri River. Since death row moved to Potosi, the security requirement has been somewhat reduced. This is partly because of the fact that Potosi Correctional Center is situated in a fairly remote part of the state, more than an hour's drive from St. Louis, nearly three hours' drive from Jefferson City, and a full day's journey from Kansas City. This has discouraged protesters and so has made perimeter security easier to manage.

At 6:00 P.M.—six hours before the normal execution time of 12:01—the superintendent carries out a final briefing of all staff, and at 6:15 P.M. they man their posts. One of the things Bill Armontrout introduced with the execution of Tiny Mercer, but which is not part of the official protocol, is a prayer service for the execution team and the rest of the prison staff. Bill told me: "One of the things that I started originally with this thing, I have a prayer service for all staff on the evening of the execution. And any staff that wants to attend can attend." In telling me this, he also added a note about his policy in assigning staff for execution duty. "Even though you think you know a lot of staff people," he said, "we make it where if a person—say I put you on a security post or whatever, and you don't believe in the death penalty—all you have to do is tell me *personally* that you don't want to be involved with it. No questions asked, and you'll be dropped. Because people do have feelings, you have to understand. And I've had a number of staff, once they've been assigned, ask not be assigned. And that's just between me and them. That's their belief, and I honor that."

From the time the staff man their posts and the inmate's last visitor is obliged to leave, every second of everyone's time is accounted for:

• 7:00 P.M. Phones in the execution room are checked. Clocks are checked and synchronized with the one in the media room.

• 7:30 P.M. The inmate is given a clean set of clothing and is offered a sedative. One of the certified operators verifies that the lethal injection machine is ready.

• 8:30 P.M. The gurney is prepared. Blinds in the death chamber are drawn.

• 10:00 P.M. During the previous ninety minutes, telephones and clocks have been checked and rechecked, as has the lethal injection machine and associated hardware. At 10:00 P.M., the execution team reports to the death chamber, and the drugs are loaded into the lethal injection machine. The assistant superintendent of programs verifies that all members of the execution team have reported. (As part of the security operation, the six key members of the execution team wear highest-priority security badges. Other staff wear badges identifying them for duty at various levels of security within the prison and at the perimeter.)

• 10:30 P.M. The chaplain reports to holding cell. Ambulance and hearse arrive at sally port. State witnesses report to employees' entrance. Missouri law requires that there be a minimum of twelve state witnesses. Six of these are normally press. Telephones are manned.

• 10:40 P.M. The director of the Division of Adult Institutions reports to parole board courtroom in the prison.

• 10:45 P.M. State witnesses report to hearing room.

• 11:00 P.M. The director of the Division of Adult Institutions reports to hearing room. The deputy director monitors the open telephone line to the attorney general.

• 11:05 P.M. The deputy director reports to main conference room.

• 11:10 P.M. Telephones are tested.

• 11:15 P.M. The doctor tests the electrocardiogram equipment.

• 11:20 P.M. The department director tests the telephones and monitors all lines. Clocks are rechecked. The department director carries a portable radio as a backup in case of telephone failure.

• 11:30 P.M. The department director telephones the governor's designated representative to check if there is any stay. The assistant superintendent of programs ensures that only authorized personnel are in execution area.

• 11:35 P.M. The inmate is escorted to the gurney and secured on it. The EKG is attached, and the IV line is set.

• 11:40 P.M. Telephones are monitored. Inmate witnesses arrive. (Missouri allows the inmate to invite five witnesses. They are the subject of a separate security operation and are segregated from state witnesses at all times.)

• 11:55 P.M. Telephones are monitored.

• 12:00 P.M. The department director telephones the superintendent to ask if there is a stay of execution. If no, the superintendent proceeds. The blinds are opened in the execution chamber.

• 12:01 A.M. The superintendent reads the death warrant. The execution commences.

During the execution, each event is timed with a stopwatch and logged by the operations officer, who is in the death chamber. The doctor monitors the EKG and signals to the operations officer that there is no sign of heart activity. The blinds are closed, and the doctor examines the inmate and establishes the time of death and signs the death certificate. After the blinds have been closed, the inmate witnesses are escorted from the prison. The state witnesses sign a Return Warrant of Execution, and the press witnesses proceed to the press area. A press conference is held, and a nominated media witness must be available for questioning by other media who did not witness the execution.

"Why," I ask Bill, "are executions always scheduled for 12:01?"

"It's not only a historical type thing," he replied. "All your other inmates are locked down. You've got everything controlled. And so you've no problem with other inmates. We've deviated from that on one because we had a stay of execution at the last minute, and so we had to wait to see what the court was going to do. The United States Supreme Court then vacated at like six o'clock that afternoon. So we actually did the execution at nine o'clock at night."

The 12:01 tradition stems not only from the extra security it affords, and the fact that it is some deterrent against demonstrators, but also because it allows the state a full twenty-four hours in which to carry out the death sentence. The death warrant does not stipulate what time of day the execution should take place. So Missouri takes the prudent step of allowing themselves a full day.

"Like I tell the staff," says Bill, "if we can't do it at one minute after midnight, we'll just wait till we can do it that day. Regardless of what it takes, you know."

Trying to imagine what it is like to be a condemned man, and to watch one's life tick away through its last hours in the certainty that the state will carry out the sentence, is impossible to do. I wondered what effect it had on Bill—the ticking of the clock inexorably toward the deliberate taking of another man's life.

Bill told me it was most difficult for him when there was a stay of execution. "It is very tough. The longer it drags out, the tougher it is. I noticed something with this last one [Maurice Byrd]. The United States Supreme Court turned this one down at five minutes till nine that evening. So, at nine o'clock that evening, we knew that we were going to be going a little after midnight. The staff were tired. We got tired just from the tension. I was very tired after that was over that evening, because I knew from nine o'clock onward, a three-hour period, I knew what we were going to do. There wasn't any wondering about it. We knew that there was no more appeals, nothing else, that this guy was going, you see."

"How does the actual killing affect you as a person?" I asked.

Bill thought for a moment and said: "I look at it this way. I've made peace with myself on this thing by knowing that the fellow that's being executed has had every chance of appeal. He's had his trials; the number of appeals the guy has had—the United States Supreme Court three times, Eighth Circuit three times, the local court of appeals three or four times. When you know that the case has been scrutinized that closely, then it makes you feel much easier. I believe in the laws of our country. I've been around the world several times. We *may* not have the most perfect criminal justice system in the world, but it's the best *I've* seen. It affords the person an ample opportunity to prove his innocence." Bill looked at me and said, with a slight trace of emotion: "So I'm at peace with myself because I know that this guy's case has been looked at a number of times. And I do personally believe in the death penalty. It may not be a deterrent for the next person, but it is for that person."

While the popular concept of lethal injection may be that it is a simple process, I was learning that it was a complex and lengthy operation. In the execution of Maurice Byrd, for instance, the execution team's log shows that fifty-one minutes elapsed from the time Byrd was placed on the gurney to the time the doctor pronounced him dead.

Byrd entered the death chamber at Potosi at 11:24 P.M. and was restrained six minutes later, at 11:30 P.M.

I asked Mark Schreiber what happened during that six-minute period.

"They're just basically talking to him and everything."

What about? I wondered. "Has anyone ever resisted?" I asked.

"We haven't had that yet," Bill told me. "We haven't been faced with that. And that's because we know our prisoners to start with. And one of the things that we do is talk to him, you know, and tell him exactly what we're going to do, what's going to happen to him. So there's no surprises. There's no scare to him, you know. He knows it's time for him to do it, and his mind is made up he's going to die, you know, because of his appeals being out or whatever. And so we explain, *step by step,* what's going to happen to him. And, so far, we have not had to manhandle an inmate to get him in there to put him down."

"I'll tell you what," said Mark. "I think it's a—it's almost an acceptance—"

Bill interrupted: "They have no animosity towards us—"

"—whereas before maybe they were a little bit full of animosity and all," Mark concluded.

In the case of Maurice Byrd, the IV line was set at 11:48 P.M., some eighteen minutes after he'd been placed on the gurney. (In my first conversation with Bill and Mark, I was unable to discover what happened during that period. I would learn later on, after talking to condemned men at Potosi.) The lethal injection machine was activated at 12:03 A.M. Mark recorded that Byrd was "apparently unconscious" four minutes later, at 12:07 A.M. At 12:08, he noted, "Visible muscular movement stopped," and "Respiration apparently stopped." Monitoring the EKG machine, Mark recorded that "cardiac complex amona" started at 12:12 A.M. Maurice Byrd was pronounced dead at 12:15 A.M.

I was curious about doctors' involvement in Missouri executions, since the American Medical Association expressly forbids their participation, except to pronounce death. Fred was always careful to use the phrase "IV technician" to refer to the person who sets the IV line and, in fact, participates in the execution. Bill told me that Missouri used a contract doctor for the Mercer execution—a physician who volunteered for the role.

Bill explained that "We don't set the IV ourselves. We have him set the IV and then we hook our lines into the T-valve. The doctor does the pronouncing of the death through an EKG machine hooked up to the person being executed. The first one we did, Tiny Mercer, the electrical impulses from the heart will show on your monitor before it flat-lines out. You'll see it for quite a while on there. It seems like forever that you see the electrical impulse from the heart before she'll flat-line out then. But the doctor monitors that continuously through the whole thing."

In some cases, the doctor's involvement in the execution goes beyond setting the IV line in the inmate and monitoring the EKG.

"With an old doper," Bill explained, "we have trouble getting a vein. We had to do an IV cutdown on one."

That inmate had been Tiny Mercer, the first man to be lethally injected in Missouri. An IV cutdown is when the vein must be surgically exposed in order for the IV to be connected. An incision is made, and the vein is lifted out with a suture so the needle may be inserted.

"The doctor does that," Mark told me.

I asked about the IV cutdown procedure on Tiny Mercer.

"Rather than do the IV cutdown in here," Bill explained, pointing to his neck, "he went to the leg, and did the IV cutdown down there." Bill pointed to his groin. "The doctor had prepared himself for it with his equipment, see? And we've found that we have a lot of different equipment there that we may never use, but in a case like this, for the IV cutdown, we had it."

"Did Tiny Mercer find it alarming?" I asked.

"No," said Bill. "It was a lot more alarming for me than it was for the inmate."

Tiny Mercer's execution took place before Missouri had built its custom-made lethal injection facility at Potosi. It was done in the old gas chamber, with the chair and door removed. I wondered how Bill and Mark felt about carrying out executions by lethal injection as opposed to lethal gas.

"It's like if you or I went to the dentist and they gave you Pentothal," said Mark. "You're gone. Good-bye."

"Oh, there's no comparison," said Bill. "I would say lethal injection is so much more humane. There is no gasping, no jerking with lethal injection. It's just going to sleep. Closing your eyes and going to sleep. With gas, there's gasping. Their eyes bulge out, they try to hold their breath. It is much more painful than lethal injection. I've never seen an execution done with electricity. I have seen them done with gunshots. But electricity to me—electrocution, if it's done properly—would probably be fairly humane, with the exception that you're going to get some burning. There's no way out. There's no way out. You're going to get some burning. See, the last electrocution they had in this country [Peewee Gaskins in South Carolina], they had to hit the guy twice. They hit him once, and they thought they had it. The doctor goes to check him, he's still alive, so they have to hit it again. That's not too humane."

I told Bill that if Fred Leuchter were facing execution, despite having invented the lethal injection machine, he would choose the electric chair.

Bill smiled. "Fred has got this stuff figured out pretty close, you know. And I would say if anybody could do electrocution in this country, Fred could probably get it down more precise than anybody could. And if I were faced, as a warden, with an electrocution of a guy, I would call Fred in as a consultant as to the voltage to use for that particular man."

Bill softened his voice and continued. His tone was one of deep concern.

"Now, everybody's different. *Everybody's* different. One of the things we do in our training sessions is pick a person that's equivalent to the size of the subject we're going to be dealing with. And we take that guy and actually put him down on a gurney and adjust the straps to him, you see, so that we know when we get the person in there that's going to be given the lethal injection, everything's going to fit for him."

Bill stood up and apologized that he had a meeting out of town, and wouldn't see me again during my present visit.

I thanked him for his time and said I hoped to see him again, perhaps after I'd learned a little bit more about the process.

"I look forward to that," he told me.

M ARK SCHREIBER offered to take me over to the old Missouri State Penitentiary to see the gas chamber. Before we left, he showed me into his office to tell me about the history of executions in Missouri—a task for which he is well suited, being an amateur historian and having researched *Somewhere in Time: A 160 Year History of Missouri Corrections*.

He opened an old leather-bound book in which he had collected photographs of the thirty-eight men and one woman who had been put to death in the gas chamber and the six men who had, so far, been executed by lethal injection. Of the thirty-nine who had been executed in the gas chamber, three were kidnappers, thirty were murderers, and six were rapists. The majority of those put to death between 1938 and 1965 were black: twenty-three, as opposed to sixteen whites—in stark contrast to Missouri's present-day death row, where whites outnumber blacks.

The book was a strange rouges' gallery of the vicious, the stupid, the unfortunate, and the obviously defective. Mark showed me a photograph of the only woman to have been executed in Missouri: Bonnie Brown

Heady. She and her partner in kidnapping, Carl Austin Hall, were executed together in the two-seater gas chamber on December 18, 1953. Mark told me that, with very few exceptions, the condemned have gone to their deaths in a dignified and stoical way. The one exception he knew of was Carl Austin Hall, who whimpered as he was strapped into the chair. Bonnie Brown Heady told him to "take it like a man" and told the executioners exactly what she thought of them.

Mark put on his jacket and we made our way out of the comfortable, air-conditioned offices to his car. By now the temperature was up around a hundred, but the day was beautifully bright and still, with hardly a cloud in the sky. He seemed more relaxed talking to me on his own, and I asked him whether he had found the Tiny Mercer execution personally difficult.

"No sir," he said. "No sir," he repeated, shaking his head. "I have some very deep feelings about things. I do not think you can be in the corrections business and not like inmates. I also understand inmates, and I know where the line can be drawn."

I found his answer intriguing. He elaborated.

"If there's anything in my opinion, in regard to the death penalty, certainly there are other people that it should be applied to—that have been lucky by one circumstance or another that they did not get the death penalty. But it really does not bother me, simply because I have worked cases myself, of people who have killed corrections officers. I don't have a feeling of animosity for those people, like where I'm going to go up to someone and say, 'I'm glad you got the death penalty.' "

Mark told me that he had experience of corrections officers who would taunt death row inmates, telling them how much they looked forward to being there when the switch was pulled.

Of death row inmates he said, "I have sympathy for their parents. They're still a mother and a father, and they have feelings the same as you or I."

He talked about his experience of being a homicide investigator at the penitentiary, and said, "Things affect me. And that's why I can't watch those police drama type of movies. It's not that you don't like your profession. But you have to have that certain curtain that you put down, and that's your psychological self protecting itself."

As we approached the old penitentiary, Mark expressed his anxiety about participating in executions, relating it to his other experiences of violent death. "I think that, as an individual, I can handle whatever the situation may be. Sure, you don't want something to happen—you don't want there to be a glitch—but if it does, then you will try to handle it in the most professional way. And humanely. It's probably never easy seeing someone die. I've seen many people die. I've been right there when many people have died. When they've been stabbed, when I was there as an investigator. Or when I was an investigator for the sheriff's department. I've seen an inmate stabbed multiple times, and you're trying to get from point A to point B to get to the infirmary to save that person's life. And that may be the sorriest inmate in the penitentiary, that you had all kinds of negative dealings with, but at that time, that's still a human being, and you do the best that you can do, you know, to try to save that person's life."

What became increasingly clear to me, as we approached the old prison, was that the Missouri Protocol helped the individual to handle his personal feelings by sharing in a collective responsibility for executions. "We all work together," Mark told me. "It's a collective thing. Everyone is properly trained. They know what they're supposed to do, and take care of business."

As we approached the forbidding stone walls, Mark told me: "My wife's third great-grandfather built this. He built the first capitol in 1827, and started the prison in 1834. By 1889, it was the largest prison in the world." We parked and entered through a pair of enormous gates and checked in. The officer behind the screen asked me what was in my bag, and I told him a notebook, camera, and tape recorder. Mark flashed his badge and told the frowning officer I had permission to bring them inside.

An officer with a heavy bunch of keys opened one of the massive internal security gates and locked us between it and another just like it. We were then admitted inside the prison, and Mark led me through dark corridors whose geography he knew intimately, and out into the yard.

The yard at Jefferson City is large and irregularly shaped. In the old days, inmates used to quarry part of it. Now it has handball courts, a weight-lifting area, and a softball field. And plenty of dark corners, making it a dangerous place to be.

Because of the good weather, hundreds of inmates were milling about.

Down near the little stone building that used to be the death house, a mixed a capella group was crooning slightly out of tune, under the direction of an earnest young black man who would stop and start them until the harmonies were right. Mostly, black and white formed their own groups. It was easy to pick out the Aryan Nation followers, with their swastika tattoos. The black prison gang, the Moors, hung together, separate from the street gangs. Both Crips and Bloods were present, keeping a wary distance from one another.

As in most American prisons, there were impressively muscled men pumping iron. Lone figures walked past, staring hard. Some smaller groups stopped what they were doing to stare with collective curiosity or contempt. Every few minutes, an inmate would come up and challenge: "Who are you?" In the afternoon I was there, rumors proliferated about my identity. I was a cop, an investigator, a reporter.

Mark and an old corrections major took me down to the death house. It is a small, rectangular stone structure with two barred steel doors, and with pointy stones set into the roof all the way around it. "This thing was built by inmates," Mark told me. The major opened the heavy, creaking door with a big key and I stepped into the cool, musty-smelling building.

In front of me was the gas chamber. It's a small steel structure that resembles a diving bell. The door is shaped like an ellipse, and it has two oblong windows on either side—one for the witnesses, one for the executioners. An exhaust pipe emerges from the top of the chamber and through the roof, to expel the cyanide gas.

Mark led me to the right of the chamber, where the executioner's controls are located. He showed me how the lever worked to lower the cyanide pellets into the hydrochloric acid, and how the ammonia and bleach were introduced into the chamber after an execution.

Inside the chamber, from which the two chairs had been removed, was the gurney on which Tiny Mercer had been executed.

To the right of the chamber was the tiny holding cell where deathwatch inmates waited to be executed. Not ten feet from the gas chamber, which the inmate contemplated throughout the deathwatch, it was barely large enough to hold a bed and a few visitors.

Adjacent to the holding cell was a room with a large sink. There were shelves to store the bottles of acid, cyanide, ammonia, and bleach. It was the room where the drugs were measured out and the syringes loaded to administer Missouri's first lethal dose.

The old major was silent. He jiggled his keys and wiped his brow under his straw hat. He`looked at me, and I supposed he wondered what I was thinking. I was busy memorizing the details of the place, and learning the movements of the executioner. I tried to imagine thirty-nine people's silent screams as they choked and gasped in the defunct tank, one by one, two by two, with the witnesses standing where I was. Even imagining it one at a time was difficult. Inside, the temperature was cool and agreeable, and my two companions remained silent, ready to answer any questions I might have. Outside, I could hear the sound of a handball thwacking against a wall, and the cheers and shouts of men watching the game.

I didn't have any questions.

Before 1989, when it was moved to Potosi Correctional Center, in a rural corner in the southeastern part of the state, death row at Missouri State Penitentiary had some of the worst prison conditions in the United States. Located in the basement of the building, it had no natural light at all. Each cell had a low-wattage bulb which made it difficult to read or write. Unless one looked at a clock, it was impossible to tell the time of day. The cells were roach infested, and subject to flooding. There was no communal area, and inmates were confined to their cells for an average of twenty-three and a half hours a day. On a maximum of three alternate days per week, they were allowed a forty-five-minute solitary exercise period on an indoor weight machine or in a small outdoor cage. There were no educational or vocational programs. Inmates took two daily meals in their cells: breakfast at 8:00 A.M. and a second meal at 2:30 P.M. Then, seventeen and a half hours without food. Medical service was poor, and dental care nonexistent.

Death row inmates filed a lawsuit in federal court and in 1986 won a consent decree which provided sixteen hours a week of out-of-cell time for "regular custody" inmates and eight hours a week for "close custody" prisoners. There was better access to health care, recreational facilities, and religious and counseling services, and an evening meal was introduced.

The major who showed me around took me back inside the main part of the prison. "What do you think?" he asked.

I told him, "For an old building, at least it's clean."

"It's a constant battle," he said.

I said it was cleaner than the waiting room of most London hospitals' emergency rooms.

He smiled, thinking I was indulging him, trying to say something agreeable. In fact, it was the truth.

"You know," he said, "we're backward here in Missouri. We're twenty years behind the times."

"I guess you've got to do the best you can with limited resources," I offered.

"Yeah," he said, wiping the sweat from his brow and stuffing his handkerchief back into his trouser pocket. "We're still backward."

The major let us out of the prison, and I thanked him for his trouble.

"Anytime," he said, with genuine warmth.

YOU WANT to go for a ride?" Mark asked me when we got in the car. "Want me to show you around?"

"Sure," I told him.

"Okay," he said. "But let's get some Coca-Cola first."

We drove to a gas station a few blocks from the prison and Mark went inside and bought two sixteen-ounce Cokes. We swigged them in the car as he set off on an unusual tour of Jefferson City and the surrounding countryside.

"Now, look at that house over there," Mark told me. He slowed down and pointed to an elegant mansion near the prison. "That used to be the warden's house."

"It's a fine house," I said.

"Sure is. But the warden doesn't live there anymore. They've had to sell it off. It's going to be renovated. Lawyers' offices."

As we drove along, Mark told me a little bit more about himself. He had started out as a teacher, then became a deputy sheriff, a corrections officer, an investigator at Missouri State Penitentiary (investigating offenses committed by corrections officers as well as inmates), and then an executive assistant in the Department of Corrections. His brother is in the prison service, and his wife works in the Jefferson City prosecutor's office. He's a Roman Catholic of German descent—one of many who settled in Missouri in the nineteenth century. (Until the turn of the century, Jefferson City had its own daily German-language newspaper.) He told me that his wife is descended from English settlers. He's traced her family tree, and they belong to a society called the Magna Carta Barons. Like Fred Leuchter, he is a member of the Sons of the American Revolution. His hero is Thomas Jefferson.

On the highway, we passed a long convoy of National Guard trucks and jeeps, and the Missouri Highway Patrol headquarters. The town soon gave way to attractive, rolling countryside and the banks of the Osage River, which branches off from the Missouri River near Bonnots Mill (near Frankenstein, Missouri) and flows into the Lake of the Ozarks. Mark turned off onto a blacktop road and we drove past Algoa Correctional Center, a medium-security prison that holds more than 1,200 men. He told me that Missouri's prison population was currently in excess of 15,000. Ten years ago, it totaled only 5,600.

He attributed much of the dramatic rise in crime to drugs. Looking around the peaceful countryside, I asked how Missouri could have a drug problem in the way that states like New York or California did.

"Easy," Mark told me. "Land is so cheap in Missouri that we're now the number two marijuana growing state in America."

While we were walking in the yard at the penitentiary, I had noticed a number of inmates wearing the colors of the two most notorious Los Angeles gangs, the Bloods and the Crips. I was surprised, first of all, to see them in Jefferson City; and, secondly, that they would be allowed to wear their colors in prison.

"As long as they don't wear them around their waist, that's all we care about," the major had said to me. "As long as they're not going to war."

Most of the Crips and Bloods had been sent to the walls for drug offenses —major trafficking, felonious assaults, or lesser murder charges—evidence that their influence has spread as far east as Kansas City and St. Louis.

As we began to follow the Osage River, Mark told me that Americans were sick and tired of violent crime, and that there was very wide support for the death penalty in Missouri.

He was pessimistic in his prognosis for the future, with a rising crime rate and with state budgets coming under increasing pressure. "I don't think you're going to see the population on death row dwindle," he said, "I think you're going to get in more at a faster rate than what you're going to execute. We're getting more all the time. Other states are as well. I think that juries and judges are becoming less hesitant in handing the death sentence out. People have gotten fed up. And I think that's true on a national scope. They're fed up, and they realize that something has to be done. Now, that something may—who knows?—it may not turn out to be the right answer. Who knows what it'll be. But they certainly have to do something."

Mark's view is that inmates in Missouri and across the United States spend too long on death row. The national average is just under eight years. Two of Missouri's capital punishment inmates, Martsay Bolder and Bobby Shaw, have been on death row for eleven years. Five have been waiting for ten years.

Mark told me: "What we need to do in this country is, they need to do something with the delays in the appeals process. Don't get me wrong. I'm not saying take away a guy's appeals—that's what makes our system what we think is a democratic system. But certainly you can cut it down to where it doesn't take eight, nine, ten years." He suggested there should be a panel of judges whose only responsibility is the review of capital cases, speeding the process up to two years from sentencing to execution.

We drove along a tiny road that had flood warning signs, and Mark told me that the Osage River often burst its banks and made the road impassable. There were tiny houses and fishing camps scattered throughout the pleasant woodland along the river, built on stilts to avoid flood damage. Mark stopped the car in front of one of them, where wood was piled beneath the raised structure. He told me a story about when he was a sheriff's deputy, and three young black inmates had escaped from Algoa. They had made their way down the railroad line that runs parallel to the river, and Mark and another deputy tracked them and had them cornered in the woodpile under the house. Nobody wanted to go under the house and flush them out, so Mark came up with a plan.

"I knew they were in there," Mark laughed. "So I drew my gun and said to my partner, 'There's a copperhead in there, I'm going to shoot it.' Well, it didn't take long for them to come out. 'Don't shoot!' they were crying. 'Don't shoot!' " He slapped his thigh and drove on.

We turned away from the river and onto higher ground. We drove along a road lined on either side with fine, mature oak trees, and Mark pointed out his house—a well-kept, ranch-style house surrounded by woodland. A little farther on, he pointed to a small, shabby house and told me another story from his deputy sheriff days, when he was working as an undercover narcotics agent.

"I'd bought some drugs from some hippies who lived in that house, and we'd gone back to make an arrest. I had some other deputies with me, and as they entered the house I heard four gunshots. I went inside, and what had happened was, the hippies kept a snake behind their sofa. They had a boa constrictor as a pet. And one of the deputies shot it!"

I said it looked like a good area for hunting. Mark said it was, and that he was an enthusiastic hunter. "There's wild turkey all around here," he said. "They eat the acorns. I've got wild turkeys come right up to my front door." He told me that Bill Armontrout was his hunting partner, and that they both sometimes hunted with a muzzle loader.

"Good sport," I remarked. "One shot."

"That's right, Steve." Mark told me he also hunted squirrels with a single-shot, bolt-action .22-caliber rifle. "I only hunt what I eat."

"You eat the squirrels?" I asked.

"They're delicious," he told me.

Later on, I met a prison officer at Potosi who'd also worked at Jefferson City, and he told me that one of the favorite pastimes on night shift was to cook up a mess of squirrels.

"What about deer?" I asked Mark.

"We've got great deer hunting in Missouri," he told me. "But you need to go a little bit south of here, down towards where you're going tomorrow, down near Potosi. Paul Delo, he's a great deer hunter."

"What about you?" I asked.

"I don't go hunting for deer," Mark told me. "I couldn't kill anything that beautiful."

AT THE end of the afternoon, we drove back to Jefferson City, and Mark offered to show me around the capitol building. He took me up steep flights of stairs for a peek into the splendid senate chamber, then down long corridors past senators' offices and group portraits of each government since Missouri became the twenty-fourth state in 1821.

I stood in the middle of the floor in the reception area, under the enormous dome, and craned my neck to read the homilies that are carved in stone:

WHERE THERE IS NO VISION THE PEOPLE PERISH

LORD GOD OF HOSTS BE WITH US YET, LEST WE FORGET

IDEAS CONTROL THE WORLD

PROPERTY IS THE FRUIT OF LABOR

THE EARTH IS THE LORD'S IN THE FULLNESS THEREOF

PARTY HONESTY IS PARTY EXPEDIENCY

Mark walked me around the permanent history exhibition in the lobby —a nicely conceived tour through Missouri history, with life-size models and artifacts. Missouri's story is a fascinating one, as the state falls just on the western side of that great dividing line between East and West, the Mississippi River, and nearly smack in the middle of America. If Missouri is not the exact geographical heart of America, it is the dividing line between west and Midwest, between southern Midwest and the Deep South.

Its earliest inhabitants were Native Americans. Explorers Louis Jolliet and Jacques Marquette came down from Canada via the Great Lakes and the Mississippi River in 1673. Nearly a decade later, René-Robert Cavelier, Sieur de la Salle, claimed the Mississippi River Valley for France.

By the eighteenth century, France had set up trading posts and small settlements to work the lead and salt deposits. The territory, largely a wilderness, was ceded to Spain in 1762 and returned to France in 1800. In 1803, the Louisiana Purchase was signed, and in the following year, Upper Louisiana became a U.S. territory. In 1812, it became the Missouri Territory. From then on, Missouri spawned one American legend after another. When frontiersman Daniel Boone lost his land claims in Kentucky, the Spanish governor of Missouri granted him 845 acres of land (Daniel Boone died in a house built by his son Nathan, near Defiance in St. Charles County, and that area of Missouri became known as the Boonslick country). At the end of the Boonslick road was the town of Franklin (later washed away by the Missouri River), which was an important stop on the Santa Fe Trail, and the boyhood home of the scout Kit Carson.

In 1797, Moses Austin built a lead mine, furnaces, shot tower, and sheet lead plant in southeastern Missouri that gave rise to the town of Potosi and made Missouri the largest lead mining area in the world. Trade relations with other areas were made possible by Lewis and Clark's exploration of the upper Missouri, and on August 10, 1821, Missouri gained statehood.

Development came fast, led by plantation owners from the Deep South who bought cheap land in the southern part of the state, where slavery was allowed. They shunned the northwest territory, where slavery was outlawed, and the issue became divisive as northerners and German immigrants began to settle in the 1830s. Just how divisive the issue was can be judged from Missouri's experience during the Civil War. Passions ran high, and 60 percent of Missourians of military age fought in the war—109,000 in the Union army, and 30,000 on the Confederate side. Casualties were steep, as was the animosity felt by the defeated Confederates toward the victorious Union army and its supporters. Missouri was ravaged by guerrilla action throughout the war.

Jesse James—perhaps Missouri's most legendary son, apart from Mark Twain—was a product of Civil War divisions in the state. Born in 1847 in Clay County, Missouri, James's family suffered at the hands of Union forces. He became an informer for the Confederate side, and at the age of fifteen he joined William C. Quantrill's "Black Flag" guerrilla force. Along with his brother Frank and their friend Cole Younger, Jesse James was part of a Quantrill raid on Lawrence, Kansas, in which more than 150 residents were killed and the town was nearly destroyed by fire. After the war, these three men were the key figures in the James Gang, who robbed and killed their way across the midwestern states. Jesse James was murdered at his home in St. Joseph, Missouri, by two members of his gang, Robert and Charles Ford, after the state governor put a bounty of $10,000 on his head, dead or alive. The life and death of Jesse James came to epitomize a peculiar split in the thinking of Americans. Many still regard him as a folk hero; but in a land which demands law and order, the James Gang did much to encourage the rise of "hanging judges" and public support for the ultimate penalty.

A S I LEFT Mark Schreiber, he said, "Be careful." I thanked him for his concern, but was slightly baffled by his parting words. The road to Potosi couldn't be that dangerous. I would later learn that "Be careful" is a Missourian way of saying good-bye—akin to "Take care," but more a genuine expression of concern in a place where people feel that caution is prudent.

I set out for Potosi from Jefferson City in the late afternoon, tracing my route on what turned out to be an inadequate road map supplied by the car rental company. Potosi is in the southeastern part of Missouri, sixty-five miles south of St. Louis, off Highway 67, the main road to Little Rock, Arkansas. It's around 130 miles from Jefferson City, and the route is slow and twisting.

I headed southeast from Jefferson City on Highway 63, over the Osage River and down through Westphalia, Freeburg, and Vienna, communities where German names are prominent on mailboxes and on the windows of small businesses. Leuchter was the German name uppermost in my mind as I reviewed all that Fred had told me about his lethal injection machine. Tomorrow I would see it installed in Missouri's death chamber, and I would talk to the first "lethal injection technicians" Fred trained, who had participated in the six executions to date. And, I thought—not without trepidation—I would be meeting some of the capital punishment inmates with short numbers, who would soon be executed on Fred's machine.

It seemed to me that Fred's greatest pride in his lethal injection machine lay not in the thing itself, but in the protocol surrounding its use. He said it recognized the humanity of the executee and the executioner. Fred had told me how traumatic it was for the warden and other corrections officers to execute an inmate they have known for years. "Prison wardens tend to think of the inmates as their wards. It's a traumatic experience to have a man that you've been responsible for for ten years be executed, and you have to be the one to do it. And nobody has ever considered this before. *I mean, you just go throw the switch and kill the bastard, and that's the end of it?*"

I was thinking about Bill Armontrout. He had spoken almost with affection about some of the inmates he knew at Jefferson City who had since been transferred to Potosi. He spoke of them with concern; and in one or two cases, of men who had murdered on death row in Jefferson City, he spoke in a way that a parent would, of a child who had done wrong, and about whom one feels responsible.

The sun was setting behind me as I headed south on a road cut through sandstone and rich mineral deposits. I could have saved myself a few miles by turning onto Highway 68 at Vichy, but the road was absent from my map. I ended up in Rolla, at the junction of Interstate 44, a stretch of the old Route 66. I stopped for gas and asked directions from the man who cleaned my windshield and filled my tank. He was a lanky, rawboned man in his fifties, with a weather-beaten face and a ready smile. He asked me where I was going, and I told him.

"Heck," he said. "This is some of the most beautiful country on earth. Why don't you go fishing instead?"

I smiled. It was a fine suggestion.

He looked at my map and shook his head.

"Have you got a better one?" I asked.

"Sure thing." He went inside and brought out a decent road map, which he spread out on the hood of my car. He pulled a stubby pencil from his shirt pocket and searched carefully for potential fishing spots. He traced a thick lead line through back roads in the Mark Twain National Forest, marking places where it would be good to stop. I allowed him to go on, half taken in by the fantasy of abandoning work for a week of fishing.

When the tank was full, I asked him how much the map would be.

"Take it," he said.

I offered him a tip for cleaning my windows and for his thoughtfulness, and he refused it graciously, without any suggestion of feeling insulted.

"Now listen," he said. "You be careful. Don't get taken hostage."

"I won't," I laughed.

He smiled, but he didn't laugh. "Be careful," he repeated. He was still waving when I checked my rearview mirror as I pulled away from the gas station.

I drove a few miles along the interstate to St. James, then turned off onto Highway 8 going south. The road was narrow, with an adverse camber and no shoulders. The sun was setting fast, and soon the trees were shrouded in gloom, from which I could occasionally spot the eyes of deer, nervous at the edges of the forest.

Potosi Correctional Center is at Mineral Point, just outside the city limits of Potosi. My destination that evening was Farmington, some twenty miles southeast of Potosi. It was the nearest place with decent accommodations. Potosi, with a population of around 2,500, had one motel. When I eventually saw it, I knew that the half-hour daily commute would be time well spent.

When I got to Flat River, it had been dark for an hour, and I got lost looking for the road that would take me to Farmington. As soon as I found the highway, I came across a two-car accident. I read in the local paper the next day that three people had died in the crash.

In the morning, I got up early and retraced my journey north on Highway 8, finding the sign for Potosi Correctional Center just before reaching the town itself. The sign directed me to Highway 0, a county road that led to the prison and the tiny community of Mineral Point, divided in half by a railway line still busy with freight trains.

My first sight of Potosi Correctional Center, the venue for executions in Missouri, was the 200-foot-tall water tower adjacent to the prison. The giant white structure dominated the landscape, providing an awesome sense of scale as the prison appeared in front of me. Built of rough gray stone, it is a low, sprawling complex surrounded by three perimeter fences. Behind the third and outermost fence is a triple roll of razor wire and a no-man's-land of red clay. The clay is dusty in summer and sticky when it rains. Either way, it clings to shoes, socks, and trousers, indelibly staining them a rusty red color. The no-man's-land is floodlit at night, and the second fence is topped with razor wire and fitted with a supersensitive alarm system which detects body mass. If anyone approaches this fence, a second layer of floodlights comes on and the computerized security system in the central control module alerts the tower, where, twenty-four hours a day, an officer equipped with binoculars and an automatic rifle with a powerful scope scans the fence inch by inch. Behind the first fence lies the prison yard, where attempts to plant grass have failed. The clay soon gives way to rock, and cannot support life. The site gives added security, since it is virtually impossible to tunnel out of the prison.

In the whole of the prison, there are no windows that open. Each cell has a thin, vertical window that throws a narrow shaft of light at the beginning or end of the day, depending on which direction the cell faces. Even the sewer system is escape-proof. The pipes narrow to a six-inch diameter at the end of their run and are capped with "rat trap" grilles. The outermost fence is surrounded by a perimeter road, patrolled round the clock by a fleet of security cars.

Potosi Correctional Center is a state-of-the-art American prison—probably the most secure prison in the United States. It is, in some ways, an elegant structure. The entrance is an imposing facade, angled at forty-five degrees. The walls of the administrative offices are plain concrete blocks painted off-white; they are no different from the walls in the inmate's recreational facilities or cells. The entire prison is air-conditioned and centrally heated, so that the temperature varies by only a few degrees the year round. It is as different from Missouri State Penitentiary as it could possibly be. By comparison, it is luxurious.

Visitors to Potosi who are acquainted with the old penitentiary, or with the Victorian prisons of other states and countries, are sometimes baffled by the reason for creating such a high-tech and well-equipped facility to house criminals who have committed the most heinous crimes. However, there is no aspect of the environment at Potosi which is not connected with high security. Since Potosi opened in 1989, there has not been a single murder in the prison (there have been a number of minor stabbings). This is an astonishing record, since the three hundred general-population inmates at Potosi all have one thing in common: they are either serving life without parole or life and fifty, or are sentenced to death. Some of them were sentenced to death for murders committed while at Missouri State Penitentiary, which, when it housed the death row population, was notorious for its violence (in 1985 alone, there were eleven murders in the Missouri prison system, the bulk of them occurring at MSP). By taking the most dangerous men out of the old penitentiary and isolating them at Potosi, Missouri has created a prison in which inmates have little to prove to one another. Each has demonstrated he is capable of murder. Any inmate picking a fight with another knows there is a good chance it would result in a killing. At MSP and other prisons which house a mixed group of medium- and maximum-security offenders, of young toughs just off the street and old convicts, the atmosphere is much more obviously threatening, as the young inmates feel they need to prove their dangerousness to earn "respect" through fear.

Potosi Correctional Center is unique in that the state acquired it for very little money. It was built by a private corporation on state land under a lease-back contract. It came fully equipped, down to the walkie-talkies carried by corrections officers. It is a far more pleasant and secure prison than ones of similar vintage built in other states with public funds. And in a state long strapped for cash, it was a necessity. In the ten years between 1980 and 1990, Missouri's prison population doubled. The same exponential growth is forecast for the year 2000 and beyond.

Driving into the prison, there is a large warning sign prohibiting the carrying of guns, knives, and other weapons, and the importation of alcohol and drugs. It is repeated again at the top of the steps that lead to the main entrance, where all visitors are subjected to a rigorous search. No one is exempted. Attorneys, state contractors, occasionally even prison staff, are required to submit to a routine set of questions which, however many times the armed officer at the door asks them, are, without exception, meant in deadly earnest. The visitor is asked if he or she is carrying a gun or knife. The contents of all pockets must be emptied onto the desk for inspection by the officer. All bags are thoroughly checked and X-rayed. The walk-through metal detector is much more sensitive than the type used at airports. It will detect the metal in the frames of a pair of glasses, a belt buckle, the underwiring in a brassiere, even the eyelets in a pair of shoes. Any of the above must be removed and passed through the X ray to gain admission to the prison. (During one of my visits to Potosi, a female attorney was refused admission on the catch-22 grounds that her bra set off the alarm; she offered to remove it, but was denied access on the grounds that all women entering the prison must wear "appropriate undergarments.") Visitors may not bring money into the prison and must carry identification at all times, in the event of being taken hostage or killed.

Security procedures were beefed up soon after the prison opened, when the angry wife of an inmate pulled a gun on the officer in charge of security. Now, anyone entering the prison is likely to have their car registration number and their name run through the state police computer. This routine check has resulted in an average of one arrest per month of visitors to the prison who are found to be the subject of felony warrants.

After stowing my wallet in a locker (though special arrangements were made for me to bring my tape recorder and camera inside the prison), I was escorted to the office of Paul Delo, the superintendent. I was surprised to find the room full of people. Paul Delo got up from his large, polished desk with a hand-carved Missouri State Seal on the front of it and came around to shake my hand. A stocky man of medium height, with short, graying hair, he moved slowly and deliberately. He was congenial, and very much at his ease. He introduced me to the other men in the room. On the sofa at one end of the office was a slight, bearded man wearing dirty white cowboy boots and an inscrutable expression. He was introduced as Gary Sutterfield, chief maintenance engineer. He eyed me warily, and I wondered why he had been invited to what I thought would be a private interview about taking responsibility for carrying out the death sentence. The other man in the room was wiry, with reddish blond hair and mustache. His eyes were fixed in a permanent half-squint, as if a cigarette were dangling from his mouth and smoke were curling around them. The skin around his eyes was wrinkled and his face was that of a man who spent a lot of time out-of-doors. A pair of crutches was resting against the arm of his chair. He was introduced as Greg Wilson, the prison investigator. He had recently been in a motorcycle accident and was recovering from a series of operations on his leg. The superintendent explained that there were two other key people I should meet, the assistant superintendents Don Roper and Phil Banks, but that they were away fishing.

I was offered a cup of coffee and a chair opposite Paul Delo's desk. I explained the purpose of my visit and watched Delo's reaction to my project. He was wary but polite, obviously expert at handling reporters. It was soon apparent that neither of us was what the other had expected. He was a far more easygoing and relaxed man than I had guessed; I was far less formal and aggressive than he might have anticipated. The fact that my questions were to be focused on process and procedure engaged everyone's attention and helped put the conversation on a more comfortable footing.

Like many men in corrections, Paul Delo comes from a military background. He is a twenty-year veteran of the army, and had also served in the air force. He first went to Vietnam in 1954, and fought there through the Tet Offensive and beyond. He was a helicopter pilot, much decorated and wounded numerous times. An unusually talented officer, he became fluent in Thai and was assigned as a military adviser in Thailand in the 1970s. After Vietnam, he worked as a highway patrol officer and sheriff's deputy. He took a job as a corrections officer and was in charge of death row at MSP in the late 1970s and 1980s. After a spell as an insurance salesman, he returned to corrections and was chosen to open Potosi. For two years before the inmates arrived, he worked with the architects and engineers to oversee the building of Missouri's securest prison.

He spoke in a quiet voice, with an ironical tone lurking under the surface, about the peculiar world I was about to enter at Potosi.

"What's a little unusual about this place," he told me, "is that we've mainstreamed our CP [capital punishment] inmates with the life and fifty in our general population. As far as I know, it's the only place in the United States where this is done."

He explained that some CP inmates prefer solitary confinement or protective custody, and that wish is granted. These inmates live in the administrative segregation unit ("the hole"), where they are locked down twenty-four hours a day in single cells, allowed out only to take a shower. If they need to visit the hospital or any other facility, they are escorted in handcuffs. General-population inmates who violate prison rules are also sent to the hole for varying lengths of time. In addition, there is a small population of extremely violent or dangerous inmates from other institutions who are kept in the hole indefinitely.

As Paul spoke, the others remained silent, watching me. After his brief introduction, Paul offered to take me on a tour of the prison and suggested we meet up with the others for lunch at 11:30. I was aware of being treated in a privileged way: Tours were normally conducted by a lieutenant, not the superintendent.

He led me through a confusing maze of white corridors to central control, which separates the inmates from the administrative block of the prison. A heavy steel door slid open, then shut behind us. Thirty feet in front was another sliding door, operated by an officer inside the ultra-secure bubble from which the security of the entire prison is monitored and controlled. From the central control tower, officers are able to observe inmates throughout the prison on closed-circuit television. From the crow's nest tower above central control, an officer observes inmate activity on television monitors and scans the perimeter fence with a pair of binoculars. While MSP has numerous towers manned by officers armed with shotguns, Potosi's high-tech design requires that only one officer, in the crow's nest above central control, be equipped with a firearm. The AK-15 is mounted above a handwritten sign that says "Fence Master."

From central control, the entire prison can be monitored electronically. A sophisticated computer system prints out all entry to and exit from the maximum-security area. On a large console is a schematic map of the prison, with warning lights to indicate any security problem. All officers working inside are issued a walkie-talkie which has a built-in "man down" alarm. If the officer is assaulted or involved in a disturbance, or if his or her walkie-talkie moves from the upright position to a forty-five-degree angle, this immediately alerts central control, and the "man down" call is sent out, along with the officer's precise location so that assistance may be rendered.

Paul pressed the button that admitted us through the second sliding door, and when it closed behind us we were standing in front of the central control bubble, with two further locked doors between us and the internal courtyard from which we would eventually gain access to the yard and housing units. The officers behind the thick, bulletproof glass wore a stern expression. One of them opened a steel trapdoor such as drive-in banks use and passed through a clipboard on which I printed my name and added my signature. Once I was cleared for entry, a large steel door popped open with a loud noise and we climbed down two short flights of stairs to a similar door, where we waited for central control to pop the lock. Paul pushed open the door and we emerged into a concrete paved area with the hospital block to the left, a sally port through which vehicles could enter in front of us, and doors to the right leading to the administrative segregation area, the yard, and housing units.

Paul pressed another buzzer and we were admitted to the yard. The weather was still sunny and hot, and there were 150 or so inmates out. At one end of the yard, a flag football game was in progress, and the sounds of colliding bodies carried across the thick air. An obvious difference from MSP is that the inmates at Potosi were an almost equal mix of black and white. Considering the sentences of the inmates at Potosi, it was shocking to see the wide variety of ages. Two of the inmates I saw looked to be around fourteen years old. I saw another in his late sixties, walking slowly along the paved path between his housing unit and the hospital.

The men were mostly hanging out in groups, though a few lone figures stood silently against a wall, smoking, or walked along the running track that circled the football field. The red earth was parched and cracked open in crazy patterns. An attempt had been made to plant grass, but the seed had taken only intermittently, and what did grow was coarse and thick. In the bright end-of-summer sun, the gray stone of the prison and its hard, geometrical shapes looked attractive—compared to the old penitentiaries and the run-down British prisons I had visited. I mentioned this to Paul, and he just smiled.

Paul seemed in no hurry and allowed me to walk around the yard, getting a feel of the place. Having made films in British prisons, I was relatively used to the company of murderers. In British prisons, I had always noticed a palpable tension between officers and inmates, and was always aware of the threat to myself. Potosi housed more murderers, and more vicious murderers, than I had ever encountered at one time. I was more than aware of the need to be on my guard, and that the relatively attractive and sedate surroundings were probably deceptive. I watched Paul and noticed that, despite his quiet and apparently relaxed manner, his body was alert, and his eyes were narrowed, taking in the movement around him.

As soon as we entered the yard, all inmates were aware of our presence. More than at MSP, there was curiosity as to who I was, and why I was there. Unlike at MSP, inmates did not simply come up and challenge me. Here, everything was slower, cooler. All movement seemed more deliberate than at MSP. Time, I would learn, passes differently for those under sentence of death or life without parole. There were only three ways out of Potosi, and two of them involved a coffin. You could be executed, or you could die while serving life without parole. The only hope of getting out alive lay in a reversal of your sentence, a most unlikely possibility. Resignation to spending the rest of one's life at Potosi bred a certain malaise.

As we walked, a number of inmates came up to Paul with complaints or requests, or simply to pass the time of day. One inmate wanted to know when Paul was going to respond to his letter protesting against a conduct violation he had received. Another wanted to know whether Paul would give him permission to marry a woman with whom he had been corresponding. Paul said he would.

I thought about the last request for a moment, and asked Paul if it was a common one.

"Yes, it is," he replied.

I wondered why a woman would marry a man who had almost no hope of ever leaving Potosi, in the certain knowledge that their physical relationship would be confined to limited kissing and hand-holding.

Paul made no comment. He just smiled again.

I asked Paul why the prison had been built at Potosi, in such a remote corner of the state.

"Well, one of the reasons is that when we decided to move death row down here, security was one of our concerns. When we executed Tiny Mercer at Jeff City, we needed a massive security presence outside the prison. We had the water patrol, the highway patrol, the capitol police, the governor's security force, helicopters, the county sheriff, the Jeff City police, and our own officers. It was a pretty expensive operation, but we had to be prepared. We didn't know how many protesters we'd have."

In the event, two hundred or so anti–death penalty protesters mounted a quiet candlelight vigil in front of the penitentiary on a cold and rainy night.

"Down here," Paul continued in his slow drawl, "we don't get many protesters. We are in a fairly rural spot, and there aren't that many willing to make the trip from Kansas City, Jeff City, or even St. Louis. So it's relatively easy to mount our security. We close off the highway, but we allow the protesters to set up on our property, near the county highway in front of the prison."

"Where did you get your prison officers from?" I asked.

"The majority of them are from the local community," he replied. He explained that when the state decides to build a maximum-security prison, local residents are usually up in arms protesting. "Here at Potosi," he told me, "they wanted the prison."

When the bottom fell out of the American lead market, Potosi became a ghost town. Other industries, such as shoemaking, had long ago left the region. Clay soil and heavy bedrock made farming difficult, and apart from small businesses, there is little to contribute to the economy of the area. Locals lobbied to have Potosi Correctional Center in their backyard because it brought three hundred jobs to the most economically deprived area of Missouri. With its $15 million payroll, the prison is the largest employer in the area (the second largest source of income in Potosi is welfare). In addition, those who make the journey to Potosi to visit friends or relatives in the prison spend money in nearby motels, restaurants, and shops, giving the local community a much-needed shot in the arm. However, while innkeepers and restaurateurs are happy about the new source of revenue, they are not always welcoming to city folk, many of whom are black, who come to visit.

The Missouri Department of Corrections is organized on paramilitary lines, and many of the senior personnel and junior corrections officers have a military background. The officers I met at Potosi are divided into two groups of inmates: Brown shirts are the more junior corrections officers (CO I, CO II); white shirts are the more senior (sergeant, lieutenant, captain, major). Paul prides himself on the rigorous professionalism of his staff, but the neatly pressed uniforms and stern demeanor of some officers are, in some cases, a front for a group of relatively uneducated people of narrow experience. Some inmates might call them hillbillies, and some of the officers may even proudly refer to themselves as rednecks. There can be no doubt that Paul Delo has created a prison that does what it sets out to do, and does it effectively. His brand of relaxed leadership, backed by a total lack of reluctance to enforce discipline when he feels the necessity, is largely responsible for the absence of prison murders to date, and the relatively low level of violence.

Paul led me across the yard to the gymnasium. There was a pickup basketball game in progress, and inside a windowed room looking out onto the court, inmates were lifting weights. Up at MSP, the weight-lifting areas were out-of-doors. Here, a number of impressively muscled men were working out. Black and white inmates seemed to mix without tension. One of the white men had an Aryan Nation swastika tattoo on his neck and was working out alongside a black inmate wearing the headdress of the Moors. In an adjacent room was a boxing ring, and I asked whether it got much use.

"We've got a few boxers here," Paul told me. "But there have been some problems with lawsuits, and so it doesn't get much use."

I told him that the idea of British inmates filing lawsuits against anyone —other inmates or the administration—was pretty farfetched. I had to remind myself that, in America, suing other people is a way of life. As I would learn, it was a habit that not only spilled over into American prisons: For some, it dominates prison life.

On our way out of the gym to visit the library, Paul showed me the two music rooms provided for inmates. Each was equipped with all the instruments and electronic paraphernalia of rock music, and he told me that there were three prison bands, each reflecting the different tastes of a very mixed group of inmates: R&B, country and western, and heavy rock.

The library was very much like that of a new high school, with the exception of the books it stocked. I scanned the shelves to find histories of organized crime, forensic texts, true crime accounts of grisly murders, and other books obviously of interest to inmates. The largest section is devoted to law and includes the proceedings of the Missouri Supreme Court. Inmates can buy a credit card to operate the photocopier, and typewriters are available for their use. Since the execution of Tiny Mercer in 1989, many death row inmates have taken a greater interest in their appeals. Since visits from public defenders or lawyers from the state's Capital Punishment Resource Center in Kansas City are rare, partly because it is a day's car journey from Potosi, many inmates have taken charge of their own defense. For many, it is an important way of structuring time—a difficult thing to do when faced with the virtual certainty of execution in ten years or less. And for some who have become proficient in the law, it is an opportunity to help other inmates who are less literate.

Apart from working on their cases, a number of inmates are dedicated to fighting the administration through a constant stream of lawsuits. These may pertain to living conditions, to a claim that a conduct violation has been wrongly issued, or to a claim against an officer for assault.

"I'm named in hundreds of lawsuits every year," Paul told me with a smile.

"But doesn't that make it difficult to run the prison, if you're always having to answer suits from inmates?"

"Not really. Most of them are bullshit. Occasionally one stands up. But I look at it like this. I'd rather have them filing lawsuits than digging tunnels."

There really was no arguing with his logic.

I remarked to Paul that, compared with most prisons I'd visited, Potosi was almost like a hotel.

"It's true that we have air-conditioning, and the facilities are just about the best you can get. I know some people regard this as a luxury, and that their tax dollars could be better spent on schools or highways. A lot of people think we should keep them in a basement."

For years, that is precisely what Missouri did. The result was a high rate of violence and an order from the federal court to improve conditions. The state had no alternative but to build Potosi.

"In corrections, you always have problems in the summer, when the weather gets a little hot. You get more violence then. I would say that the air-conditioning here goes a long way to keeping the violence down."

Paul said it was just about time for lunch, and so we made our way back through central control to his office, where Gary Sutterfield, the plant maintenance engineer, and Greg Wilson, the prison investigator, were waiting.

"You want to ride with Red?" Paul asked me, a mischievous smile playing at his lips.

Greg laughed, and I realized that Red was his nickname. But I didn't know what the joke was.

Greg was stuffing an old police .38 with a well-worn grip into the waistband of his trousers. "I've got something to do first. I'll see you over there."

We drove back out to Highway 8 in an old but immaculate Ford LTD, Paul's official car. I noticed that it had more than 100,000 miles on the clock, and he explained that it had formerly been used by the chancellor of Missouri State University. The Department of Corrections has a homely sense of housekeeping, and keeps costs down by purchasing secondhand cars from within the state sector, often from the Highway Patrol.

We drove half a mile toward Potosi, where we parked in front of a family restaurant where the administration lunched most days. The restaurant had three rooms, and Paul led us to his usual table in the back—the table at which the most important meetings about the running of the prison were held, and where many decisions were made.

The waitress brought big glasses of iced tea, and everyone ordered the lunch special: all the soup, salad bar, and chicken wings you could eat for $4.99.

There was a lot of banter with the waitresses, and everyone made two trips to the food bar, leaving the table piled high with chicken bones. Greg Wilson came in while we were on our second helping of wings.

Gary Sutterfield pulled out a chair. "Hey, bud, take a seat," he said.

Greg positioned himself alongside the chair, held both crutches in his left hand, and steadied himself with his right while sitting down. He was scowling.

"What's the problem, Red?" Paul asks.

"I got a guy. I know he's got dope up his ass, and the doctor won't X-ray him for me."

"Why not?" Paul inquires mildly.

"Says it's not his job."

"Aw hell," says Paul, disappointed at the lack of cooperation. "We all work together."

"Yeah," says Red, disgusted. "But he doesn't see it that way."

Paul thinks for a minute and tells a story. "When I was in the highway patrol, I was out on Sixty-seven one morning and this guy comes by, out-of-state plates, doing sixty-five. I didn't have anything else to do, so I pulled him over. He's wearing a suit. Mr. Businessman. I ask to see his license, and I write him a ticket. I hand it to him and I ask him to sign at the bottom. 'I'm not signing anything,' the guy tells me. I explain to him that, since he's from out of state, he's got to acknowledge that he's received the ticket and will either pay a fine or make a court appearance. 'I'm not signing anything,' the guy insists. Standing on his rights. So I tell him to park his car, lock it, and give me the keys. I ask him if there's a garage around here that he particularly likes. The guy looks at me and says, 'What do you mean?' 'It's simple,' I tell him. 'If you don't sign this ticket, and you drive away, I've got no way to guarantee you're going to pay the fine or go to court. So I'm taking you to jail.' The guy signed the ticket.''

The table laughs appreciatively.

"Which asshole is it?" Paul asks Red.

Red tells him the name of the inmate.

"Okay, Red," Paul says matter-of-factly. "You're a sheriff's deputy, right?"

"Right."

"Then tell the doctor if he doesn't do the X ray for you he's under arrest. Take him over to the county jail."

Sometimes the smile that concludes one of Paul's anecdotes is more like a large, horizontal zipper opening.

Paul and Gary got up to leave. Paul suggested I get a ride back with Greg.

I waited while Greg negotiated the food bar with his crutches. When he returned, he told me with a rueful grin, "There's one or two things that're real difficult to do on crutches."

I asked him about how he came to be the investigator at Potosi. He told me a little about his career. He had served long tours of duty in Vietnam, and he talked about it with a wistful look in his eye. I had never heard anyone speak of his time in Vietnam as if it were something he now missed. Greg mentioned nothing of the battles in which he'd fought; he didn't tell any stories about his time there; it was simply that Vietnam had been an important part of his life, and now it was over forever. (I learned many months later, from one of his colleagues, that Greg had fought in the battle of Hamburger Hill.)

After Vietnam, he had been a police officer in St. Louis, and an investigator at MSP. When Paul Delo was chosen to open Potosi, he was allowed to handpick his own team. Greg was one of the names at the top of his list.

"My job is to investigate everything that goes on in the prison, whether it's inmates or staff," he told me.

Knowing that, so far, there had been no murders and only a handful of assaults at Potosi, I asked him what most of his investigations concerned.

"Drugs," he said. "There's a drug problem everywhere, and here is no different."

He explained that, within the closed system of the prison, drugs cause the same problems they do on the outside, but in an exaggerated way. Marijuana, cocaine, heroin, are all imported into the prison in relatively small amounts, compared to what is available on the street. They are sold for absurdly inflated prices, and problems arise when inmates fall into debt. In prison, there are many ways to repay a debt, from providing sexual services to carrying out a killing on behalf of the dealer. In prison, no debt is ever forgotten. Greg's job in stopping drug traffic is primarily about preventing opportunities for violence from arising.

"How do most of the drugs get into the prison?" I asked. "Visitors?"

"Primarily. They bring it inside in, uh, body cavities, and we can't strip-search everyone. But we've got a problem with staff, too."

I thought that Greg's job must be a lonely one. If no one in the prison was above suspicion, it must be difficult to be anyone's friend.

"So how do you handle suspected staff violations?" I asked.

"Searches. Polygraph tests."

"How do you begin to suspect someone?"

"It's like with any investigation. They're never the same. People are different, and you've got to treat each one individually. But if I see an officer on basic pay who turns up one day in a new car, or has a new bass boat, or is taking expensive vacations, I've got to think about that." Greg's eyes narrowed as he talked. "It's easy to be tempted. A little bit of dope can be worth a lot of money in prison."

"But surely," I said, "people know that it's not worth risking their jobs, and that with the kind of security you've got in the prison, they're bound to get caught."

"There's more to it than just greed," Greg told me. "It's real easy to be conned by inmates. They've got all the time in the world to sit there figuring out how to run a game on you. And some of them are great con artists. They can take an officer, get him or her feeling sorry for them. It starts with getting them to bring some little thing into the prison, and goes on from there."

My first impression of watching inmates and officers suggested there was little love lost between them; I wondered how that worked.

"We've got a number of female corrections officers working here, and some of them have been susceptible to inmates. You know, they fall in love. We've caught some giving sexual favors. In the prison up at Farmington, they recently fired five women for fooling around with inmates in the kitchen."

"Does your job mean that you've even got to suspect Paul? If you think he's up to something, that you've got to investigate him?"

"Yes, it does."

Greg told me that he loved his work. He liked the challenge of an investigation, of finding the right way to handle an inmate to find out the information he needed. "You know, inmates like to think that they hate a snitch. But everybody's got a story to tell, and you've just got to figure out the right way to get them to tell it."

Greg changed the subject and asked me questions about where I lived in England, and how I liked it. We were talking about the problems of maintaining a steady home life while working long hours, and he told me that he and his wife had broken up a few weeks previously. I asked him how long he'd been married, and he told me, "fifteen years." Her decision came out of the blue for Greg, and had affected him deeply. There was a hint of despair in his voice as he reflected on how fifteen years of shared effort could add up to nothing.

The waitresses joked with Greg as I paid the bill, and I followed him out into the parking lot.

"What kind of car do you drive?" Greg asked.

"A Fiat."

"It's probably nicer than my car." He stopped in front of a broken-down Ford van. It was a dull, rusty hulk of a vehicle, with a half-gallon plastic bleach bottle tied to the front. "Radiator overflow," Greg explained.

I climbed in and Greg showed me the sofa he'd fitted in the back. I looked down at my feet and could see daylight through the floor of the van.

"The heater doesn't work too good," he mentioned.

"I guess that doesn't matter today," I said.

"No, it doesn't," he agreed. The engine sparked grudgingly, and we drove back to the prison.

P

AUL DELO and Gary Sutterfield were waiting for me when Greg and I returned. My tour was to continue with a visit to the execution chamber, and we made our way through the elaborate security checkpoints and out into the walled courtyard by which the hospital was entered.

As we were walking, Gary began to explain the lethal injection machine in detail. I mentioned that I had spent a week with Fred Leuchter, and had a pretty good grounding in the basics.

"What'd you think of Fred?" Gary asked bluntly. He'd been eyeing me suspiciously ever since I'd arrived in the prison.

"He's unusual," I said.

Paul smiled broadly.

"He's kind of strange, don't you think?" said Gary.

"Yeah."

"Did you meet his wife?" he asked.

I said I had.

Paul opened the door for us.

We entered the hospital, which had a red cross and a no smoking sign on it. Just to the right of the door was a bench. Two nurses were seated on it, smoking. Staff call it "the liar's bench."

The main door gave way to a corridor, to the right of which was another door leading to the inmate waiting area. If an inmate wishes to visit the hospital, he needs written permission. The administration has up to eight days to respond to the request. When the request is granted, the inmate is given a slip of paper, which he takes into the waiting room. The waiting room is separated from the nurse's station by thick security glass. When the inmate is called, he slides his medical slip under a door at the other end of the waiting room. The door leading from the waiting room to the hospital itself is manned by an officer who checks the slip, then admits the inmate. He is searched before being allowed into the treatment room, which is opposite the nurse's station. The treatment room is modern, clean, bright. It looks like the emergency room of a modern hospital, and is fitted with three gurneys.

"Only two people have keys to the death chamber," Gary told me. "Paul and myself."

Gary led the way. Adjacent to the treatment room was a folding door, directly opposite the nurse's station. Gary pulled it back and closed it quickly behind him. We were standing in a short, dark corridor, and to the left was a door numbered A-025. It was marked OUT OF BOUNDS. Paul rocked on his heels while Gary unlocked the door. He switched on the light and held the door as I entered, then closed it behind us.

I was standing in a room that, at first glance, was like any other in the hospital block. The only difference was that minor modifications had been made to convert it to the purpose of executions. It measured about eighteen by twelve feet and, like everywhere else in the prison, had white-painted cinder-block walls, a linoleum-tiled floor, and fluorescent lights overhead. There were windows on three sides of the room, looking out onto the corridors. They were covered on the outside by Venetian blinds, and on the inside by roller blinds. On the wall opposite the door by which I'd entered the death chamber was another door, fitted with a one-way mirror. In one corner of the room was a small sink. Opposite the door by which we entered, a gray steel box was mounted on the wall: the delivery module of the lethal injection machine. The locked box had a handle on the front of it, and a small brass plate that said "Fred A. Leuchter Associates, Inc., Boston MA." On the right-hand side of the machine were three sets of amber, green, and red lights. Beneath the delivery module there was a hole in the wall, about two inches in diameter. In the corner opposite the sink, draped with a pink bed sheet, stood the control module of Missouri's lethal injection machine. Next to it was a red tool cart, such as car mechanics use. Inside were various tools required to maintain the lethal injection machine, and spare IV lines and clamps.

In the middle of the room was the gurney which had been used in the executions of Gerald Smith, Leonard Laws, George Gilmore, Winford Stokes, and Maurice Byrd. It was a basic-model hospital gurney that had been customized for the purpose of executions. In the top right corner, near where the executed man's head would rest, was an IV drip stand. The condemned man lies on a gray hospital blanket folded lengthwise. The same hospital blanket had been used for all five executions to date at Potosi. I looked at the coarse fabric and noticed that it was stained. I looked away.

A set of four nylon-webbed restraints with Velcro fastenings was rolled neatly at either side of the gurney. And a more recent addition, two stout leather straps with buckles, to ensure maximum restraint. During an execution at Potosi, witnesses never see the restraints. The condemned man is draped in a white sheet which covers his feet and is folded back under his chin, leaving only his face visible.

"On execution night," Gary explained, "I'm responsible for getting everything ready.

He began to describe his part in the Missouri Protocol. "When we get a death warrant that looks like it's a good one, I start to prepare. I check the machine, make sure everything's functioning smoothly. I check the drugs, all three of them, and make sure we have enough, and that they haven't passed their expiration date. About forty-eight hours before the execution, we'll have a full rehearsal. I set up the machine, and everyone who participates in the execution goes through the drill. We put someone on the gurney, an officer, who is about the same size as the inmate. We make sure everything is functioning smoothly. We don't leave anything to chance. On the day of the execution, I'm here from about seven-fifteen in the morning. I'm making sure everything's ready to go. We have various

Fred Leuchter in the basement of his home in Malden, Massachusetts, with the control module of his lethal injection machine. (Photo: Stephen Trombley.)

Fred A. Leuchter Associates' state of the art electric chair at River Bend Maximum Security Institution, Nashville, Tennessee. (Photo: Stephen Trombley.)

The gas chamber at Missouri State Penitentiary. Inside is the gurney on which Tiny Mercer was laid for the first ever lethal injection execution using Fred Leuchter's machine, on January 6, 1989. (Photo: Stephen Trombley.)

Mark Schreiber, coauthor of the Missouri Protocol—the state's execution plan. He is seen here in the yard at Jefferson City Correctional Center (formerly Missouri State Penitentiary), talking with inmates. (Photo: Stephen Trombley.)

Bobby Shaw, CP#7. Convicted in the 1980 murder of a corrections officer at Missouri State Penitentiary, Shaw has been on death row for nearly twelve years. Diagnosed as having organic brain damage, questions have been raised about his competency to face execution. (Photo: Stephen Trombley.)

Stephen Trombley (right) with A. J. Bannister at the door of his cell in Housing Unit 5, Potosi Correctional Center. (Photo: Lukasz Jogalla.)

Potosi Correctional Center. Located sixty-five miles southwest of St. Louis, all three hundred general population inmates are convicted of capital murder. Nearly one hundred have the death sentence. The remainder have life without parole or life without the possibility of parole for fifty years. (Photo: Lukasz Jogalla.)

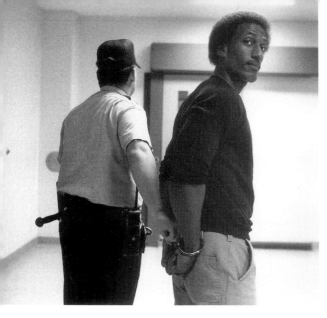

Walter Blair being led back to administrative segregation, or "the hole," after an interview with the author. In the three years Blair has been at Potosi, he has spent the majority of his time in solitary confinement.
(Photo: Lukasz Jogalla.)

Paul Delo, superintendent of Potosi Correctional Center. After a distinguished military career, Delo worked at Missouri State Penitentiary before opening Potosi. (Photo: Lukasz Jogalla.)

RIGHT: Bill Armontrout with the old gas chamber at Missouri State Penitentiary. (Photo: Lukasz Jogalla.)

CENTER: Potosi Correctional Center Chaplain, Gary Tune. (Photo: Lukasz Jogalla.)

BELOW:
Typical cell on Missouri's old death row at Jefferson City Correctional Center (formerly Missouri State Penitentiary). Cramped, squalid, cold in the winter and hot in the summer, death row inmates described it as hell on earth. (Photo: Lukasz Jogalla.)

RIGHT: Doyle Williams, CP#14. Sentenced to death in 1981, Williams came within three hours of being executed in March 1990. (Photo: Lukasz Jogalla.)

LEFT: Joe Amrine, CP#48. Amrine is thirty-six years old and has served six years on death row. (Photo: Lukasz Jogalla.)

BELOW: Lloyd Schlup, CP#42. Thirty-one-year-old Schlup was sentenced to death in 1986. This photo was taken hours after he received a stay of execution while on deathwatch. (Photo: Lukasz Jogalla.)

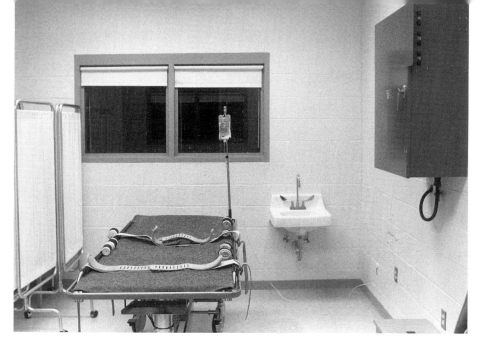

The death chamber at Potosi Correctional Center. It is located in the hospital block. The doctor monitors the dying inmate's heart from behind the screen (left). The operations officer stands in the corner of the room (front right) and coordinates the execution via a radio headset. He can watch the lights on the delivery module of the lethal injection machine mounted on the wall, which signify that each of the three drugs is being injected. (Photo: Lukasz Jogalla.)

The control panel of the lethal injection machine is placed in the dental storage area in the room next to the execution chamber. Mounted on the wall (top right) are the manual override pulls, in the event that the automatic or manual electric modes fail. (Photo: Lukasz Jogalla.)

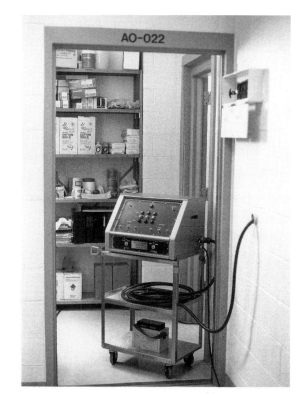

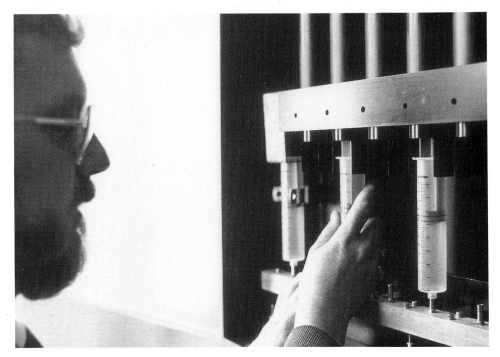

Gary Sutterfield, in charge of plant maintenance at Potosi Correctional Center. He ensures that the lethal injection machine is maintained and functional. On the night of the execution, he prepares and arms the machine. Here he is loading the lethal chemicals into the delivery module. (Photo: Lukasz Jogalla.)

RIGHT: Tiny and Christy Mercer. They married at Missouri State Penitentiary. Christy Mercer was present at her husband's execution on January 6, 1989. (Photo: By permission of Christy Mercer.)

meetings in the afternoon, and then I have some of my staff set up the witness areas."

Gary showed me the three witness areas, each of which is set up with specially made two-tiered bleachers, on which are mounted plastic chairs. In Missouri, there are usually twelve state witnesses, including press, who are seated in two connecting areas in front of the windows to the right of the door. Under the Missouri capital punishment statute, the inmate may invite five witnesses to his execution. These are escorted into the prison through a different entrance than the state witnesses, and they are kept segregated throughout the evening. The inmate witnesses' seats are mounted behind the head of the condemned man, so that the last view each has of the other is upside down.

Gary showed me how the machine is set up, and explained in detail how it works. He unlocked the door with the one-way-mirror window and we entered the storage cupboard of the dental clinic. Gary wheeled in the control module and pulled off the dust sheet. He placed it near the hole in the wall separating the death chamber from the dental area. He unfurled a thick, black cable connected to the bottom of the control module and fed it through the wall. I followed him around to the other side and watched while he screwed the fitting in place. He showed me how the twelve-volt battery was connected.

"I built this special tray to hold the syringes," Gary explained, showing me a piece of wood with six grooves in it. He unwrapped six fat plastic syringes and laid them carefully onto the tray. He then opened some bags of saline solution and neatly filled the syringes in order to demonstrate how the machine was loaded. We returned to the execution chamber, where Gary climbed up on a pair of gray-painted wooden steps and unlocked the door of the delivery module. It swung open to reveal the business end of Fred's machine, the part that no one ever sees while an execution is in progress. Inside were the six weighted pistons Fred had told me about. On either side were the two syringes filled with saline solution which are used to flush the machine clean after an execution. Gary delicately fitted each of the six syringes into the machine. He pulled out one of the pistons and handed it to me. "Feel the weight of that," he said.

As I was holding it, he explained that he had made many modifications to the machine Missouri had acquired from Fred. "I replaced his steel pistons with these stainless steel ones," he told me. He also detailed other changes he'd made to Fred's timing system, so that each syringe is depressed much more quickly than in the original specification, which Fred argues is designed to respond to the aqueous pressure in the inmate's body. Instead of Fred's recommended one-minute interval between the administration of each of the three lethal drugs, Gary has set the machine so that there is a thirty-second interval between the injection of the sodium pentothal and the pancuronium bromide, and a sixty-second interval before the release of the final drug, potassium chloride.

"The one thing you've got to be careful of when loading the syringes and fitting them into the machine," he told me, "is to make sure there are no air bubbles in the syringes or in the IV line. You get air in there, it'll kill a man.

"Before the execution begins," Gary continued, "I remove these safety pins which hold the pistons in place." He removed the six steel pins and placed them in the pocket of his Western-cut corduroy jacket. "Then I close the cabinet and lock the door. Only Paul and I have the keys," he reminded me.

He showed me how the inmate is attached to the lethal injection machine. "About forty minutes before the execution, we have a contract nurse who is an expert in anesthetics, and he comes in and places the IV in the inmate's arm. If we need to do an IV cutdown in the neck or groin, he does that. We take the IV line from the saline drip, and the IV line that comes out of the bottom of the delivery module, and we hook these together with a Y-joint to the IV line coming out of the inmate's body. I clamp off the IV leading from the machine, and when the execution is ready to begin, I take that off, which allows the drugs to flow through the line."

Having prepared the machine and the inmate, Gary waits until midnight, when his next task is to raise the blinds inside the execution chamber. "Paul then reads the death warrant, and we go behind the door and the execution is ready to begin."

I looked around the room. It was a cold space. It was the essence of what lethal injection is about. Sanitized. Impersonal. Clean. At least, on the surface.

Gary and Paul took me through the door with the one-way mirror which led to the dental storage area.

"On execution nights," Gary told me, "we remove this door here." He placed his hand on a door which separated the storage area from the small dental clinic itself.

I nodded, and walked into the dental clinic. There were two dentist's chairs. On the instrument tray over one of them was a cast for a set of false teeth.

"So," Gary continued, anxious that I should pay close attention. "Let's look at the operation of the machine itself."

I stood next to him in front of the control module.

"I don't actually press the button. I just arm the machine. When I arm the machine, it's ready to go. I place a key in each of these switches, and I arm the machine. The machine decides which of the button pressers actually performs the execution."

Gary checked to see if I was following his explanation.

"Okay. Now the executioners, if you will, depress the buttons simultaneously on a count of three."

"Who does the counting?" I asked.

"One of the button pushers," Gary replied. "And they do it like this." He stood behind the machine, so that I could see, and placed a thumb on each button. He showed how the buttons are not simply pressed; the buttons are depressed, and the executioners slide their thumbs off the buttons so that they snap back with a loud report.

"Once the machine is activated," Gary told me, "everything is automatic. The light will come on. The first piston will drop. When all three lights come on, the second piston will kick in, and so forth. Any questions?"

I shook my head.

"Okay. Now, if anything goes wrong with the automatic sequence, we go to the electrical backup. You see, I'm timing the sequence with a stopwatch, and if the lights don't come on at the right time, to tell me that any of the syringes have not been activated, then we know to go to the electrical backup."

Paul explained that the operations officer in the death chamber with the inmate also has a stopwatch and is monitoring the sequence of lights on the delivery module. Also, Mark Schreiber holds a stopwatch and keeps a log in the area where the control module is.

"To go to the electrical backup system," Gary continued, "we use these three switches here." He demonstrated the two sets of three toggle switches, one for each executioner. "We count off the thirty-second and sixty-second intervals, and on command, the switches are thrown. Now, if that doesn't work—if there's some kind of problem with the electrical system—we go to the manual backup."

Gary reached up to a rectangular wooden box mounted on the wall above the hole through which the cable connected the control module to the delivery module. It was sealed with a padlock, which he opened, and the front of the box swung down to reveal six pull rods, with handles like an oversize manual choke on a car.

"This is our third backup system, and it will ensure that the execution takes place even if all the other systems fail. Once again, we count it down with our stopwatches, and each of the pull rods is pulled simultaneously by the two persons." He grasped two of the handles to show how it would be done. "Any questions?"

"Not so far," I said.

"Okay, let's run it through one time. I've armed the machine and it's ready to go. Now I'll press the buttons."

Gary depressed the buttons simultaneously with both of his thumbs. As they snapped back into place, there was a brief interval in which Gary's tension was evident. Then the lights for the sodium pentothal sequence switched on, and I could hear a surprisingly loud report, even through the thick concrete walls, as the piston was loosed from its cradle and fell onto the plunger of the first syringe. Gary kept his eye on the dentist's clock as we waited for the second sequence, and he nodded as the lights and the piston performed. The third sequence was completed, and Gary said: "When you're waiting for these sequences to happen, when you're waiting and hoping that everything is going to go smoothly, a minute seems like a lifetime."

It was clear that Gary took his responsibility for the machine extremely seriously. In fact, it was clear that his responsibility for the lethal injection machine singled Gary out as unique among any other employee at Potosi. "I am the only one in the state of Missouri trained on this machine," he told me. "I haven't trained anyone else.

"I've got two full sets of syringes up there, so I can show you how the manual pulls work," Gary told me. "I don't have a stopwatch on me, but you'll get the idea."

Gary stood in front of the manual override panel. His white cowboy boots were planted square to the wall. He shrugged his shoulders and loosened the sleeves of his jacket so that his clothing did not restrict his movements. I was standing alongside him, and as his hands moved in to grasp the pull rods I could see them reflected in the photosensitive aviator-style glasses he wore, and in the glint of his jewelry. He wore an expensive gold watch which glittered madly in his glasses, and on the same hand he wore two chunky gold rings set with diamonds. He pulled the first two rods, and two sounds followed almost simultaneously: the loud clunk of the pulled rods and the punchy, metallic sound of the piston falling in the box on the other side of the wall.

"What happens when the execution is over?" I asked. "What do you do then?"

"As soon as the doctor signals to the operations officer that the execution is complete, the blinds are drawn and the witnesses are escorted from the area. As soon as the order goes out to stand down, I reverse the process," said Gary. "I flush the machine out with saline to clean it, and put everything away. I tidy up the room, take down the bleachers, and store them for next time. Then I go upstairs, and that's it."

What passed for professionalism in Gary gave clues to the almost military-inspired feeling of a chain of command and a set of procedures that ensured that an execution went smoothly, but only partly took account of the feelings of the people who conducted it. I wanted to ask about that, but Paul was looking at his watch, and it was clear that everyone felt it was time to leave the death chamber.

Gary was keen to show me the engineering department of the prison, and Paul said good-bye for the afternoon. "Whatever you want to do tomorrow, just let us know, and we'll set it up for you," he told me. I thanked him while Gary finished locking up the death chamber. As soon as everything was squared away, he suggested we go outside and smoke a cigarette.

We joined the nurses and officers who were smoking outside the hospital entrance.

"Sure is a beautiful day," said Gary.

GARY AND I walked over to the maintenance area. He explained the extent of his operation, that he had twenty people working under him. He took a great deal of pride in his responsibility for maintaining the sophisticated air-handling and security systems at Potosi.

"Security is everything," he told me. "These are dangerous criminals here, the most dangerous in the state. You've got to be security-minded all the time. If you drop your guard for a moment, you're in trouble. They'll make a weapon out of anything, and somebody'll get killed. We don't leave any tools out in the shop, we don't let inmates handle tools. We have to stay right on top of any outside contractors who come to work here, and make sure they don't leave tools lying around, and that they take away all their garbage when they're done. All it takes is a little piece of metal for a blade, and some tape for a handle, and you've got a knife that will kill a man."

We entered the maintenance shop, and two of Gary's men were repairing a large coffee urn.

"I want to show you something," Gary said. He called out to one of the men working on the coffee urn, "Is my machine still down here?"

The maintenance man looked confused for a moment. "Oh, *your* machine? *That* machine."

"Yeah," said Gary. "My machine."

"I think so."

While the maintenance man went off to look for "the machine," Gary explained what it was.

"Last year, I went up to Illinois and helped them with an execution. They hadn't had one for a long time. They had bought one of Fred's machines, but it needed servicing, and I know that Fred had some problems there in Illinois, so they had me come up on a contract and do it for them."

I was aware of the background to the Charles Walker execution, but not of the fact that Gary Sutterfield had traveled from Missouri to do it. After the fallout from the Carnes memo and *The Leuchter Report,* Illinois had canceled its contract with Fred. Fred explained to me that he was a victim of "Jewish legislators who wanted to keep me out of their state."

The Walker execution, which took place on September 12, 1990, at Stateville Correctional Center near Joliet, was controversial because even though Walker had abandoned his appeals, other death row inmates filed a lawsuit against the state in which they argued that execution by Fred Leuchter's lethal injection machine was a cruel and unusual punishment. They claimed that the Illinois lethal injection statute authorized the use of two chemical agents, a barbiturate and a paralytic agent. Because the Leuchter machine employs three chemicals, the inmates claimed, its use would be in violation of the state statute. The inmates also presented an affidavit from Dr. Edward Brunner, chairman of the Department of Anesthesia at Northwestern University Medical School, who claimed that the Leuchter machine and protocol "create the substantial risk that plaintiffs will strangle or suffer excruciating pain during the three-chemical injection, but will be prevented by the paralytic agent from communicating their distress."

I had discussed the Brunner affidavit with Fred over Labor Day, and he told me: "As to whether or not the potassium chloride causes pain, I'm not a physiologist and I don't know that. But I will say this much—that by

the time the potassium chloride is introduced there is sufficient brain damage so that there would be no pain. So I do not believe that the potassium
chloride causes pain if the person is either brain-damaged or totally asleep.
But it may well cause pain if it were administered without the other chemicals.''

When Illinois fired Fred, the press jumped on the story and left state
prison officials feeling exposed and anxious. Since the only other state that
had used Fred's machine was Missouri, the superintendent of Stateville
contacted Potosi. Gary received a contract from the Illinois Department of
Corrections, effective from August 25, 1990, to November 25, 1990. He
was paid a daily rate of five hundred dollars plus expenses for his participation in the execution of Charles Walker.

The maintenance man brought in a machine of wood, Plexiglas, and
steel and set it up on the workbench next to the broken coffee urn.

"This is my baby," Gary told me. "When they had that problem up in
Illinois, there was some question about whether Fred's machine could be
used. Paul asked me whether that problem could happen here in Missouri,
and of course we didn't know. So, to be safe, I built my own machine. It's
fully manual, but it would get the job done. I call it my twenty-nine ninety-
five machine, as opposed to Fred's twenty-nine ninety-five machine.''

"You mean, $29.95 as opposed to $29,095.00?''

"That's right.''

Gary looked at his watch. "Four-thirty. Quittin' time.'' He escorted me
back through central control and past Paul's office. "You going to be
around for a while?'' he asked.

I said I would be.

"How about we drink some beer tomorrow night?''

I said that would be fine.

After I said good night to Paul, Greg Wilson came by.

Paul called out, "Get that X ray you wanted?''

"No problem,'' Red replied.

"Find what you were looking for?''

"Yes sir.''

HE NEXT morning, I arrived early at the prison, and not without a little apprehension. My plan was to begin interviewing death row inmates. I had requested that I be allowed to speak with them in a room alone, with the door closed so that no corrections officers or prison staff could hear what was said. Paul Delo had agreed to this and offered to let me use a room in the building where the caseworkers' offices were located, in the yard just next door to Housing Unit 5.

One of the caseworkers, Fred Johnson, came up to escort me inside. A rosy-cheeked good ol' boy with a college education and a slow drawl, he asked me who I wanted to see. I had no way of knowing which of the condemned inmates would make for a strong interview, or even if any of them would want to talk to me. Having studied the list of condemned men I'd been given in Jefferson City, I had decided to start with two extremes, youth and age.

Missouri has the oldest man and woman on death row in the United States, Ray and Faye Copeland. Ray was born in 1914, Faye in 1921. They had been sentenced to death three months previously, in June. I'd read about their case, which involved the murders of five men who had been lured to work on the Copeland farm in Chillicothe, Missouri, where bank accounts were set up in the five men's names. The Copelands would buy cattle with bad checks drawn on the workers' accounts, then kill the men. All were shot with a .22-caliber rifle.

Missouri also had one of the youngest men on death row, Heath Wilkins. Age sixteen when he committed the crime that brought him the death sentence, he had turned twenty-two just before Labor Day.

Fred Johnson had made a list of some other death row inmates he thought I might wish to interview, including some who were getting close to an execution date. He was also concerned that he introduce a selection of black and white inmates. He cleared his desk to make room for me and my tape recorder, and called over to Ray Copeland's housing unit for him to be sent down.

Despite his age, Ray Copeland is a tall and sturdy man. He was dressed in prison grays and wore a hat, which he took off when he shook my hand.

I asked him how he was doing. He didn't respond, and then he told me that he was very hard of hearing, and that I'd have to talk into his good ear. I came around from behind the desk and pulled up a chair next to him. I asked the question again, and he told me in a voice that was at once husky and frail that he was fine. I asked him if he was settling in okay and he said he was. I asked him if he'd been in prison before, and he told me that, as a young man, he had been.

I asked if he had heard from his wife, and he began to weep. The whole idea of this interview seemed to be a bad one, as I watched the old man wipe the tears with his sleeve.

"I'm innocent," he told me.

"What happened?" I asked.

He handed me a grubby manila envelope and asked if I would read the papers inside. He said they proved his innocence.

In the envelope was a pile of papers in disarray. There were old pages of court transcript and other items relating to his case, all in an unintelligible jumble.

"I'm innocent," he said. "And that proves it."

I had told myself before I arrived at Potosi that it would be unwise to focus my attention on the details of anyone's case. There was no way that I could assume responsibility to assist in anyone's appeal. More important, I felt, if there is an ultimate objection to be made to the death penalty, it does not rest on the argument that the death penalty is a bad thing because the state may execute an innocent person; if executions are undesirable in a civilized society, they are undesirable in relation to the guilty as well as the innocent. The life and fifty or life without parole sentence as applied in Missouri makes it nearly 100 percent certain that the inmate will never reenter society.

I asked Ray if he was feeling fit, and he told me: "I bench-pressed two hundred ninety pounds yesterday. I can take just about any man in this place. I told them I'd like to be put to work, but they don't have any jobs for me."

When the interview was over, I mentioned this to Fred Johnson, who commented that it might make people nervous for Ray to be seen with a shovel in his hand.

"Hey," he added. "Did you hear that Mr. Copeland is writing a book?"

"No, I didn't know that."

"Yeah. It's called *How to Run a Farm on a Skeleton Crew*."

H

EATH WILKINS has achieved a dubious fame in his short life. He is one of the youngest men on death row in the United States (the youngest in Missouri). And he was the subject of a landmark court decision, *Wilkins* v. *Missouri* (1989), in which the U.S. Supreme Court ruled that the execution of sixteen- and seventeen-year-old offenders is permissible under the Constitution of the United States.

He sat down and presented a bundle of contradictions. When he shook my hand, there was a boyish quality about him, though it was mixed with a wariness that no adult who has not spent years in prison ever learns. Blond, slender, and lightly tanned, Heath was dressed in a muscle shirt and shorts and was trying, with modest success, to grow a beard. If the circumstances of our meeting had been different, it would be difficult to pick Heath out from any number of American kids of similar appearance as someone considered by the state to be too dangerous to live.

A man-child who had been raised in various institutions since the age of eight, Heath had experienced only six months of liberty in his short life before being convicted of capital murder. Raised in Little Rock, Arkansas, Heath was severely beaten by both of his parents from infancy. When he was two, his father left home. His mother, who was then a regular drug user, continued the beatings. Heath's mother's brother lived with the family, and Heath testified at his own trial that the brother had given him drugs from the time he was six years old. The mother's boyfriend also beat Heath and his brother.

As a child, Heath was caught vandalizing a tractor, starting small fires, and committing petty thefts. When he was ten years old, he attempted to murder his mother and her boyfriend by lacing Tylenol capsules with poison. He was sent to a mental institution for six months. At the age of ten, he made the first of three suicide attempts by throwing himself off a bridge into the path of an oncoming truck, which avoided him. His next three years were spent in another institution in which he was diagnosed as having a "schizotypal personality" and was placed on Mellaril. His second and third failed suicide attempts involved drugs and alcohol. He was moved to a foster home, then another institution (where he was placed on Thorazine), and yet another foster home. In 1985, he was returned to his mother's care, but she refused to let him live with her.

From May 1985 until he committed murder in July 1985, Heath lived on the streets in Kansas City, Missouri. He, his girlfriend Midget, and two friends called Bo and Shades lived in Penguin Park, a run-down children's attraction featuring three-story-high concrete animals on an acre of scrubby grass. Heath and his girlfriend lived in the concrete penguin's pouch. They passed the time drinking peach schnapps and taking black dragon, a homemade LSD substitute. They would hang out at a nearby shopping center, and take turns shoplifting food when they were hungry.

Heath had got it into his head that if he had enough money to buy a motorcycle, his life would change. He and his friend Bo went to a convenience store in Avondale, Missouri, shortly before 11:00 P.M. on July 27, 1985. Heath had planned the murder in advance. Bo would hide in the bathroom while Heath ordered a sandwich. When Heath pulled a double-edge "butterfly" knife on the store clerk, Nancy Allen, Bo emerged from the bathroom and held her arms. Midget and Shades were waiting nearby with a change of clothes. Heath stabbed Nancy Allen while Bo held her. Then, while Bo cleaned out the cash register, Heath stabbed her in the back, chest, and heart. While she pleaded in vain for her life, Heath stabbed her a further four times in the neck. He later said he had stabbed her in the neck to stop the sound of her pleas.

I asked Heath, "When you committed your crime, did you have any thoughts about the consequences in terms of going to prison?"

"Yeah, I did. I thought I'd die, though. I thought they'd kill me."

"But were you surprised when the court handed down a death sentence on someone as young as you were at the time?"

Heath was patient with my obvious lack of understanding. When he spoke, his voice was soft and boyish, but the words he had to say were beyond the experience of most people. "No," he told me. "I asked for it. I was real concerned about living the rest of my life in pri. on. I was trying to kill myself and I kept chickening out just before I'd lose consciousness. So I thought, I'll push myself. It's like walking closer to the edge of a cliff. I thought, if I got the death penalty, then I would know there's *no* way I could get out of it. Then I could do it."

"You'd made other suicide attempts in the past, and they failed?"

Heath nodded.

"And by taking someone else's life, you were putting yourself in a position where you hoped yours would be taken?"

Heath said that was the case.

Heath told me about living in state facilities from early childhood, and about how he was feeling at the time of the murder.

"I always carried a weapon on me. I thought I'd get some money so I could buy a motorcycle, so I could at least get out of there, go do something. I had some boots on. I'd walked holes through these boots looking for a job."

As he told me the story, small details rose out of his drugged past and lodged in my mind like objects in a weird still life. The knife. The boots. The old Harley-Davidson owned by a friend, which Heath viewed as a means of leaving his miserable existence behind. The ordinary significance of these objects was transformed by circumstance and the confusion of an injured and frightened adolescent mind, and an innocent woman had become the opportunity for that nightmarish transformation to occur.

I didn't ask Heath about his mental condition, but he explained how, "When I was arrested, they took me and they certified me." Then, "Someone came up with the idea of pleading guilty and everything."

But Heath was not to be deterred from his suicidal plan. He fired his attorney and, at the age of sixteen, represented himself on a capital murder charge.

"How long did the trial last?" I asked.

"There was no jury," Heath replied, jumping ahead to the heart of the story. "I didn't want a jury trial."

"How long did it take?"

"They stretched it over, but they did the bulk of it in a day."

I wondered how a judge could allow a minor to demand the death penalty without legal representation. I asked Heath if the judge had made any effort to dissuade him from abandoning his life.

"At first they were concerned, and I saw it. But I knew that . . ." Heath's face was twisted in a confused and painful expression. He was frustrated, at a loss for words. "You know what I'm saying? He didn't say, 'Listen,' too many times, 'uh, I don't think you should, uh . . .' " Heath's voice trailed off as he thought of the judge. "He was doing it because he thought he had to."

Heath was taken to death row at MSP. I asked him what that had been like.

"It's a lot better now. It used to be real bad. We were locked in our cells. We had very few visits. Maybe once every other month. I was terrorized. Here I was this young, skinny kid, and all these huge guys."

I asked how he found Potosi compared with MSP.

"This place is a gift of God," he said without hesitation. "It's clean. I used to get bugs in my tea at MSP." Looking back at the nightmare of MSP, Heath's voice assumed a bright, boyish tone, and he grinned broadly. "I used to have mice jump on my face. They'd live in your TV."

But the bright, open smile disappeared after a moment and was replaced with a painful look. "Jefferson City was a real negative atmosphere."

Heath told me that he'd changed a great deal from the adolescent who had committed a murder. "I used to think that being cruel was a strength," he said.

Potosi was full of cruel people, Heath reflected. Some people—officers and inmates alike—thrive in prison because of the opportunities for cruelty it presents; others are made cruel by the environment they find themselves in. "One time," he recalled, "a guard came to MSP to work there, and I told him, 'Get yourself a job someplace else. Even if it pays less. You don't want this job. It'll ruin your personal character, it'll ruin your family life.' " He shook his head. "Is it possible for guys to come here and work and be so cruel and not be that way on the streets? And even when you're here, you know what I'm saying, things happen? You get mad. You react. You start dealing with it. And that's the way you deal with it under a cruel environment, is to be cruel."

"What happened to that officer?" I asked.

"The man's still working. He's moved from MSP and he's down here now. He's lost his wife and everything."

Heath went on to explain something I would hear later from staff at Potosi. Working in a prison, particularly in a maximum-security prison, is so stressful that it is often difficult to relate to people outside of that industry. Domestic life often suffers. Current divorces are a major topic of conversation at Potosi.

Since coming to death row, Heath said, he had become a Christian, and spent much of his time studying the Bible.

I asked him about the chapel at Potosi.

"Believe it or not, not many go. Only about ten or twelve, at tops, twenty people. There's a lot of guys though, who God's dealt with, but they're back-slipping."

"What kind of man is the prison chaplain?"

"He's an administrator. He's one of them. He's like the guards."

"Isn't the chaplain in an odd position, having to participate in executions here?"

Heath's face showed no expression. "Like you say, he's in an odd position."

For years, when I had thought about the death penalty, I had wondered how it was possible to structure time if you knew that your life was going to be taken in the foreseeable future. Doing time in prison was one thing; but doing time when there was very little chance of ever getting out, and every chance that you would be executed, seemed an impossibility. To have started a death sentence as a child seemed doubly impossible.

"At first," Heath said, "you separate yourself from reality. All of a sudden one day I woke up and I said, 'I have done *four* years in prison.' " Heath sought pen friends and had intimate correspondence with two women, one from New York and one from Los Angeles. He eventually married the woman from Los Angeles, and she visits him at Potosi.

"An example of how the guards can be cruel," Heath started to tell me. "Man. You know, sometimes they strip-search visitors to this place? To come in here, you have to sign a paper that says you agree to a strip search. When that happens, they take you in a little room, and you take off all your clothes. They check in your hair, behind your ears, in your mouth, and in your, you know . . ."

I nodded.

"That's a violation, man. I told my wife, I said, 'Babe, you sign that, go ahead. But if they ever want to strip-search you for any reason, don't come in.' They can do anything they want to me. But if they try to do it to her, I couldn't stand it. And I've had guards go up and insult my wife in the visiting room."

The caseworker had told me that Heath's wife is a very attractive woman, and that "ol' Heath likes to get his hand up her skirt."

"The visiting room is a *privilege*. And the guys that get a lot of visits are really in the palms of their hands," Heath said.

We talked about the physical environment at Potosi. Heath had just come back from the gym, and I remarked how fit he looked.

"Yeah, compared to Jeff City . . ."

At moments, it seems as though Heath can hardly believe he left MSP, or that Potosi is real. The definition of comfort depends very much on an experience of comfort. For Heath, Potosi is the closest thing to a home that he's known.

"There's a window in your cell, which makes a big difference, you know what I mean?"

"What can you see from your window?"

"There's trees and lakes and everything on the other side of the fence."

I asked if anyone ever thought about trying to escape from Potosi.

Heath laughed. "Have you seen the fence around this place? There ain't nobody going anywhere. If anybody got out of this place, it'd be *obvious*. It'd be a helicopter right into the courtyard. They used to use barbed wire. But then they started using razor wire. And now they don't even use razor wire. That stuff out there's concertina wire. It'll grab ahold of you, know what I'm saying, it won't let go of you. The yard has a fence around it plus there's two perimeter fences, plus they're putting a third perimeter fence with sensors on it."

We talked about Heath's appeals, and what his chances of success were.

For some time, he hadn't bothered with his appeals. But his conversion to Christianity and his marriage had altered his view of his own life. He now pursues his appeals, but he takes a hard moral line about how they are pursued, based on his view of Christianity.

"In the past, they would lie in my appeals and say I was innocent." Heath looked me straight in the eyes and said: "If you lie in an appeal and you lose, and you die . . ."

Heath's belief in a life after death, the quality of which would be determined by how he behaved now, left me silent.

He was tolerant of my lack of response, and reiterated his point. "I would refuse to let them file the appeals. I'd say, 'No, man, you're lying all the time. Cut all that stuff out. You guys can say anything, but don't say I'm not guilty.' "

I wondered how Heath regarded his death sentence now. "When you were at Jeff City," I began, "and you were satisfied that you'd got the death penalty . . ."

I was searching for the right way to ask a very difficult question.

Heath let out a terrible sigh and said, "Yeah . . ."

"Did you worry about it?"

"About being executed?"

"Yes."

"Oh, man . . . Some of the guys here who have it now don't even think about it. The guys in here that, if they thought that, you know what I'm saying?"

"No."

"Some of them really aren't altogether there, you know what I mean? If, uh, for some reason a situation came up and they felt they had to kill somebody, they'd still do it. Even if they were told . . . they'd just do it. You don't think about your death penalty until they're taking you into that little cell and locking you in there, and they're going to strap you to the table."

"Do you think about that?"

"Do I think about the death penalty?"

"I mean, in relation to you."

"No."

"Do you think they might come for you one day?"

"No." He paused and then asked himself the question. "Do I think they will? I really don't know. I don't believe so. But, you know what I'm saying, time will tell."

Heath steered the conversation away from himself to talk about the death penalty in general. He prefaced his thoughts by telling me, "I feel kind of hypocritical saying this, because it doesn't really matter, because of my position. But it's wrong. It's vengeance in its purest form. It really makes prosecutors . . . They really think it's a big deal. They get off on the death penalty."

Heath told me that, on the other hand, he could see why people supported the death penalty. "If somebody killed my mom or my wife—you know what I'm saying, and killed them horribly? Man, I'd just . . . I could understand how they'd feel. I'd want that person dead, I'd be so upset. Maybe by the grace of God I'd be able to forgive that person. But still, just because I forgive that person doesn't mean I want them back out on the streets either. So, life without parole, I can see that, but not the death penalty."

"What if you'd received life without instead of the death sentence?"

"You know, if you get a life sentence, that means you go for parole every year. That doesn't mean they have to let you out. They can keep you in prison for the rest of your life. So if you're a menace to society, they can keep you in there. But life without parole is basically saying, *We don't care whether you change or not.*"

"If you have to be executed," I asked Heath, "what do you think about lethal injection as the method?"

"I don't like the idea of being laid down on the table. I don't want to have to be laid down. I'd rather be sitting up."

Lying down to be executed seemed to Heath the final indignity.

"Another thing that really distresses me," Heath said, "is that they give you a shot before they take you in and execute you. And I don't know if it's, you know, if they have to force it on you or what. But they put you out so that you don't fight and everything like that. I don't know if that's mandatory, though, or not. Some guys say it's not, and some say it is."

Heath told me that, if he has to face execution, he wants to have a clear mind when it is happening to him.

"Believe this or not," Heath told me, stroking the fuzzy growth on his chin, "this may sound kind of corny, and people do think it's corny—but I don't want to die. For my wife's sake, or for my mom's sake. If there was nobody out there who would care, then I wouldn't mind. But there are a lot of people out there who care, and that's why I don't want to die."

I asked Heath what effect executions had on other death row inmates at Potosi.

"It bothers me, personally. First of all, I know these guys. I've lived with these guys. I've seen these guys do funny things. I've laughed with these guys. I've seen these guys be angry. Of course, you sit around with them for years, you get to know them. And, uh, not necessarily sympathize with them." Heath gave out a little laugh. "But you get to know them."

"How do the officers act around the time of an execution?"

"A lot of the guards, they say the strangest things. A lot of these guards —and that's not the white shirts, you know, they're totally detached from this—but all the guards feel real bad about the executions. As a matter of fact, they look for any weakness in a guard, and then they try to weed them out. Any guard that is against the death penalty. I've had guards come by and ask me how I was doing, and I say, '*Look, are you serious?*' He's one of the ones who's going to execute this last guy."

Heath told me a story, intended as an analogy of how he views the participation of corrections officers in executions—as accessories to killing. "There's a guy in here who's on death row for holding a guard, and somebody else stabbed the guard and killed him. He didn't know if the guy was going to stab him and kill him. He knew the guy was going to beat him up. But he didn't know he was going to whip out a shank and stab him. And he got the death penalty for that. I heard a"—Heath laughed and shook his head—"a guard tell me once, 'You know, this isn't personal, we're not really . . . we're just *holding you.*' "

Heath knows that the "white shirts" are more closely involved in executions, and he reserves a special dislike for them.

"The white shirts, many of them actually enjoy it because they are— and this is not me just saying this or making this up—I had a guard tell me one time, 'I can't wait to'—talking about me, telling another guard—'I can't wait to execute that guy. When they do, I want to be standing right there.' "

Heath told me that he notices a party atmosphere among some officers on the day of an execution. In Missouri, as elsewhere, executions may be less of a Roman holiday than a public hanging would be, but they are nevertheless a public event, put on by the state.

"What do they do?" I asked.

"They have a table. What they do is, you know the visiting room?"

"Yes."

"They pull in a long table so they can put coffee and drinks—not alcoholic drinks, of course—but coffee and stuff. And, you know, snacks and everything. Because all these bigwigs come and they stand around and they need refreshments. It turns into a little get-together, a little party. Were you there when Byrd was executed?"

"No."

"You ought to try and come by one time, see what it's like. If they'll let you around. I'm pretty sure they will. Just check out the atmosphere. And look at their faces and see. It's really a bummer. But that's the way it is."

"How do people feel about going to the hospital here?" I asked.

"First of all, we have . . . Guys do not have *any* good feelings towards that place. If you went over there, and it cost him . . ."

"Him?"

". . . you know, the doctor. If it cost him something to help you out . . . Do you know what lay-in is?"

"No."

"If you have an injury, you know that keeps you from playing sports, you stay in your unit and they bring you food. But what they use it as, is if you complain about something, they say, 'Well, we're going to keep you locked in your cell. *You can't come out.*' It's like, I was having back problems, and they were going to keep me locked in my cell. They said, 'Well, you can't run or work out.' Well, I can still go out to chapel. It's hypocritical the way they describe it, so we're real leery about which problems we go there with. And also, a lot of times they won't treat you."

"Does everyone here know where the death chamber is?"

"Yes."

"Does that seem a little insensitive to you?"

Heath laughs. "No, it doesn't. Because you got to think that every time we want to go visit our wife and our family, they can make them go through a strip search."

I thought that probably no one can spend all their time on death row reflecting on their execution and the circumstances in which it will happen. Daily indignities loom larger. But I repeated my question, about what people thought of the death chamber being in the prison hospital.

Heath's face clouded over with exasperation and helplessness.

"That is kind of . . ."

It's a question to which Heath didn't really have an answer. His brow furrowed and his eyes were glazed with incomprehension.

"The nurses in there, you know what I'm saying? I don't know. I guess it's . . . they know something more than we will. Even though we're the ones that's being killed."

WHAT ABOUT ol' Heath?" one of the caseworkers said as we walked across the yard and back up to Paul Delo's office. "Ain't he a beaut?"

A parade of inmates from five houses streamed out of the door next to the caseworkers' office at 11:30 precisely, heading for lunch.

"Do you know how to tell when an inmate's lying?" the caseworker asked.

I took the question seriously. "I think so," I said.

"You can tell he's lying," said the caseworker, "if his lips are moving."

*   *   *

My first sight of A. J. Bannister was from the window of the caseworkers' office. He entered the waiting room in a slow, deliberate way. My first impression was of impressive physical bulk. His walk spelled arrogance and defiance. When he sat down on the molded plastic seating in the waiting room, I thought his expression was one of fixed disdain. He is thirty-four. He looks older.

The caseworkers' brief summary of A. J. Bannister was that he was a pervert, and a violent, dangerous inmate.

A.J. came into the room and we shook hands. Standing about six foot one, and weighing enough to play tight end for the Chicago Bears, he seemed both curious and wary about why I'd asked to see him. He was dressed in a prison-issue gray shirt with his number, CP24, written in faded black Magic Marker over his heart, and a pair of shorts and training shoes.

"Take a seat," I offered.

A. J. Bannister's physical presence was more powerful than that of any other person I'd encountered at Potosi. He wasn't the largest man there, by any means. Nor did he have the sculpted physique that many of the inmates cultivated. He was fleshy, with a slight paunch, but my instincts told me that he was potentially one of the most dangerous men at Potosi. He was the kind of man who, if you met him on the outside, you might move several stools down the bar to accommodate.

"What's this for?" he asked, referring to our interview. His eyes narrowed and fixed on me in a naked challenge. One eye was slightly closed in a permanent squint.

When he spoke, I was astonished at the contrast between his overwhelming physical presence and the deep and cultivated tone of his speech. His accent wasn't the broad drawl of Missouri or Arkansas, though it was unmistakably midwestern. His voice was an intelligent one, and its depth was not simply a matter of pitch. It was full of a quiet anger tinged with sadness. The contrast was overwhelming and confusing. A.J. had been advertised as a violent criminal, a cold-blooded contract killer who would just as soon kill you as look at you. But even half a dozen words from him gave the lie to so glib a dismissal.

I told him why I was at Potosi, and the kinds of questions I wanted to ask. He liked the idea of using a focus on process and procedure to get the administration to talk openly about the death penalty and about carrying out executions.

We looked at each other, and I thought that A.J. was weighing up how much he could afford to tell me; how much he could afford to trust me to represent accurately and fairly what he said. My assumption was right.

"A lot of reporters come down here, looking for a story," he said slowly. "Looking for headlines. And we're never represented fairly. We're always portrayed as monsters. And it just isn't like that."

A.J. didn't know whether or not I was familiar with his case, and he didn't ask. I knew nothing about him except that he was described by the administration as a "contract killer." For reasons of his own, A.J. decided that he would tell me part of his story, and the moment of decision was apparent. His face relaxed, his eyes lost much of their suspicion, and he began in a deep, clear voice: "I was arrested August twenty-first, 1982. I was sentenced on March fourteenth, 1983. I was twenty-four years old when I was arrested. I was assigned a public defender, and he didn't put up much of a defense. The trial lasted five days. I was six years at MSP."

"How did you find MSP?" I asked.

"It leaves a great deal to be desired."

"At the time of committing your crime, did you think you might end up on death row at MSP?"

"I hadn't even considered that I'd ever be sent there."

"And when you were?"

"I was expecting to see all these murderers scowling and skulking around corners and looking for something to kill," he said in a soft voice, heavy with irony. "And it just wasn't like that. The conditions at Jefferson City were deplorable. We had water on the floors any time it rained. Dust, dirt, cockroaches. The food was cold. We didn't have access to our dining hall, like the rest of the people there. We were completely isolated, segregated. And we were generally . . . we were in the basement, and forgotten."

"Since Missouri wasn't executing people at that time, did you think they were serious? Did it seem real to you?"

"At that point, no."

"When did that change?"

"Before George Mercer's execution. He was my next-door neighbor."

A.J. looked to me for recognition of who Tiny Mercer was and noted it. Later, as our relationship developed, his answers to my questions would become lengthy, and marked by pauses of ten or fifteen seconds in which he would consider what he was saying, and give narrative shape to the events of his life on death row. At our first meeting, I didn't know A.J.

well enough to let those silences happen. I wanted to know much more about his relationship with Tiny Mercer, but the look on his face when Mercer's name was mentioned told me that it was a painful and sensitive area, and I resolved to let A.J. take the lead about how much he wanted to tell me. I steered the Tiny Mercer story onto a more impersonal level.

"Did the setting of Tiny Mercer's execution date come out of the blue?" I asked.

A.J. explained that a number of death warrants had been issued, and stays given. But when the last warrant came, everyone, including Tiny Mercer, knew it was the end. "It woke a lot of people up," A.J. told me. "We had thought that these appeals would drag on forever. It isn't like that. In fact, I just got turned down last month, and I'm not real happy about that." A.J. explained that he's had eight appeals, and that very few avenues now remain open to him.

"My lawyer just told me that the worst-case scenario is that I've got between twelve and eighteen months left to live."

I calculated that A.J. had been on death row for nearly eight and a half years. His time was growing short. He had already been waiting for the executioner a year longer than the average man on death row in America.

"Justice just doesn't happen unless you have the money," said A.J. "If you have that, you don't get the death penalty. It's basically the blacks and people that are at or below the poverty line, that can't afford legal representation from the start. And when the quality of your defense depends on your station in life, that's inherently unfair."

I asked if Missouri's decision to switch from gas to lethal injection as a means of execution had a great effect on death row inmates at MSP.

A.J. nodded and looked at me as if to say, "Okay, let's get to the meat of this thing." He rested one foot on his knee, and I could see a jailhouse tattoo on the other knee that said "A.J.," like a monogram on a shirt or a handkerchief.

"There was a lot that built up to that. Tiny and I had a number of debates over lethal injection as opposed to gas. And he and his wife, and some of their friends, were supportive of the Missouri legislature switching over to lethal injection. A painless way to die, I suppose. It was thought that while the gas chamber is being used, there's going to be horror stories that come out following this. And the public gets to hear of how someone gagged for eight, ten, twelve minutes; tongue swollen, eyes popping out, things like that. And that's gruesome. And if they're borderline on their feelings on capital punishment, if they read about this, that could sway them *against* it. But, the way it is now, with lethal injection, the state wants that because it's like putting a dog to sleep at the veterinarian's."

A.J. delivered the last line in a long drawl and ended in a sigh that summed up the state's intention and his own frustration. His words hung in the air-conditioned room, and the only sound was the buzzing of the fluorescent lights and the distant hum of the air-handling plant on the roof of the prison.

"You get the first shot, you drift off to sleep," he continued after a pause. "You get the second one, your lungs stop. Third one, your heart stops. People witness executions that are . . ."

A.J. was at a loss for words. He held his enormous hands in front of his face as if he were trying to grab hold of an understanding, or at least a phrase to make his frustration something tangible that he could pull out of the air and hand to me, so I could understand.

". . . it's impersonal," he said, letting his hands fall into his lap. "They're going to sleep. That's all these people see. They don't see the mental anguish that goes on beforehand, knowing that this is going to take place. And they also don't know about the fact that, before a man's executed, he's being held in that hospital over there. And there's a doctor here who nobody particularly cares for, who gives him an examination, searching for a vein beforehand. They put a catheter in your penis and a plug in your ass so you don't shit all over yourself in front of their witnesses, because that would just *ruin* the sterile effect of execution."

The expression of fixed disdain which A.J. wore when he first came into the room made sense. It was permanent. It was how I would feel if I lived at Potosi, facing execution.

"I just wanted to see the gas chamber kept in effect. Not because it was a pleasant way to go—I don't think there's any easy way to die when you know it's happening months and months in advance, and you're watching the time right down to the last minute. If the gas chamber was kept in effect, some of us might have lived. And it caused a lot of bad feelings between us and some of the groups that are working to abolish the death penalty, because their feeling was, they supported lethal injection because it's an easier way for the man to go, and for his family. And I just could not understand this thinking. You're equally dead. At least have some benefit come out of it for the rest of us who don't support this. And yet they did. And they just lost credibility with us. If you're against the death penalty, you cannot support a method. That's just a contradiction in terms."

We discussed how lethal injection was a particularly modern method of killing someone: "clean," "humane." Relatively quick. Painless, perhaps; though no one would ever be able to say with certainty.

"What do inmates think about the fact that the death house is in the hospital?" I asked.

A.J. laughed bitterly. "Not much. In past years at MSP, they had a little . . . a death chamber, where the gas chamber was located, and two isolation cells. It was in a separate building."

I told A.J. that I'd been there. He shook his head grimly.

"Here, it's . . ." He took a deep breath and let it out very slowly. "They simply don't have the facility here to . . . have that. Because it's sort of a symbol to have a *death house*. To put it over in the hospital, it doesn't carry the same significance. You're not allowed to see that part of the building until that time . . . until you're put to death. And they go out of their way to make sure you don't."

We talked about how Potosi was a showcase prison compared to MSP or, indeed, most of the recently built prisons in the United States. I asked A.J. how the mainstreaming of death row and life and fifty inmates had worked from the point of view of men with the death sentence.

A.J. smiled at this. "When we moved up here, we weren't incorporated in the general population right away. That came earlier this year. It wasn't brought about by any compassion on the administration's or the state's part. We hit them over the head with a consent decree. They had to, without admitting guilt, change conditions. Which at MSP were real bad. We were supposed to come here with some of those same elements intact. And as soon as we got here, they started changing it. They decided they weren't bound by it. But, as long as we were kept segregated, even here, there weren't enough of us to fill up one entire housing unit. So they decided in their infinite wisdom that we're going to incorporate these people with general population and, that way, we can make use of every cell we've got here. And they built this place and Cameron—Western Missouri Correctional Center—and told the taxpayers, 'Look, we just spent a hundred million dollars but this is going to solve all prison overcrowding through 1995, *don't worry about it.*' And now it's 1991 and they're out of space. *Again.* Now they're having to change the statutes to where Class A and B felonies are getting their sentences shortened by way of good time. And it has an effect on the taxpayers, which affects the politicians that get into office. Because they use the platform, 'Get Tough on Crime.' And that impresses some people, because people are scared. They don't go on to explain that we're tying up your tax dollars for years and years to come. And it's coming in from the highways, it's coming from the schools. And now it's getting to the point where they're realizing that these guys with a life and fifty sentence, or natural life, they're going to be here, under these current statutes, *for life.* And as these men get older, you're going to end up with an old folks' home. And now they want to alter that. But they're not sure how to do that *and* keep the death penalty. And with the tax dollars coming away from the schools, and the highways and every-thing, our system of education in the United States is going downhill rapidly. If you ask school kids, they think your Neville Chamberlain is a miniseries."

I asked A.J. about the level of illiteracy among inmates.

"It's not like that on death row. It's there in general population. And a lot of these guys that have natural life, a lot of them plead guilty to escape the death penalty. Prosecutors use that as leverage. They threaten these young men, they say, 'Come on, we're going to give you the death penalty unless you plead guilty.' And it scares the hell out of them. Because some of them are first-time offenders. They haven't got the slightest idea what's going on. They're just awestruck by the judicial process. There's a sixteen-year-old seven cells down from me. He's been here for two years. He's got a life and fifty."

A.J. made no attempt to suggest he wasn't guilty of a murder. But he objected strongly to the arbitrary way in which two men who commit a very similar crime can receive either a death sentence or life and fifty. He spoke with contempt of an inmate he'd known who faced five murder charges and who, in exchange for telling the prosecutor where he had buried the bodies, received a life sentence.

"You *can't* put a value on one murder against five—it's equally bad. But I could understand how the prosecutor would want to make a deal because of how the families of those victims felt. They wanted to put them to rest, and know where they were. Not have to wonder for years and years what field they're lying in, what ditch they're lying in. But when you start bartering like that, it sends a message to the next man. 'Well, you hide your victims, and you don't tell us where they're at, and you can make a deal on that.' " A.J. slaps his knee and throws his hands in the air. " 'We'll go for it.' And in my case, initially they brought a plea bargain. If I plead guilty, life and fifty. I thought, No, I can't do that, because I was twenty-four years old at the time. I don't think I'm going to see seventy-four in prison, so you're just going to have to take me to trial. Went to trial, and I basically got the death sentence because I exercised my so-called constitutional right to a trial by jury."

Much of the research work that anti–death penalty groups had done tended to focus heavily on race as a key factor in the capricious or arbitrary handing down of death sentences. A.J.'s case was different. He was white, with a white victim. He came from a working-class background, but not one of abject poverty.

"What sentence you get depends on all kinds of things. It even depends upon what time of year it is. If it's election year. Oh yeah, that's the big one. Is there an incumbent? Do they have a challenger? The way that politics affects capital punishment in America is tragic. Bush appointees to the federal courts are conservative. These federal judges, and even Supreme Court justices, do not necessarily vote their conscience anymore. They vote the conscience of the party that put them into that prestigious position. They're there for life, and it changes the entire complexion of American justice. In the past ten years, there's been the drive-by shootings, the L.A. gangs, the Jamaican posses—the American public is just scared to death. No place in America is safe from this. Drugs are everywhere. Now they've got this war on drugs, and they're fighting it. But to do that, they have to build more prisons. Now they're going to introduce the death penalty on the federal level for drug trafficking of major proportions. Noriega's in prison down in Florida. Sure, he was running Panama, siphoning drugs through channels into the States and making a lot of money. But they don't tell the American public that we put him in power basically, funded him, coddled him for years and years. They don't tell them that. But we're getting off the track here," said A.J.

I wanted to return to the question of what effect executions had on other inmates.

"In Mercer's execution, the first one, we were all at MSP. Jefferson City. In different wings, where the CPs and the general population didn't have contact with each other. That evening, they ran a number of videos on the closed-circuit channel. A sex video, right at midnight; so a number of people would be watching this, and wouldn't be thinking about what was taking place, a couple of hundred yards away. Tiny was respected by nearly everyone over there. I had known him for years. It was a sense of loss. Here at Potosi, it always happens at 12:01. I mean, you have to do the dirty deed in the middle of the night. On the day preceding the execution, everyone knows it's going to take place. And everyone's sort of hoping that a court is going to step in. But everyone knows that's pretty much . . . Odds are it's going to take place. They take us to the evening meal between five and six, and once we come back to our housing units, we're locked down. And that's so they can free up their guards and go out and patrol, and make a big show of it for what few supporters and protesters show up out in the parking lot. And I can understand their fear that if we were out at the time, somebody might just go off the deep end. But they show videos here, too. Till three, four, five o'clock in the morning, hoping to take the men's minds off of what's taking place in our hospital, seventy-five yards away."

A.J.'s face darkened and he looked long and hard at me, and then down at the floor.

"You wonder what's going on at that very moment, when it's going to be you over there. You wonder what it must be like, because you're isolated. You have a guard watching over you twenty-four hours a day for the four or five days preceding your execution. And here, this so-called deterrent effect, because they couldn't counter the fact that the murder rate *rises* after an execution. I mean, they just can't explain that. And now, they're basically saying that it's retaliation. It's society fighting back against violent crime."

The caseworkers were gathered in the lobby, and one of them was pointing at his watch and mouthing through the window that it was time to go. A.J. said he was surprised that I was allowed to talk with him alone and in total confidence. I said I was too.

The caseworker gave us five more minutes, so we went outside to smoke a cigarette. A.J. and I both found it slightly odd that we were left alone, that no one stood by to keep an eye on us. I offered A.J. one of my cigarettes, but he preferred to smoke his own brand—generic nonfilters. I asked about his next appeal.

"It basically depends on the luck of the draw. What three-judge panel I get assigned to. Whether they were appointed by Carter, Nixon, Ford— my life depends on who put them in office. Republicans. That's not a good sign."

A.J. let out a massive sigh. I felt exhausted from the interview. To listen to someone focus hard for two hours on their own impending death was a strange experience for me. I couldn't imagine how it would be to live that way. When it was time to go, we shook hands. I told A.J. that I would probably have a lot of questions after I returned to London, and asked if I could put them to him in a letter.

"Sure," he said. "I look forward to it."

THAT NIGHT, Paul Delo and some of his staff had arranged to take me out for the evening. Gary Sutterfield met me at my hotel, and we went over to the local Elks Lodge.

"There's not too many places to go drinking around here," said Gary, "if you just want to have a quiet drink. Most of the bars around here, I don't go in unless I'm carrying. Otherwise you're likely to have to fight your way out."

The Elks Lodge was a bunkerlike structure with a big parking lot. There was a big oval-shaped bar with tables around it. Off the bar were two rooms. One had a crowded bingo game in progress. The other had a pool table.

Paul Delo and his wife, Sharon, were there, along with a couple of the maintenance people and some other prison staff. We drank beer and played pool until late.

"Well, Steve," Paul asked me, "did you get what you wanted?"

I said I had made a start. I was on my way to Nashville in the morning to look at Fred Leuchter's newest electric chair.

Paul asked if I'd be coming back, and I said it looked as though I would be there for Missouri's next execution.

"It shouldn't be too long," he told me.

PART TWO/THANKSGIVING

RETURNING TO London from Missouri was a strange experience. After twenty years of traveling back and forth between the United States and England, the differences between the two, while well appreciated, didn't take much adjusting to. After returning from my first journey inside America's execution industry, England had a weird shimmer of normality that I'd experienced when returning from difficult assignments, such as working in South African townships in the mid-1980s, or in the *favelas* of Salvador, Bahia, in the northeast of Brazil. The America that I'd just visited was an unknown country.

On my return, I wrote to A.J. with a long list of questions. I told him a little bit about my life and my childhood in upstate New York. On October 21, I received a letter from him that was dated October 4 and that had been posted on October 16. The envelope was written in a beautiful copperplate script and carried A.J.'s full mailing address in the upper left-hand corner:

A. J. Bannister C.P.#24 5B-37
Potosi Correctional Center
Rte 2 Box 2222
Mineral Point, Missouri 63660
USA

The letter arrived on a sunny day, and it took a moment to adjust to the world from which it had been sent, where part of an inmate's name is his number in line to die, and his housing unit and cell number.

The ten-page letter was written on very fine airmail paper and included two other documents: a copy of a letter to A.J. from his attorney, and a copy of a judgment from the U.S. District Court, dated August 23. The court judgment was on a standard form which had been typed in by the clerk of the court. It was headed "Alan J. Bannister, Petitioner, v. Bill Armontrout, et al., Respondents." The form had two boxes, "Jury Verdict" and "Decision by Court." The second box had been marked with an X and carried the news of what was very likely A.J.'s penultimate appeal. I read: "Decision by Court. This action came to consideration before the Court. The issues have been considered and a decision has been rendered. It is ordered and adjudged that Bannister's Second Amended Habeas Corpus Petition is denied."

In her letter, A.J.'s attorney wrote that the denial "came as quite a surprise to me as I'm sure it does to you." The letter ends, "Try not to get too discouraged."

I put the legal documents aside and began to read.

"Dear Stephen,

"Greetings from the colonies! I received your letter this evening. I've been looking forward to hearing from you. As for the $5 you enclosed for postage, they confiscated it and are requiring me to send it out to someone within 30 days or 'donate' it to a charity of their choice, which generally means their billfolds, so I'll have it sent to my mother. I appreciate the thought.

"So, you have two thousand questions you'd like to ask. I agree, it is difficult from a distance. But, while you're getting the funding together for this documentary, please feel free to ask as many questions as you'd like and I'll do my level best to answer them to the best of my ability.

"Your first question was about George 'Tiny' Mercer, what kind of person he was and what I remember of him. I met Tiny in May/June of 1983 when I was moved into cell 15—he was in cell 16. He initially struck me as a rather odd individual. He slept on the floor rather than in his bunk, and his entire cell was decorated with religious artifacts—crosses on the wall, paintings of Jesus and several Bibles. He had married a gal by the name of Christy in 1980 or 1981, and she lived right there in Jefferson City. He'd lift weights every morning, get a visit from his wife nearly every afternoon, and in the evening would write her, do sit ups and read his Bible. A number of people thought his 'Christianity' was a ruse to possibly fool the authorities. But in all the years I knew him, I never saw him falter in his beliefs. His wife is equally religious, nearly to the point of being fanatical. It is only my opinion, but I believe he was sincere about his religion. However, over the years I've seen a number of men turn to religion as a form of mentally escaping the reality of 'prison' or their crime. Some men immerse themselves into learning about the law, others go full tilt into lifting weights and improving their physiques, yet others 'do' their time by trying to circumvent every rule. Tiny's escape was religion and lifting weights. He was a very giving person. He and his wife were both this way and would help any of us any way they could. At that time, we were not allowed to have TVs in our cells, only on the walkway outside. Tiny and I shared a TV—made a table with wheels on it and a tether to pull it back and forth to change channels. One of my fondest memories of Tiny was that he and I had a favorite movie that we must've watched 50 times—it was Mel Gibson's 'Road Warrior.' Both of us would get to laughing hysterically at the one scene with the small boy and the boomerang. To this day I don't know 'why,' but it always struck us funny.

"Your next question was about the day and night he was executed, and how the procedures were different that day, and what I know of the execution itself. To start with, he was taken off the walk 4 or 5 days prior to his execution. I recall how I was back in the weightroom at the time. He packed his stuff and came back to say 'goodbye' to the 4 or 5 of us in the weightroom. He knew, as did all of us, that it was going to take place and this is the last we'd see of him. It was an eerie moment. He was in manufactured good spirits. We all shook hands with him, and I remember one guy saying 'see ya later' and realizing how out of place that was. Tiny just smiled and said 'in Heaven.' It was a moment like no other, Stephen. Having spent better than 6 years in close proximity to him, there was a feeling of frustration and helplessness, and there was also a sense of pride. Tiny showed no fear and had come to terms with his fate. I don't know if you're familiar with his case, but, the short and quick of it is that he was a biker. Supposedly a friend of his brought him a gal for his birthday and he choked her to death during the course of having sex with her. It's entirely possible that Tiny was innocent of this, but, he knew who had committed the crime and his code of principles wouldn't allow him to point the finger. He told me of the crime, and I consider myself a fairly good judge of who's lying and who's not when it comes to proclaiming their innocence. The media portrayed the victim to be an upstanding citizen and pure as driven snow [. . .]. Of course, her lifestyle is irrelevant. The bottom line is she was the victim of a heinous crime—and somebody had to pay. Tiny's co-defendant, who testified against him for a lighter sentence, was coincidentally released from prison only a few months after Tiny's execution. On Jan 5th 1989, we were all kept on lockdown status all day long, as a security precaution. Tiny was well liked by the guards at MSP too, and they were visibly troubled by his pending execution. At 7 P.M. that evening they began showing movies on the closed circuit channel. At 11 P.M. they aired a light porno movie. It was clear to all of us that they thought this would take our minds off what was taking place. It was quiet that night. I watched the news and it reported at 12:20 A.M. that Missouri had held its first execution in nearly 24 years, that Tiny Mercer had been put to death. As for the execution itself, his wife and a friend of theirs were there to witness it. As they injected the sodium pentothal he mouthed the words 'I love you' to her, and went unconscious. There was some twitching as the other drugs were injected. I'm not supposed to know this, but they added 3 straps to the execution gurney following his execution to keep the twitching to a minimum. He had requested that he be buried in his leather jacket— and was refused. What I'm about to tell you isn't commonly known, but Christy dug up his casket to put his leather jacket on him—and was caught. It was kept quiet. Also, I believe I'd told you how one of their procedures is to fit the condemned man with a rectal plug and catheter (so as not to upset the witnesses to an execution). Well, rather than remove the catheter they broke it off.

"Your third question was how this initial execution affected me, and the others on death row in light of how it hadn't been carried out in this state for so long, and what, if anything, it caused me to think of my own sentence? I have always known the state is very serious about carrying out executions. I had thought they were going to execute him from that previous October. He was prepared for it then also. A great many of my peers were snapped to reality that night. They'd convinced themselves that it just wasn't going to take place, that somehow the state was just kidding about it. It was a rude awakening. Not only did they have to accept that it had taken place, but also had to rethink their contrived 'can't happen to me' false sense of securities. Many of them were in a daze for weeks after. All of a sudden there was a renewed effort on their parts to get involved in their appellate litigation. This didn't last long. Couple of months at best. As for what his execution caused me to think about in regards to my own sentence. In the aftermath of his execution the media really portrayed him in the worst possible light, and I couldn't help but wonder what they'd say about me following my execution? The general public wasn't given an accurate portrayal of him. The media and state would have all the voting public believe us all to be frothing at the mouth, beady eyed killers just waiting to kill them! To hear them tell it, we're all blathering idiots, psychopaths that must be put to death to save the public at large from our murderous rampages. It troubles me deeply when they portray me even indirectly in this fashion. It's not at all accurate. I'm still somewhat surprised they allowed you and I to talk. The administration here is familiar with my outspoken ways. They generally handpick those inmates for the various media outlets to interview—and they select the 'snivelers', and ones who'll continue to profess their innocence in spite of an overwhelming preponderance of evidence. We have several individuals here that only lend credence to the state's version of 'us,' but they've all been told in no uncertain terms not to agree to any interview that may cast us all in a poor light.

"Your fourth question was about the other 5 men who've been executed and how things have changed with executions being more frequent. The second man executed was Gerald Smith. He and I were pinochle partners for many years. Gerald *was* innocent of the crime he was put to death for. His brother actually committed it. Gerald was protecting his younger brother. But he and another C.P. murdered an inmate at MSP in 1985, for which they both received an additional death sentence. Gerald was very easily manipulated. I compare him to a guided missile just waiting to be aimed. I believe he was manic depressive. He'd waived, and resumed his appeals several times in the years I knew him. Finally, he ran out of time. The procedure was identical to Tiny Mercer's—they removed him several days in advance and placed him in an isolation room over in the hospital, and ran movies on the eve of his execution. And the entire prison was locked down immediately after the evening meal. Gerald was put to death Jan 18th, 1990, which coincidentally, is the same day the Rumanian government which ousted Ceausescu outlawed capital punishment. Then, in May 1990—12th & 13th—Winford Stokes and Leonard Laws went in quick succession. On Stokes, he was disliked by everyone here, and we were let off lockdown status 10 minutes after his execution. I found this very tacky. Sure, he wasn't liked, but he was still a human being. With Leonard Laws, his execution is the one that affected me the most. He was a very soft spoken individual, and would give a person the shirt off his back. What troubled me with his death is that a couple years earlier the courts had ruled in his favor—for a life sentence, and the state appealed this and got a higher court to reverse the favorable ruling—and reinstate the death penalty. It broke his spirit. He simply gave up. The night of his death I actually cried in frustration as I thought of how this man had trudged through the rice paddies of Vietnam, survived the densest of jungles, only to return to the United States and be put to death like a dog at the veterinarian's being 'put to sleep.' Oh, Winford Stokes broke down at the end and begged and pleaded for his life to be spared. Next was George Gilmore. There was no public sympathy for him due to the brutal nature of his crimes. He robbed the elderly, murdered them and set their residence on fire to try and cover the crime. George struggled at the end, and I've heard rumors that several of the guards continued to strike him even after he was securely strapped to the gurney. George and I got along, but he, for all his timidity, was dangerous. I knew him to be the type that would run from a fistfight, but outside of here, with a gun in his hand—thoroughly dangerous. And then there's Maurice Byrd this past August 23rd. Maurice may have been innocent, I really don't know. The night of his execution, I couldn't help but think of how he is C.P.#21 and how if things had gone just a little differently, it could've just as easily been me that night. There's not a great deal of difference timewise between #21 and my #24. I'd been 4 years at one stage in the appellate process, and unfortunately that same day—August 23rd, my Writ of Habeas was denied. I didn't even learn of it till August 24th—got a large manila envelope from my lawyer, and as I wasn't expecting anything, I opened it right away. All I had to do was read the cover letter. I'll enclose a copy of it and the first page of the ruling. Suffice it to say, it wasn't good news. The day before we spoke, I'd gotten a visit from a lawyer working on my case and he had told me that I've got approximately 12–18 months before I'm put to death in a worst-case scenario. So, when we spoke, that was still weighing heavily on my mind, and I apologize for any distracted impressions I may have given you. I'm usually a very good conversationalist, but as I sat there I could hear myself tripping over words and such.

"Now, as for your fifth question. The offense that got me the death penalty, my trial and ensuing appeals. To start with Stephen, I am not innocent. However, the degree of my guilt was embellished by the authorities. According to the state, I allegedly assassinated a man for money. This was not the case at all. Got to tell you, I feel very uncomfortable talking about my case, not because I have anything to hide, but because I've not come to terms with what I've done. I'll attempt to explain."

The state's presentation of the Bannister case is summed up by a 1989 report on Missouri's death row in the *St. Louis Post-Dispatch*: "Alan Jeffrey Bannister was convicted of the contract killing of Darrell Ruestman of Joplin in August 1982. Bannister was paid $4,000 for the murder by a man who said his wife had left him for Ruestman. Bannister had earlier convictions for rape, armed robbery, deviate sexual assault and burglary."

In his letter, A.J. told me his version of how he killed Darrell Ruestman.

"It began in June 1982. I was offered the opportunity to make some quick money by selling some drugs for a guy I'd known for years. I took him up on the offer, but felt uneasy about it. Well, the opportunity to travel to Phoenix arose, and I took it—I still had some cocaine—couldn't find the guy to return it to him, so I gave it to a mutual friend of ours to give to him—and left. Well, the man I'd entrusted to return the drugs, went on a week long drunk, and it appeared to everyone that I'd run off with these drugs (I hadn't). They were eventually returned to the guy, but not before he'd slandered me in a big way, and at this time I'm unaware of any of this confusion. When I do hear of it I called him immediately, and it had been straightened out already—or so I thought. Turns out he'd talked so badly about me that he couldn't bring himself to admit his mistake, and on July 9th, 1982 I was attacked by 3 men in the parking lot of the Cactus Club in Paradise City, Arizona. I was stabbed 6 times in the back and left for dead.

I vaguely recognized one of them, and they thought I was done and made a comment about 'he won't rip nobody else off.' I was taken by helicopter to the hospital—and survived. I cannot express the anger I felt. I returned to Illinois. On the way back I had time to cool off and realize how it could've looked as if I'd stolen those drugs. But still, he'd misled me, and I knew there had to be somebody else involved. Upon my arrival back in Illinois, the entire area was abuzz with anticipation of a confrontation between him and I, and the tension was unmistakable. I was more concerned with recuperating at that time, but someone took a shot at me with a rifle as I sat on a seawall along the banks of the Illinois River. Enough was enough so I set up a meeting with the guy for that evening. He insisted he had nothing to do with my being shot at, and then he went on to tell me how bad he felt over my being stabbed, how his supplier had set it up and he didn't know about it till it was too late to warn me. It all seemed plausible to me, even though I knew he was shifting the burden of guilt. So I asked him who this supplier was, and he gave me the name and address of a man in Missouri. His story was that this guy had moved when he heard I hadn't died and was returning. I thought about it and decided I was going to make this guy feel the same pain I'd gone through. I'm ashamed to tell you this, but my first thought was to stab him. I quickly discarded this idea, and decided I was going to shoot him in the kneecaps and cripple him. I wasn't hiding my anger or plans at all, and left for Missouri. I got here and located the man, and confirmed that he'd just moved here from Illinois. I sat at the trailer next to his and he drove up. It was a tense moment as I thought he'd recognize me and panic. He didn't. Walked right past me and even said 'hello,' and he didn't look to me to be any drug dealer. So I returned to my motel, called the guy who'd given me his name, and he assured me it was this guy. I had a .22-caliber revolver that had been given to me. So, I returned to this trailer park, and sat there thinking about everything. I realized I couldn't shoot this guy in the kneecaps. The image of a TV series flashed through my mind—where a man was shot in the leg, and bled to death. So I went through this trailer park looking for a baseball bat, to beat him with. Couldn't find one, so I returned to my little spot and did some thinking, and came up with what I thought was the solution—to tell this guy the whole story and how I'd been given his name and address by his so called partner. I figured this would create strife between them, and I'd be in the clear. I had been carrying this gun tucked into the front of my pants. I moved it around to my left rear pocket, just in case he tried to knee me, and I went up and knocked at the door. He answered, and I froze. All I could think of to say was 'I'm from Illinois and want to know why.' He was on me instantly. He was 40–50 pounds heavier than me, and I was only 6 weeks out of ICU and in no shape to be fighting. I cupped the revolver in my left hand and swung it at his jaw. He had a good hold on me with his right arm. As I swung, he tried to block it—and did, and to this day I don't know if it was his forearm or the heel of my hand that hit the hammer causing the gun to fire. But it did, and it was like it all happened in slow motion. It's forever etched in my mind. He loosened his hold on me, there was no look of pain on his face, quite the opposite, almost a peaceful expression as he calmly turned around and walked back in the trailer. I panicked and ran as I was sure he was going for a gun. I wasn't even sure if he'd been hit. I was trying to figure out where I was going to go. I firmly believed he'd be coming for me, and obviously had the power to track me down in Arizona from Illinois. At 5:10 A.M. the next morning I was sitting in a bus station when I heard a TV report of a man being murdered the night before in this trailer park. It was a sick feeling Stephen. I knew they were talking about Darrell Ruestman, and it froze me. Yet, there was also a feeling of relief that he wouldn't be coming after me. I was arrested 20 minutes later. I was familiar enough with the law not to say anything, but when I heard they were calling it a contract killing—I couldn't believe it. As it turned out, the slug had entered about 4 inches above his right nipple and traveled at a 60° downward angle—piercing his pericardial sac. It didn't take me long to find out some things that really leveled me. Turns out that Darrell Ruestman was no drug dealer, and had absolutely nothing to do with my getting stabbed. Yes, he had just left Illinois. Why? Because the estranged husband of his girlfriend was hassling them and had been paying people to assault him. It was the worst case of mistaken identities imaginable. He must've thought I was yet another person hassling him, and I thought he was the man behind my being stabbed. We both lost. He lost his life and I've lost my freedom, and, quite possibly my life. Even though his death was accidental, I can't discard my responsibility in the loss of his life. If I could bring him back by forfeiting my life, I'd gladly do so. As for my trial, it was a farce. Even as it was, there was no physical evidence against me. The state's attorney for that county was up for re-election, and even though he knew it wasn't a contract murder, he pursued it as if it were. To get the conviction, several police officers took the stand and testified that I made incriminating remarks. Truth is, I didn't. But who's a jury going to believe?! Their local law enforcement officials or a long haired criminal type from another state! Even their perjury wasn't well thought out. The sheriff testified how I'd told him I sat on a bluff overlooking the highway to confirm the 'hit' by 'watching the meatwagon drive by slowly.' Problem is, I couldn't possibly have done this as I was positively identified by another of the state's witnesses as being 26 blocks away at virtually the same time! I pointed out this flaw to my court appointed attorney, and he simply glossed right over it. I also wanted him to emphasize to the jury that the angle of the gunshot was not such that it could be done intentionally. He didn't say a word. Instead, the prosecutor told the jury I was 'ambidextrous' to explain this. Truth is, I'm strictly right handed. And not one word was said about my being stabbed, or of the drug deal. This would've muddled their theory of a contract killing. Yet, it was common knowledge to literally hundreds of people in Illinois. There's a great many other inconsistencies, all of which I can refute, and prove by documentation—*their* documentation. But its moot. All in all, I'm not guilty of capital murder, but I am guilty of either 2nd degree murder or manslaughter, neither of which is punishable with death. Eventually, I will be executed Stephen. But this punishment by the state, excessive as it is, is nothing by comparison to the self-inflicted punishment of a tortured conscience. Maybe now you can understand why this is a difficult subject for me to discuss."

A.J. went on to talk about disparity of sentencing in murder cases, and closed with some pages about his childhood, finding some humor in the fact that I had been a truant and he a regular school attender. He talked about the British television programs he enjoyed watching, and ended, "I'll be looking forward to your return to good ol' Potosi. Please don't hesitate to ask any questions. Take care."

I answered A.J.'s letter, and meanwhile there was business to conduct in preparation for the film I was making. TV2 in Sweden was first to lend financial support to the project. In the United Kingdom, there was a great resistance to it. Some television executives found a focus on the executioners themselves a violation of good taste. Others took a harder moral line and found the project voyeuristic, appealing to an audience's basest motives for watching. The United States proved more receptive, and two channels bid for the film. One, a large pay-TV service, offered a considerably larger sum than the other channel. Intense telephone negotiations took place during October, and before Thanksgiving I traveled to the United States, on my way to Potosi, to finalize the contract. The negotiations were uncomfortable in many ways, but were concluded on a handshake. I returned to the broadcaster's office the next day to sign the heads of agreement, and found that a new clause had been added, saying that I would guarantee that an execution in Missouri would take place by a certain date; otherwise I would be in breach of contract.

I patiently explained an obvious fact: that the Missouri Supreme Court sets execution dates, and it was impossible to predict how any man's appeal would go in advance, and what the court's decision might be. Of course, delivery of the film was an important contractual issue. However, the film was unusual in that it dealt with issues of life and death as they happened, and the film schedule would have to follow that of the judicial process. To my astonishment, the issue could not be resolved. We resumed successful negotiations with another broadcaster able to square its commercial needs with an understanding of the subject, and a belief in the importance of the debate.

I kept thinking of something that Paul Delo had told me. He made a comparison between his role in executions and his military experience. He talked about being in a state of "battle preparedness." The difference between war and a state execution, of course, is that in the latter, everyone knows in advance who will do the killing and who will die. However, it is the certainty of that event for which one must prepare psychologically, in the most private depths of one's self. In a way, there was a war going on: the war on crime, the war on drugs. There were many casualties, many victims. It was a war in which prisoners were taken, and some of them were to be executed. Waiting was the name of the game, and as each day passed, I found myself more and more a part of it.

WHILE I WAS in New York, Fred Leuchter hit the headlines again. On September 27, the *Jewish Chronicle* in London had carried a front-page story headed "NUS Backs Call to Ban Leuchter." (NUS stands for the National Union of Students.) I knew that David Irving was planning a series of meetings in Germany, France, and Britain at which Fred was to speak about *The Leuchter Report*. The *Jewish Chronicle* article said that a number of groups and the chairman of the House of Commons Select Committee on Home Affairs had appealed to the Home Secretary to ban Fred from entering the United Kingdom. The following week, Fred was the main headline in the *Jewish Chronicle*: "Home Secretary Bans Holocaust Revisionist from Entering Britain." The then Home Secretary, Kenneth Baker, said that he had decided to keep Leuchter out because his "deeply repugnant" views were an offense to British Jews and "his presence here would not be conducive to the public good."

I called Fred to ask what was happening, and he told me that he thought the whole thing was a hoax. I asked if he'd received a notice from the Home Office advising him that he was banned. He said that a document had arrived, but had been sent to his father's address. He thought it suspicious.

"Why?" I asked.

"Because it's got no reference number on it. That part of the form letter isn't filled in."

I asked Fred to fax me a copy. It was dated October 1, 1991, and it read:

"Dear Mr Leuchter

"I am directed by the Home Secretary to inform you that he has given directions that you should not be given entry to the United Kingdom on the grounds that your presence here would not be conducive to the public good.

"As these directions have been given by the Home Secretary personally, in accordance with Section 13 (5) of the Immigration Act 1971, you are not entitled to exercise the right of appeal that would otherwise be available under Section 13 of that Act.

"If you attempt to travel to the United Kingdom you will therefore be refused entry."

The letter was signed by a Home Office official. I telephoned the Immigration and Nationality Department to find out if it was a valid order or whether, as Fred suspected, it was the work of a "radical Jewish group." The Home Office confirmed that the order was genuine, and I told Fred of my conversation.

"Well, it doesn't stop me going to Germany," he said.

Fred did go to Germany, where he addressed right-wing political meetings. Then, driving a German rental car, he and Caroline managed to enter Britain undetected, by sea, through the port of Dover. The successful illegal entry to Britain was planned by Irving, who later refused to tell reporters how he smuggled Fred into Britain, saying that "he planned to use the same route in future."

On November 15, Fred turned up with Irving and the French revisionist Robert Faurisson to address a meeting at Chelsea Town Hall in London. Irving introduced Fred as "an American gas chamber specialist" and shook his hand as he welcomed him to the platform. Fred had just started his talk when Irving remounted the platform and whispered into his ear: "There's a gentleman here to see you." The gentleman turned out to be an inspector from the Metropolitan Police.

Fred was arrested, and he and Caroline were taken to a police station.

Fred was held in a cell for fourteen hours, while Caroline waited in the lobby of the police station. Fred claimed that he had entered Britain legally, holding up his stamped passport as evidence. He claimed that he had not been banned from the United Kingdom, but that, apparently, his father had. Fred's illegal entry caused a minor row after it had been reported to the Home Office by John Marshall, the Member of Parliament for Hendon South. He told reporters: "It is very worrying that an individual against whom an exclusion order has been issued can waltz in without any subterfuge. It raises very grave questions about the conscientiousness of some officials." A Home Office spokesman responded: "The system didn't balls up, it worked correctly. He was not here for long." Fred sought help from the U.S. Embassy in London, but his appeal fell on deaf ears.

Fred said that the police who arrested and detained him were "only doing their job," but he complained that he was given only a single cup of coffee and no food during his fourteen hours in the police cell. Leaving the police station en route to the airport, Fred released a statement to the press which said: "I was incarcerated in a frigid cell with known felons (a dangerous and potentially lethal place for a maker of execution equipment)." At Heathrow, he was handed a one-way ticket back to Boston, courtesy of Her Majesty's Government.

WHEN I returned to Potosi the week before Thanksgiving, the temperature had plunged to freezing and the leaves had fallen from the trees. I returned to a different landscape. Significant landmarks of St. Francis and Washington counties were etched in my memory from the summer; but now they were framed against a hard, gray sky. The trees, water towers, abandoned lead mines, had a flat, stark appearance; but in the gray light, the rich ore through which Highway 8 had been cut showed blue and green, and glistened with the water that ran off the scrubby hills and down the rock face.

Paul Delo greeted me on my arrival at the prison. I said hello to the other members of the execution team I'd met on my first visit, and the main topic of conversation in the prison was deer hunting. Paul had been out with his muzzle loader and spotted a deer, but couldn't get a clean shot. Throughout the prison that morning, as the shifts arrived for work, the greeting was, "Get Bambi?"

Paul introduced his two assistant superintendents, Don Roper and Phil

Banks. Both were key members of the execution team, who switched between two roles. Phil was currently the operations officer, which meant that apart from the doctor and the condemned inmate, he was the only other person in the death chamber while the execution took place; he was also the only other person, apart from the inmate, visible to the witnesses. The other role, currently performed by Don Roper, was to escort the state witnesses and look after the brass who came down from Jefferson City for an execution.

Don Roper is a native of southern Missouri. Stocky, with a full beard, he is an ebullient character with an easy smile and a limitless stock of jokes. Known for his brightly colored shirts and ties, his easygoing manner has behind it a deadly seriousness. His creed is, "Every time you go inside, you've got to remember where you are. These guys are killers. They'd kill you or me in a moment if they thought it would be to their advantage."

He took me into his office and poured some coffee. Don is an experienced corrections administrator, and is relaxed and comfortable in his job. He put his feet on the desk and I drew attention to the embroidered sleeve patches which filled his bulletin board. Each represented a deer kill, and indicated how many points the buck had. There were snapshots of him standing with his prey, hunting bow in one hand, antlers in the other. Bow hunting is very popular in southeastern Missouri, and I'd heard that Don was nationally ranked as an archer.

"Did you get one this year?" I asked.

Don scowled and said he hadn't had any luck so far. "First year ever I haven't had one yet."

We began to talk about the kind of inmates housed at Potosi, and he told me: "Let's face it. The guys we got out here, it's too late for them. We're baby-sitting them for the rest of their lives, whenever the end of that life comes—either by execution, or if the guy's got life and fifty, and he's fifty years old, there's no way he's going to live to be a hundred years old. So we're just going to have to put up with them and baby-sit them, whatever that takes. And there's aspects of the program that's going to create its own problems as we go down the line."

"You mean, it'll turn into an old folks' home?" I asked.

"That's right. And we'll have all kinds of problems. It'll be staff-intensive, and medical's going to go sky high."

"So," I asked, "Missouri's prison population doubled in the past ten years, and it's set to double again. What's the answer?"

He shrugged his shoulders. "I don't know. You tell me."

He began talking about the philosophy behind Potosi Correctional Center, spelling it out in a simple form. "These guys are classified C-Five, our highest security classification. But we took them and said, 'We're going to give you the best food, the best recreation the state can provide. Air-conditioning. It's like the carrot and the stick, and that's the carrot. You can have this semi-freedom. But right across the hall here, in administrative segregation, we've got the stick. We're going to leave it up to you. If you choose to be a butthole, an aggressive, assaultive-behaviored inmate, then we've got the stick.' I think that's got their attention. Certainly, the capital punishment inmates."

"What was it like when the prison first opened, and the capital punishment inmates started to arrive?"

Don poured out some more coffee and said, "You know, it was ironic. When we opened them up the first time and allowed them to have Fourth of July without restraints, and these guys were playing volleyball, some of them for the first time in ten years without leg irons and restraints, they couldn't move." He leaned forward and said, "They still shuffled. Because they'd learned to walk with leg irons on, they still shuffled. So, they knew what the stick was all about."

I wondered if there was any initial tension between the condemned men and the life and fifty inmates.

Don said there wasn't, because they were both at Potosi for the same type of crime. "The only difference between those with the death sentence and those with life and fifty is that some of them had good lawyers, and some of them didn't. Or one of them had a super prosecutor, and got death rather than life." He shrugged his shoulders.

"It's worked," he said. "We spent over forty thousand dollars on a law library. We installed cable TV. And there's a lot of people in this county that can't afford it. Hey, I'd rather see this guy laying in his cell watching a flick than out fighting, digging tunnels, or trying to scale the fences. I'd rather see them watching an X-rated movie on TV and taking care of their sexual problems that way than raping some little punk out here."

Don reminded me how little violence had occurred at Potosi since the prison opened, and looked about for some wood to knock on. "You know the old adage, 'If you chain a dog, you make him mean'? I think you can extend that to humans. And there's been no cross-violence between death and life and fifty inmates. There have been stabbings within the groups. But, hey, you put five hundred sailors on a ship and you'll have as many fights as we have."

I asked Don if he had been involved in the execution of Tiny Mercer at MSP. He told me that he was part of the original execution team trained by Fred Leuchter, but at the Mercer execution he was an observer. He told me that, since the death penalty had been moved to Potosi, it had become a flawlessly functioning procedure, about which everyone was proud. He said the key to successful executions at Potosi rested on the decision made by the head office to let Paul Delo run the prison without interference. "The upper echelons said, 'We're giving you the responsibility and the authority to take care of it, and we're going to stay out of your way.' And it's been done that way. It's been done by the people at mid-management level. We keep the bigwigs out of it, the ones that are responsible directly to the politicians. Leave it to the guys who are hands-on in middle management."

I asked Don about his role in executions, and he told me: "My responsibility as the operations officer is to make sure that the nuts and bolts of the operation are taken care of. Me or Phil Banks."

Before we got further into his role in executions, Don raised a question that other people had put to him, about whether carrying out executions was a difficult, stressful assignment. He said, "I'm a Vietnam vet, but I don't suffer from post-traumatic stress disorder. I didn't really know what it was until I went to a seminar about it."

He told me about a Department of Corrections stress seminar he attended with the prison psychologist, Betty Weber, and some other staff from Potosi. There were six groups in all, from prisons around the state. "There was a worry that people involved in executions would suffer from it," he said. "So at this seminar, each of the groups had to list, in order of priority, the six most stressful work situations they could think of. In my group, the first one was being taken hostage by inmates. The second was watching a fellow staff member get killed or raped. There were a few more. And we couldn't figure out number six, so we put down, *going through an execution*. Out of the six groups, the other five felt that going through an execution was number one. But none of them were from Potosi, and none had any experience. When it's done as professionally as we do it here at Potosi, there's very little stress. There's much more stress when there's a stay."

"It doesn't bother you at all?" I asked.

He looked me in the eye and said it didn't. "I don't know if that's the calloused individuals in us, or what. I don't know. People say, 'Well, you're right there in the execution chamber with them. I mean, you're the last person to see them draw breath. You're the last person that gives him a cigarette and lets him smoke. Does it bother you?' And I say no. And it doesn't bother me. Sure, I take it for what it is. And I *know* where I'm at. And as a professional in the Department of Corrections, I know my duty. These people killed somebody. I didn't. All I'm doing is a job that the state says I should do."

We talked about stress and working in corrections, and Don told me, "Our general population are the worst of the worst. They have committed very hideous crimes. And in dealing with the inmates you have to be on your toes all the time, one hundred percent of the time. I think that's what makes it a high-stress job. Probably the divorce rate in corrections and fire fighters and police officers and law enforcement overall is very high. I think the reason for that is because you have high stress."

Don's healthy respect for the ever-present danger that lurked inside Potosi spilled over into fear. Not a crude fear of physical assault, although he pointed out that you would be crazy not to have it, but a fear of being used by inmates. "If you ever let your guard down, one time . . ." he began. He shifted in his chair and leaned forward to explain. "These inmates are in here twenty-four hours a day, figuring out a way to circumvent the system. And if they can use you as a correctional officer to do that, they are going to do it. And they are good at it. Their byline is con, and yeah, they can con you out of your shorts. They don't have to do it immediately; they can do it over the next ten years and do it so slowly, and so easily. It's kind of like the bullfrog in boiling water: He doesn't even realize he's in boiling water until he's dead. And that same thing happens in corrections. These guys are *so* smooth, and over a period of time they've got you doing things for them."

"What about fear for your own physical safety?" I asked.

"Absolutely," said Don. "You know, people ask me, 'Well, aren't you ever scared?' And I say, 'Yes sir. I'm scared every time I go in there.' But it's the control of fear that makes the difference between a good officer and not a good officer. Some of the officers probably wouldn't tell you that they fear. They have fear at times, but I think they have good control of their fear. I think that makes the difference between a mediocre or a bad officer, and a good officer. He knows that he's scared, and he knows how to control it. And he knows how to keep himself out of a bad situation."

"Does fear create anger? Does that lead to difficult situations?"

"Sure. We had an incident here just in the last month or so where we had some fluids being thrown on officers and officers being spat on. There is no doubt in my mind that if someone spits on me, my anger is going to flare, because I'm a human being. And I'm afraid somebody is going to get the crap knocked out of them. It might be me but, hey, if somebody spits on me I'm just that type of guy. You don't spit on me and get away with it. So certainly those officers, in my mind, have the right to be angry when someone throws body fluids or spits on them. And, yeah, there's times when possibly there is an excessive use of force because of an incident where an inmate spits on someone."

I asked Don about why the local people were so eager for the prison to be built in their community. He told me he'd been involved in setting up three different prisons during his tenure in corrections. "I can remember my first experience, they burned the sign at Missouri Eastern Correctional Center 'cause they didn't want the prison there. And then I came to Farmington and helped set that up, and there was some opposition there. But when I was invited to come to the ground breaking at Potosi Correctional Center, it was a totally different atmosphere. They had brass bands, they had the high school band playing, and they had politicians making speeches. People were wearing hats that said 'Yes to Potosi Prison.' It was the first time I had actually seen a community bonded together in a lobbying body to get a prison in their community. It was a different atmosphere altogether."

"But," I asked, "even though Washington County is one of the most depressed parts of the state, why would anyone want a maximum-security prison designed to house people for life or execute them?"

"It's a nonconsumptive industry, a nonpolluting type of industry," Don told me. "You're not putting chemicals in the air or into the streams. This particular county had the highest unemployment rate of all counties around. So it was a step in the direction that they needed to improve their economy and get something here for the local community to be able to have employment."

"What about your role in executions," I asked. "How do you fit into the Missouri Protocol?"

"Protocol in regard to executions. The execution warrant is handed down from the Missouri Supreme Court, then it's usually faxed to us via the attorney general's office to Mr. Delo's secretary. At that time, Mr. Delo usually calls myself and the other assistant in, and we evaluate whether it's got some potential. Normally, Mr. Delo is on the telephone quite a bit to the attorney general's office to see what kind of substantiation and validity the execution warrant has. When we determine that it does have some real sound validity, and there is the possibility that the execution will be carried out, then we start according to our post orders and according to the execution procedures."

"What's the next step in the procedure?"

"Mr. Delo, myself, and the other assistant superintendent take the death warrant to the individual and hand it to him personally. At that time, we normally give the inmate the option of going into the holding cell or staying out. That depends on the inmate. We also depend highly on our psychologist to determine if the guy's of the mental state to be able to handle being still out. So, there are a number of people that we talk to. We talk to the caseworkers. And Mr. Delo and myself and Mr. Banks evaluate the information that we receive. We then make the determination at what point or at what stage we should put the condemned inmate in the holding cell. One of the inmates we put in as long as a week prior to—"

"Why?"

"Okay. Because he was quite unstable, and he let us know that he was. So we felt for our staff's protection, as well as his own, that we should put him in the holding cell. The past one we just done—"

"Maurice Byrd?"

Don nodded. "Basically, a pretty good inmate. We didn't put him in the holding cell until approximately forty-eight hours prior to the execution."

"Once the inmate is in the holding cell," I asked, "what happens to him?"

"We allow him to take all of his property. In particular, we allow him to take all of his legal documents. He has free access to the telephone; unlimited access, whereby he can talk to his attorney to check on any kind of last-minute appeals, or any kind of Supreme Court rulings.

"He is watched continuously, under twenty-four-hour supervision by correctional officers. By policy, Mr. Delo and myself or Mr. Banks, the other assistant superintendent, visit with him at least every twenty-four hours. We allow him pretty well free access to the canteen and the items that he needs in regard to snacks or soda—those sorts of things. We try to make it as professional and as comfortable as possible in those last few hours of his life."

"Tell me about the location of the holding cell, in relation to the death chamber. Where is it geographically within the institution?"

"The holding cell is in proximity to the medical unit and is quite close to the actual death chamber itself. It's just a few feet away. It's in proximity to Housing Unit One, which is a total lock-down unit. So he is fairly isolated within the unit."

"What are the deathwatch officer's responsibilities while he's in the holding cell?"

"It's an open room subdivided down the middle with a wire mesh. The officer sits on one side of it with a typewriter and telephone, and he documents everything that happens in chronological order. And I mean everything. Every telephone call, what he's eating, his attitude—everything is put on the chronological. And Mr. Delo and myself are in constant contact with the officer and the inmate."

"So," I said. "You've got the inmate in the holding cell. What next?"

"From that point we go into the execution mode. Approximately forty-eight hours prior to the execution, we do a complete thorough run-through. We do everything, step by step. Lock, stock, and barrel. If it's an i to be dotted, we dot the i. We go through it and say, 'Hey, this is what's going to happen that night. This is what we are going to do that night.' And we take it all the way down to even putting an individual on the gurney. We also check our machine in that run-through. We do all the exterior perimeter security. We do internal security. We do all the operations posts, all the security posts. We run through the witnesses—staff witnesses as well as the press witnesses, and make people aware of what's going to happen. I think the key to making this thing run as smoothly as it does is that people know what's going to happen. They know exactly how to react when a situation comes, and they act very professionally."

"And on the day of the execution?"

"The morning of the execution, we start closing the institution down gradually. We start closing down any traffic into the institution. We also start making places in the parking lot for head office staff, witnesses, and the news media who come. We have our staff park in the lower end of the parking lot so all the dignitaries and folks that are coming can have up-front parking—those sort of issues are covered right away that morning. The operations officer starts a morning chronological of everything that happens in regards to the execution itself, in addition to the chronological that's ongoing with the officer in the holding cell. Any oddity, any news-paper people that call—this is what the chronological is for. It's to record what's transpiring in regards to the news media and the press."

"When do people start to man their posts?" I asked.

"The bulk of the people don't come on until approximately three-thirty on the afternoon prior to the execution, which is held at twelve oh-one. We have our first briefing for those individuals at three, and then we have another briefing at six. Outside security comes on at three, and we do that briefing and post those individuals. During all this process, we have individuals to call the news, individuals to call all law enforcement agencies connected with the execution. We have other emergency squads coming from other institutions, and they are set up in the main command headquarters outside in case there is something out of the norm that transpires, such as an enormous amount of protesters, or an enormous amount of people that are for the execution. We've had a few of both, so we have people on hand to take care of any situation that might exist. We start closing the institution down gradually to where it is real tight. In fact, as you come under the viaduct, into the institutional grounds, you're challenged at that point. And if you have no reason to be here, you're turned away. All deliveries are stopped. All outside traffic is stopped. The only people that are allowed on the institution grounds at that time are people that are directly involved with the execution or have a work assignment for the evening shift.

"At six we have our briefing for all of the security posts, and those individuals that are involved directly in the proximity of the execution chamber. Everyone receives their post orders, and they will receive the badge for the particular post that they are assigned to."

A top-secret part of the Missouri Protocol is the security system whereby each key execution-duty post has a color-coded badge.

"What happens after that final briefing?"

"Everybody is dismissed, and shortly after that briefing we have a chaplain service where anybody can volunteer, if they like, to hear a little message by the chaplain, a prayer service. That's for all staff. Then everybody is assigned to their post and they shortly thereafter go to that particular post. The inside security is buttoned up real tight. The control center doesn't allow anyone to enter if they don't have the right color badge on, or if they're not in the right position."

"What is happening down in the execution chamber at this point?"

"The area is blocked off from the actual medical unit itself with curtains. We don't want to interfere with the medical unit, because the institution is still running. So, if we have medical problems, they have to be able to take care of them. We have one exterior door operator who makes sure anybody that goes in behind the curtain itself is cleared to be there. We have three individuals that are technicians, that are sergeants and lieutenants, that make sure the internal security is adhered to. Once again, they are very professional individuals that will be in contact with state witnesses and press witnesses in that particular area.

"Inside the actual chamber itself, the plant maintenance engineer and his entourage is making sure once again that the machine is operational, and all of the vials are filled correctly with the right amount and the proper chemical. We have two or three individuals that are in that area making sure that the telephones work, that the manual systems are in operation, making sure that the blinds are operational. The doctor is there, checking the machines and checking to make sure that all the proper equipment— IVs, tubes, and everything—is there and ready to go. We also have on contract a nurse that does the actual setting of the IV. That individual is there to make sure, once again, that the proper equipment is available and ready to be utilized. The psychologist and the chaplain are on hand also in that area, if someone needs to talk. They have free access to the inmate, the condemned inmate, at that time. So, once again, we do this in a very professional manner, and we try to keep everybody abreast of what's transpiring."

"While all these preparations are going on, what is happening to the inmate?"

"From about seven things really start to speed up. All of the appeals are still in process. He's in contact with his attorney. We are in contact with the attorney general's office, who is in contact with wherever the appeal might be—either in the Eighth Circuit Court, or the U.S. Supreme Court. At seven, he is offered a sedative, and that sedative is at his option. That's not a forced sedative. Once again, he determines if he wants it or not. Generally, they accept the sedative. We continue in the execution mode at that time.

"Usually, Mr. Delo or myself visits with the inmate around that time. We have made exceptions to the visiting policy and allowed visitors to stay with the inmate right up to nine or nine-thirty, but after nine-thirty, things really start to happen. Everything is set in the execution mode. Everything is open and ready to go at that time. Our director usually comes on site at that time. All of the press and state witnesses are called in for a briefing. We require approximately fourteen witnesses, whether they be press or regular state witnesses. They come into the assembly room and are briefed on what to expect. Then, at approximately eleven, they are taken downstairs for a special briefing with the director of the Department of Corrections, Mr. Dick Moore, and George Lombardi, the director of Adult Institutions. They are told to choose a spokesman out of the group, to relay the turn of events that transpire in the next hour back to the rest of the news media waiting upstairs. They have an opportunity to sit around and chitchat."

"And the inmate?"

"Back in the holding cell, the inmate is constantly observed and watched."

Don's voice was quiet and precise as he related, from his own experience as a key member of the execution team, what happens to a condemned man in the final forty-five minutes of his life.

"At approximately eleven thirty-five, the inmate is taken into the actual execution chamber, where he is strapped down to the gurney. Shortly thereafter, the IV is placed in the arm."

He leaned forward and looked directly at me. "That last twenty-five minutes, when you're standing in the execution chamber as an operations officer, documenting, logging the things that transpire—a minute is a life-time. Seriously. And it's very serious throughout the institution. We do not take any of this execution procedure lightly. But certainly, that last thirty minutes, when you're in preparation of actually taking a human life—you have to look into your own self and say, 'I'm an instrument of the state. I have a job to do, and I chose to do it. I never killed anybody, but this individual has been convicted thereof. And so this is the ultimate penalty that will be carried out, and we are the instruments whereby it's carried out.' "

Don had turned his walkie-talkie off at the start of our interview, so it was quiet in his windowless office. The only sound was the muffled clatter-ing of a word processor on the other side of the closed door.

"In the chamber itself," he continued, "you have the operations officer, Mr. Banks or myself, actually in the chamber documenting everything that transpires. The plant maintenance engineer is in there in regard to any last-minute preparations for the machine. There are four other individuals be-hind closed doors that do the actual pushing of the button per se, when you're at the last few minutes of the execution mode. Mr. Sutterfield, Mr. Delo, Mr. Armontrout, Mark Schreiber, those are the key individuals in regard to making sure that everything . . . that the proper information comes from the director to them, and they give the word to the operations officer, who initiates the command for execution. There are a couple of other individuals that are in constant telephone contact with the telephone operator upstairs to make sure that we have lines open if there's ever a last-minute stay. We even call the governor to see if he's going to give the guy clemency, or if he wants to stay the execution."

Since executions recommenced in Missouri in 1989, Governor John Ash-croft has denied all appeals for clemency.

Don then went on to describe the chain of command in the final mo-ments before an execution, from the death chamber itself, all the way up to the governor's mansion in Jefferson City, and described his role as the one who actually orders the executioners to begin.

"At twelve, all systems are checked. All the way from the execution chamber itself, we talk to the director, who in turn talks to his legal counsel, and the legal counsel for the governor, to see if there is any change at all in the upcoming execution. At twelve midnight, the order is given to commence the execution itself, and at that time the operations officer receives word through the protocol and chain of command, and gives the word to proceed. The machine is activated at that time. Then the buttons are pushed, and the execution commences. It takes approximately four and a half minutes from the time that the first chemical is dropped until permanent death occurs. There's three chemicals that are dropped through IV tubes into the individual's body. It's basically very painless, very swift. The individual goes to sleep."

"What do you experience personally during an execution?"

"As the operations officer, I am the last individual to be visible in the execution chamber. I take note of everything that transpires. We offer the individual to say any last requests or anything; he has that option to speak, if he would like. At twelve, the individual normally looks at his visitors or just kind of looks around. It's very anticlimactic, and there's no convulsions, screaming, or paranoia. There's basically never been any of that. The individual, generally speaking, has accepted that they're sort of like a terminally ill person, and they have accepted their fate. Once again, it's the ultimate penalty for the crimes that they committed. And they basically . . . the eyes just close, and they're dead."

"What do you hear?" I asked.

"Quiet. It is *real* quiet. Probably, I could hear my own heart beating more than anything else that I'm conscious of in that last three, four, five minutes after the execution warrant has been read, and the green light has been given to proceed with the execution."

"What is the doctor doing?"

"The doctor himself is behind a screen and he's constantly watching the heart monitor to pronounce the individual dead. It takes about four minutes, and as soon as that time arrives, he gives the word that the individual is deceased, and we close the blinds at that time and disconnect the condemned inmate."

"And what is going on outside the death chamber?"

"Probably a little bit more involved than just what's inside. The state and press witnesses are dismissed, but prior to their dismissal, they have to sign a notarized return warrant of execution. That takes place right after the execution itself, and then they're dismissed to go back upstairs and to tell the rest of the news media what transpired. Mr. Dick Moore also goes up to the press area and gives a statement, usually from the governor or from the governor's office, in regard to what's transpired."

"What happens in the death chamber after the execution?"

"Within the chamber itself, the inmate, the deceased inmate at that time, is fingerprinted. It is verified that this is the individual that was executed by law. And after all those determinations are made, then the local coroner comes in and takes the body."

"If the purpose of the fingerprinting is to make a positive identification of the inmate, why don't you fingerprint him before you execute him?"

"We are very . . . we know exactly who the inmate is prior to him going in there. But we need the fingerprints to go with the execution warrant, where it is thereby verified that this inmate is the one that's deceased. They are attached to the execution warrant, which goes to central office and then to the judicial system, whereby it's filed. It's on file that the inmate was executed in accordance with Missouri state law."

"What is it like after an execution? Not just for you, but for the other members of the team?"

"Very relieved. Very calm, cool, and collected. Very professional." Don leaned back in his chair and said, "We anticipated a lot of stress in regard to executions. That has not been the case. People have met the challenge, if you will, and have taken the stress in stride and moved right along. Very professionally. And once an execution is over, people just basically go home. In regard to myself, I generally pack everything up and close my office about two in the morning, and go home. Normally, my wife is up, and we sit down, we talk and discuss, and I go to sleep. I don't have a problem going to sleep after an execution."

While Don goes home after an execution, the rest of the team holds a party.

We agreed it was a good moment to pause for a cigarette. It was cold outside, and Highway O, where it snaked off toward Mineral Point, was shrouded in a light mist. A freight train screeched and clanked cautiously along the tracks that cut through Mineral Point, blowing its whistle.

When we went back inside, I asked Don to tell me about the five executions that had taken place at Potosi.

"Okay. Our first execution at Potosi, done in January of 1990, was

Gerald Smith. The next execution was done in May of 1990, which was Winford Stokes, and we done another one also in May of 1990, Leonard Laws. Then, August of 1990 was George Gilmore, and our last execution, done in August of 1991, was Maurice Byrd. Now, all of those executions were done very professional."

I asked if any of the executions had made a particular impact on him.

"The one that I recall more so than Gerald Smith was Leonard Laws," said Don. "Leonard Laws was a past vet and there were a couple of last-minute stays for Leonard Laws in regard to his military background. And possibly his involvement in Vietnam had an impact on the crime that he had committed. As far as a bond between Leonard and myself because he was a veteran, I never did feel that. Leonard Laws basically was a good inmate, and he was not disruptive or destructive. He was not assaultive or aggressive towards the staff. Leonard Laws was probably, from the community standpoint—because he was from this local community—was a pretty good boy that had went bad."

Leonard Laws was a native of Mineral Point. He had burned the house of his victims. I had seen the ruins of the house in which he had been raised; ironically, it had burned to the ground. It was almost directly across the road from Paul Delo's house.

"Leonard assisted in and was charged with the killing of four elderly people—one being in a wheelchair—for a few dollars and then burnt their home. Of course, they all died in it. He was charged with four counts of capital murder," Don told me.

The fact that Leonard Laws had been a Vietnam veteran, just like the key members of the execution team, made me think of Paul Delo's metaphor of "battle preparedness" in getting ready to carry out an execution. I asked Don whether he thought his military experience contributed to his ability to function smoothly as part of a group which deliberately set out to take a life.

"Certainly from the standpoint of protocol, of chain of command, it certainly aligns itself with the military chain of command. And I have heard Paul numerous times refer to it as a battle, or possibly preparing for a particular initiative, or a particular battle. And I think there's some validity behind that, even from my own standpoint, of when I went to Vietnam. I knew there was a job to do, and knew what job I had to do. And I knew that people were going to be killed. I knew that up front. So I think the preparedness that I go through might be something similar. I don't consciously think about Vietnam because I pretty well put up a mental block and let that be past history, and to forget about it. But, yeah, I know where my chain of command lies. I know what is expected of me. I've prepared for it. I've practiced for it. And in order to make Mr. Delo look good, I'm going to do my job a hundred and ten percent. And I think all of that works together."

"What about the machine? Does it make a difference, compared to giving a lethal injection by hand, like they do in Texas? Does it really make any difference to the button pressers which of them activated the machine?"

"Many people are familiar with the Texas mode of execution, which is just a syringe, and they give the guy a shot. This machine itself is a computerized machine that is triggered by weighted pistons on a cylinder which pushes a vial of chemical into an IV tube that then flows into the individual's veins. The individual loses consciousness within seconds after the first chemical is passed into the IV tube. Once again, quite a complicated machine. It's not just a simple syringe and needle. It's more than that, much more. It takes out almost . . . virtually all human error. And it also takes out the doubt of who actually pushes the button, because it works off of a computer rotating mechanism whereby there is always a doubt in the individual's mind that pushed the button whether he was the one that started the lethal injection rolling or not. So you have that external doubt whereby it probably gives someone a protective mechanism to say, 'I don't know that I did.' "

"But if you were pressing one of the buttons, would the dual control system make any difference to you? Would it make any difference to you whether you knew or not?"

"No. To me it wouldn't make any difference whatsoever. I, once again, have made up my mind that I am a tool of the state and I perform these as a penalty, the ultimate penalty being the death penalty. And it would not bother me whatsoever to push the button. These individuals have been charged and convicted of capital, and in many instances, multi-capital, crimes."

ON MY FIRST visit, Paul Delo had suggested that I talk to the prison psychologist, Betty Weber. He told me that after executions had started at Potosi, she carried out a survey designed to measure the psychological effects on staff. Betty was away on a fishing trip during my first visit, but she responded to a letter I sent from England, and enclosed a copy of her questionnaire and the results.

Thirty-four staff at Potosi responded to the survey, including twenty-four corrections officers and six management. The survey, carried out in June 1990, consisted of fourteen yes/no questions and was prefaced by a statement of purpose: "The following questionnaire has been devised in order to more accurately evaluate staff's thoughts and feelings related to our execution process and procedure. The purpose of the questionnaire is to allow us to better assess the total procedure and to determine if staff concerns and needs are being adequately addressed and met. Your input would greatly enhance our ability to accurately assess your concerns and to be able to plan for future executional procedures accordingly."

After collating the responses, Betty Weber reported that "the overall consensus of opinion was that the problems expected, i.e. stress, guilt, depression, etc. did not occur following the executions." The survey showed that five staff had second thoughts about accepting a work assignment on execution night (one did not answer); two experienced family problems as a result of their involvement; four staff said they would not volunteer for a specific execution assignment (one did not answer); eight said they did not understand the appeals process in death penalty cases (two said they understood it "somewhat"); eighteen said they would benefit from training relating to the appeals process (though thirteen did not answer this question); five had reservations about the guilt of condemned inmates; and four staff said they needed to talk with someone after an execution.

Betty circulated the results to staff, along with a note which read: "In view of the fact that we are interested in everyone's thoughts and feelings concerning the execution procedure and the related responsibilities we have accepted, we feel that open communication is necessary and will enhance our cooperative efforts to perform in a competent, professional manner. At the same time, our goal is also to provide support for fellow workers and to maintain empathy, compassion and concern for all involved."

Betty and I met at Potosi during the week before Thanksgiving. A large, outgoing lady who wears flowing floral-print dresses, she is, like her mentor Bill Armontrout, a native of Oklahoma. She's had seventeen years experience in corrections and has worked in every type of prison. Bill Armontrout first hired her to work at MSP, and they have had a close relationship ever since. She was at MSP for the execution of Tiny Mercer, and she met Fred Leuchter when he came to install his lethal injection machine and to train the Missouri execution team.

Betty is a key part of the execution team. While she is not involved in the chain of command or in the actual operation of the lethal injection machine, her presence is an essential part of Missouri's approach to carrying out executions. Paul Delo and Bill Armontrout both feel it is important that a psychologist be present to deal with any staff problems which may arise, or to talk with the condemned inmate during his last hours, if he so wishes. During the time of an execution, Betty works closely with Gary

Tune, the prison chaplain, and they share a pastoral or counseling role. I was interested to know, from her standpoint as a professional, what the Missouri Protocol meant for her. I began by asking what her duties were.

One of the most difficult, she told me, was competency determinations. The purpose of a competency determination is to declare that the inmate is "mentally competent" to be executed. It is a controversial issue, and one that piques abolitionists. They argue that if there is a question as to the mental competence of a condemned person, he or she should not be on death row in the first place. If the condemned person is insane, they argue, he or she should not have been convicted of capital murder. Along with the execution of minors, or those given a death sentence while under the age of eighteen, the execution of retarded or mentally incompetent persons is also the focus of fierce criticism from anti–death penalty groups and the liberal press.

One of the problems in competency determinations is who should be appointed to give a professional opinion. Betty told me: "If our person does it, then the inmate's attorney is saying, 'They're promoting their point of view to kill that person.' If their attorney arranges it, why, everybody's saying, 'They're trying to get him off.' "

I knew that the competency issue had come to a head during the last few weeks, in the case of Bobby Shaw. Bobby Shaw is CP#7. He's been on death row since 1980, and most of the staff at Potosi were expecting him to be next in line for execution.

In July 1979, Shaw was serving a life sentence for murder at MSP when he stabbed a sixty-one-year-old corrections officer to death. The stabbing occurred in the prison kitchen, and Shaw was cornered in the yard at MSP. The order was given to an officer in the tower to shoot, but was refused. Shaw was eventually disarmed by an officer wielding a baseball bat, and was struck in the head.

While I had yet to meet Bobby Shaw, I was aware of the feeling that corrections officers had for an inmate who had killed one of their own. Most stated baldly that they were looking forward to the execution.

I had spoken to Paul Delo about Bobby Shaw, and asked if I could interview him.

"Sure. You can try," Paul said, "but Bobby Shaw hasn't had much to say to anybody for years."

"What do you think?" I asked Paul. "Do you think he's competent to be executed?"

Paul smiled, and answered the question the best way he knew how. "I don't think Bobby Shaw's any stupider now than the day he came to prison."

I asked Betty whether she had been involved in competency determinations in the case of Bobby Shaw.

She said she had, and told me: "I think the major contention there—originally, and even now—is mental retardation."

"Is he mentally retarded?" I asked.

"There's some there," she said. "But how do we know that was not caused when they took the weapon away from him?"

"When they used force to subdue him?"

"Yeah. There was a head problem."

Betty sighed in resignation. "He, like so many inmates . . . they show you one side, which they want you to see. And I've sat and talked with him long enough to know that he's a depressed individual."

I asked Betty whether, in her opinion, Bobby Shaw would agree to talk to me.

"I think so," she said. She warned that conversation, when it happened, was very difficult. "So you have to sit down and spend some time. Coach him a little bit. Listen to what he's saying. Allot whatever time is necessary. You don't jump in there."

"What's his IQ?" I asked.

"Probably borderline," Betty replied. "He has organic brain damage. Granted, a lot of them do have organic brain damage. But a lot of people out running around, a lot of the staff, have some. But that does not mean that you are incompetent or nonfunctional. But they're making a big issue out of *'This makes him incompetent.'* "

I asked Betty for more general impressions of Bobby Shaw.

"He mostly just sits there with a hangdog expression," she said.

"Has he been close to being executed?"

"Yes," said Betty. "He got a stay the day before."

"Was he fully aware of what was going on?"

"Yes."

I pressed Betty for more. She said he was "a passive guy who kills."

"How do you interpret that passivity?"

"For all outward appearances, as far as functioning here, anybody who is that passive, that much of a loner on the surface, has got to be having a lot of pent-up frustration, anger." She nodded her head to emphasize the point. "Oh yeah. . . ."

I was interested to hear Betty's view of A. J. Bannister. "Tell me about your meetings with him," I asked.

"They've all been congenial. Really, about the only time I've spent with him has been kind of game playing. Tennis. You know, bat the ball, see what he can get out of you, and where you're coming from. Seldom a serious conversation."

I suggested that inmates might be wary of Betty, and I asked whether that made her job difficult.

Betty was blunt. "They see me as the enemy here, for the most part. They think, 'You want anything, all she's going to do is put you to death.' "

The fact that Potosi Correctional Center is a purpose-built capital punishment facility means that everyone working there is part of the execution process. Betty finds that this does inhibit her ability to function.

"It sometimes makes it difficult to do my job," she told me. "There is always a worry, on their part, about confidentiality."

Betty admitted that confidentiality was a problem for her also. If she learns of things that could affect the security of the institution, or pose a threat to another inmate or staff, she feels a responsibility to make that information known, so that appropriate action may be taken. As with the chaplain and the doctor, Betty's first responsibility is to ensure the security of the institution.

We spoke about the difficulties in treating people who had no future outside of prison. What is the point of working toward rehabilitation when the state has already decided that the offender is incorrigible, and will either be executed or incarcerated until his death?

"With long-term offenders," said Betty, "my goal is not cure. It's stabilization. All I do is fight fires, basically." She regretted the fact that she lacked the opportunity to use all of her skills to design treatment programs and carry out research. "But," she said, "it was my choice to come here. Ain't nobody's fault but my own."

"What about staff problems?" I asked. "Do you get very involved in that?"

"It has taken up a lot of my time," Betty told me. "It goes in spurts. There are a lot of problems at home."

"Caused by the job?"

"It's hard to say in a lot of these cases which càme first, the chicken or the egg. Did the job cause the problems at home, or were there problems at home initially; and when the job got to be an issue, you know, everything just kind of came to a head. I find a lot of problems with alcohol. And there is peer pressure that causes problems at home."

Betty also said that she came across a lot of domestic violence among staff. I asked if she thought that was a direct result of the job they were in. She said that, in her view, most of the people with violence problems had them before they came to work at Potosi.

"Do staff problems ever become serious enough that you have to consider whether that person should continue to be employed at the prison?"

"What I usually do is, I check mental status. And if I see anything that is affecting their job from the security point of view, then I get hold of their supervisor. Otherwise I might say, okay, I think this person is dealing with their situation; or it's a situation we can deal with in a couple of sessions."

But treatment of very serious staff problems would have to be referred outside the prison, Betty told me. "If I were to have a long-term situation —and this has happened—I might become a threat to that person because I know too much."

We discussed Betty's role in the execution process, and she told me that from the time a death warrant is issued, she is on call. During the final forty-eight hours of a deathwatch, she works closely with the chaplain, making herself available to staff and the condemned inmate. On the day of an execution, she and the chaplain tour the housing units, letting inmates know they are available if anyone would like to talk. As the execution itself approaches, Betty and the chaplain are in the execution area, where they remain until the procedure is completed. To date, their services have not been much in demand. But their presence seems to be an important part of the ritual of the Missouri Protocol.

I wanted to return to the survey that Betty had designed. Since it confined itself to yes/no answers, I wondered if she thought there were staff concerns beyond what a brief questionnaire could address.

"Everybody says we ought to have all these problems. I've always said no, I don't think so. Because we can opt out at any time and not participate. We are not *made* to do executions. And that security alone helps out a whole lot."

"But wasn't there a lot of anxiety on the part of those who had no experience of executions?"

"Curiosity overrides a lot of that initially. You know, they want to see what's going on. This is an unknown thing."

"What about you?" I asked. "How did you react when you became involved in the process of taking a life? Did it have any effect on you?"

"Not really. I have a very clear-cut and secure feeling. I did not make the decision to execute the inmate. I have nothing to do with that. I am there to provide what comfort is possible, and support."

Betty had been present at the execution of Tiny Mercer at MSP, and at all of the executions carried out at Potosi. She said that Fred Leuchter's machine and the Missouri Protocol do much to reduce the level of stress associated with an execution. The constant practice, the breaking down of the process into specific roles, the clear understanding on the part of staff precisely what their role is, all made for a procedure which she called competent, professional, and stress-free.

AFTER MY interview with Betty Weber, I took her to lunch at the local restaurant. When we arrived, Paul Delo and some of his staff were finishing their lunch at the next table. I was talking with Betty when Paul came over and said hello.

"I'm afraid I won't be able to let you go inside this afternoon," he said.

I was worried that something had gone wrong—that I had inadvertently transgressed some rule, and that Paul was telling me I would have to leave. Also, I had arranged to talk with A.J. that afternoon, and I was hoping to meet Bobby Shaw. I was anxious that I wouldn't be able to get word to them.

"You can stop by the admin block this afternoon and talk to any staff you want to. But most of them'll be tied up in a meeting this afternoon."

"Okay," I said.

"All right," said Paul. "I'll talk to you later."

"Do you know what that's about?" I asked Betty.

"Unh-uh," she said. "I have no idea."

I felt uneasy throughout lunch, and when I drove Betty back to the prison, Paul was having a cigarette in front of the main entrance.

"I'll tell you what it is, Steve." He looked at his watch. "I'm going to have to make an announcement to the staff, and then to the press, this afternoon. You'll have to promise to keep this confidential until tomorrow."

I said I would.

"I'm announcing that we're going to mainstream the HIV-positive inmates in general population."

"I see."

"I'll inform the inmates this afternoon. And just as a precaution, in case we do have any trouble, I'd rather you didn't go inside this afternoon."

I thanked Paul for his explanation, and told him that I had been worried.

"No problem," he said. "Come back tomorrow and do whatever you want."

That morning, there had been a concert in the prison featuring the inmate bands, and a St. Louis television station had come down to do a story. That evening I stayed in my room, watching for news from Potosi, but there was no mention of either the concert or the new HIV policy.

*   *   *

The next day, I went to visit the caseworker who had taken my request for an interview with Bobby Shaw. I had very little hope that Shaw would consent; but to my surprise, and that of the caseworker, he did.

Bobby Shaw shuffled into the interview room. He was dressed in prison grays. Unlike most inmates, he had no item of clothing which lent some personal style or identity. I had heard that Bobby was probably the poorest inmate at Potosi. He had no radio, no TV, virtually no possessions at all. He wore his hair in an uncombed Afro that dated from the time of his offense, ten years earlier. His eyes were heavy-lidded and his movements slow. When I shook his hand, it was limp. When he spoke, it was like a record played at the wrong speed. He sat down in the chair I offered, and he fixed his eyes at a forty-five-degree angle looking at the ceiling while I explained the purpose of my visit. My first impression of Bobby Shaw was that he was severely withdrawn. However, he listened carefully to what I had to say, and he answered the questions I put to him.

I asked about his previous execution date, and he told me that the courts had stepped in.

"Are you getting much help from your lawyers?"

"I don't know," Bobby said. "I haven't heard from them."

"Do they ever come down to see you?"

"Not recently."

"Is there anyone here that you're particularly close to?"

"No. Not real close socially."

I asked Bobby how he spent most of his time.

"It's cold out there," he said.

"Sure is," I said.

Winter in Potosi could be brutally cold, and the design of the prison was such that the wind whipped along the walls. There were very few inmates out in the yard.

"I don't know. Read sometimes. Papers and stuff like that. I just got a brochure from an organization that's opposed to the death penalty. Read my Bible."

I asked Bobby if he had been a Christian before coming to prison. He said he had been raised as one, but hadn't been a churchgoer.

"How did you come to read the Bible?"

"I don't know. Chapel. A Bible course."

I asked Bobby how he got along with the guards at Potosi.

He looked at the ceiling and didn't answer.

I asked if he thought he had a chance with his appeals.

"I don't know. I couldn't tell you that." He laughed. "I wouldn't know."

When I asked Bobby whether he would agree to a film interview, he responded in a brighter and stronger voice, his speech quicker and more animated than before.

"What you going to do, try to air it in America, or over there in London?"

I told him the film would be shown in the United States and in Europe.

Bobby's decision was firm. "I really wouldn't like to be on television. Some of them would."

A. **J. BANNISTER** was in good spirits when he came into the caseworkers' building, and seemed glad to see me. We spent half an hour telling each other more about ourselves and our personal lives, and discussing current affairs. He was amused about the story of Britain's director of public prosecutions, who was caught by police soliciting a prostitute from his car in a seedy London back street. Faced with the difficult job of evaluating the police report on his own case and deciding whether he should prosecute himself, he had no option but to resign. Less amusing to A.J. was the appointment of Clarence Thomas as the newest member of the U.S. Supreme Court. We discussed how he had faced hundreds of questions about his stand on abortion, and how, without giving a straight answer to any of them, he nevertheless had his nomination confirmed. He had been asked one question on capital punishment, and promptly replied that he did not think it was unconstitutional.

Despite the cold weather, A.J. was dressed in a short-sleeved shirt. I asked him why he wasn't wearing a coat, and he told me that, some time ago, a guard had made him walk across the yard without his coat, so now he refused to wear one, ever.

I explained why I couldn't make our meeting the previous day, and he smiled. I asked if the decision had caused any problems among the inmates.

"Not really. A few years ago, the HIV inmates broke out of their locked unit at MSP, and that caused a stir. But we know who they are down here."

I asked A.J. how his appeal was going, and he told me there was no news. We began talking about the appeals process and stressed how the rules of the game kept changing.

A.J. said: "The *Barefoot* ruling [*Barefoot* v. *Estelle,* 1983] put an end to CP inmates holding back points of appeal so that they always had a fresh point to make. Winford Stokes was doing this, and it backfired on him. Executions are set for one minute after midnight. He had got a stay that evening, just prior to his execution. The attorney general's office from this state went and got that lifted, and they executed him like nine-thirty on a Friday evening. They knew that they had that entire day. Twelve oh-one is not a set time. That's just when it can begin. But they got his stay lifted, locked us down at six that evening, executed him at nine-thirty, and let us back out at about nine forty-five."

A.J. spoke in an angry voice, and he wanted to be sure that I understood his anger over the Stokes execution, despite the fact that he had a personal dislike for his fellow inmate.

"There were some really bizarre things that were being said that night. People talking about throwing a party afterwards, and that's just . . . People had that much dislike for him. Celebrating the death of one of their peers."

I knew that, in the execution of Winford Stokes, his wife had driven across the state to be at the prison. When the stay was granted, and it appeared as though the execution would not take place, she drove back to Kansas City. Her husband was executed while she was driving home. She learned of it on the car radio.

A.J. said that the life of condemned men at Potosi wasn't always gloomy, that there were humorous moments. He told me about how one of the larger officers was strolling down his walk, singing "Killing Me Softly with His Song" in a falsetto voice.

"I just heard that and I started laughing," A.J. said. "And he wasn't sure why."

A.J. told me, "There's some funny things that go on here, little moments. We were sitting at dinner one night talking about computers and Nintendo, and a guy talks about wanting to get some 'sloppy disks.' And he was dead serious they were 'sloppy disks.' And it's moments like that, that sort of break the tension. And the way we tease each other. When they had the gas chamber—I mean this is sort of morbid humor—but one of the big sayings back then was, 'Take a deep breath.' And that was said in jest. But that's teasing among ourselves. There's nothing bad meant by it."

I could see why A.J. laughed at the officer singing on his walk; but I wondered how he viewed their attitude toward executions.

"A few of them have that sort of mentality that they're killing something that is socially unacceptable to anyone else. But the vast majority of guards here are following orders. And I think that's how they justify taking part in that exercise in the perimeter that evening, or watching over a locked down housing unit, even though they're aware that they are powerless to do anything about it. The thing I've noticed is that the ones who are sensitive to it, they're given a position as far away as possible. The ones that are staunch supporters of it are the ones that are strapping that man to the gurney."

A.J. was concerned that I should be clear about the arbitrary nature of the death penalty and capital murder appeals process. He told me that Martsay Bolder (who is CP#5) had been granted a reversal, which had later been taken away from him.

"What about James Schnick?" I asked.

A.J. shook his head in resignation.

James Schnick is a dairy farmer from Elkland, Missouri. In 1987, he was charged with murdering his wife and six other members of his family. It was the worst mass slaying in Missouri history. He was given the death penalty for three of the murders. Schnick is a Vietnam veteran, and he was said to have been suffering from post-traumatic stress disorder. Earlier that day, Schnick had been granted a reversal of his death sentence. I asked Paul Delo what would happen to him next.

"Oh, they'll take him to the county jail. But he's got enough murders that we'll see him back here eventually."

"The thing about Schnick," said A.J., "is that other people got angry because he got a reversal on a legal point denied to other inmates in the past. It's all down to the arbitrariness of the court makeup, and which judge is prepared to listen to what argument."

He continued: "Bobby Shaw is a case in point. Bobby Shaw killed a guard. Bobby Shaw is black. He should have the same rights in the court on the same issues as everyone else. If a white man with a seventy IQ can get his case reduced for that reason, then a black man with an IQ of seventy should get it reduced."

A.J. told me that he and a few other inmates look after Bobby. "He doesn't have much money," said A.J., "so we give him cigarettes and soda." I learned from Paul and from Betty that while Bobby Shaw came from a large family, he'd had almost no visits since arriving at Potosi. The only visit anyone could remember was from a brother who lived in California and was passing through Missouri.

The disparity of sentencing in capital murder cases is an issue with which A.J. is obsessed, since his life depends upon it. He explained: "It's frustrating because we all know that this is taking place. And a lot of people complain and gripe about it, but then the outside world looks, and sees where we're at. And they expect us to complain and gripe, to make things up. *Well, you're probably guilty anyway.*

"It's used as a political tool by prosecutors. Two people can commit the identical crime—murder, obviously. In one county, the prosecutor might decide, 'Oh, this doesn't warrant the death penalty,' and charge this man with second-degree murder. And, in doing so, knows that with the conviction and the ultimate sentence, the largest sentence available at second degree, that this man's going to be out in ten or eleven years. Whereas, in the next county, same set of circumstances, the man, for whatever reason —maybe he doesn't have family in that area, or the victim is someone of standing—that man is charged with first-degree or capital murder, and receives the death penalty. It's prosecutorial discretion which to charge an individual with. There's no uniform set of rules governing this. It's at *their* discretion how they charge, and how vigorously they pursue that. And they use it as a means to get their name in print in the newspapers. It's big news when they pursue the death penalty, and they know it's going to get them a lot of lines. It's a sad state of affairs here in the United States as far as capital punishment goes, because the rich people don't get it—those that are represented by competent attorneys. I had a public defender who was representing everyone in that county who couldn't afford an attorney. And he had no previous capital litigation experience. It's a rough way to go. What sort of tickled me is they told me beforehand that I was going to get the death penalty. They made such a three-ring circus out of it that they invited the local high school civics class to sit in on one day of the trial."

A.J.'s anger filled the room.

"And once you're convicted, and you're facing the appellate process, the burden of proof is shifted onto the defendant. And it's hard to prove that, because we don't have the same resources that the attorney general's office and the state does. I don't have five million dollars to devote to investigators, and tracing down this paperwork and that."

A.J.'s anger made me aware of his past record of violence, and I wanted to ask him about it. I had seen his police record, and between 1975 and 1983, he had been charged with numerous offenses: unlawful use of weapons, burglary, battery, possession of cannabis, contributing to the sexual delinquency of a child, assault, unlawful restraint, armed robbery, unlawful use of weapons, rape, leaving the scene of an accident, illegal transportation of alcohol, fleeing the police, obstructing a police officer, and deviate sexual assault. I asked him about the offenses he'd been found guilty of before he was convicted of the killing of Darrell Ruestman.

"There was an armed robbery. The way that went down was, me and another guy picked up a hooker. Paid her. He got some head from her, and afterwards we robbed her. And that's armed robbery and deviate sexual assault. It all comes back to haunt you."

"You've done a lot of violent things," I said. "People think you're dangerous. Are you?"

"Ten years ago, I had that potential. I had a quick temper and I had a streak of violence that, if provoked, it would come out. But, since that time —not that this place has rehabilitated me or changed me, just the fact that I've grown up and it's just a little bit too late. I had a rough start, and I don't blame anyone for it, but I first went to prison when I was seventeen for a crime that I didn't actually commit, but knew about, and it's been a revolving door since then."

A.J.'s first conviction was for stealing car radios. He told me that he wasn't guilty of the particular instance he'd been charged with, but that it had been his primary means of support when he was seventeen.

"I didn't want to see my friend go to prison by himself, 'cause prison was a scary thought. So I took my lumps right along with him."

A.J., who was raised in Peoria, Illinois, was sent to the state penitentiary at Menard.

"It was like a big summer camp," he told me. "I did nine months and then got parole. I was going to finish high school. I had to wait two months before the next semester began. And in prison I'd heard stories from older cons. About the crimes these men had committed, the money they had, the women they had, the cars they had. I wanted that. I ended up breaking into a house and stole a safe, and while peeling the door off the safe I ended up injuring an eye. And got caught, and got resentenced. I never made it back to high school. And it just seemed that, every time I got out, I had the best intentions. But then I got out and I looked at friends I went to high school with, that had gone on and were starting to buy houses and own cars, and I wanted that. I wanted to have that same thing. But I just couldn't see that the slow route was the best route. So I'd get involved in something else."

A.J. let out a long, slow breath. "That just kept leading me back to penitentiaries. And I knew this was my fault. I just didn't know how to start over and go about it slowly. And," he said, "there's no way anybody's going to give you a job if you're an admitted felon. And rehabilitation is an old concept now. Now it's punishment. It's warehousing now."

I felt that A.J. hadn't really answered my question. "Are you dangerous now?" I asked.

"As far as me being dangerous now? I've grown up. My values have changed. My principles have changed." A.J. laughed. "I've gotten some now, whereas I didn't have many before. And I know that I'm never going to be happy in places like this. And now, just wanting to have a slow, sedate, boring *life,* has great value to me. Has great meaning to me. But it's also something I know that I'm not going to have, so . . ."

His voice trailed off with the virtual certainty of that.

"And it hurts to think about that, what I might have had." His voice became heavy with irony: "Because people tell me, 'Well, you had *such* potential.' " The irony gave way to real anger. "Well, it's a little late to tell me that now."

There was nothing to say in response. Nearly a minute passed before either of us spoke.

Then A.J. said: "Now it's just a matter of trying to duck out gracefully. That's something I think about."

There was more silence.

"I don't know how I'll react when it gets right down to that last moment, when . . . I'm already of the opinion that it's going to happen. I have to be realistic about that. But when it comes right down to 'Will you hop up on the gurney, A.J.?' "

When A.J. tells me how he thinks his last minutes will be, his breathing is fast, his face tight, his voice like a clenched fist.

"I just don't know what I'm going to do. My senses tell me, 'Fuck you, I'm punching you in the nose. *Don't ask me a silly question like that.*' But then there's also the realization that, afterwards, people will say, 'Oh, what a chickenshit, he was afraid to go.' *Come on, I was 'afraid to go.'* "

A.J.'s voice was soft and low, but vehement. His body was tensed with the anger and helplessness he felt at his impending execution.

Before he spoke again, he reined in his frustration.

"I know that, doing something like that, they're still going to get me on there. And I don't really want to get beat up while strapped to a gurney. But then again, at that point, what difference does it make? A few bruises . . ."

A.J. laughed in disgust. "It's not going to hurt for long. And I'm sure a lot of these other men wonder how they're going to react when it gets right down to that point."

The conversation was unlike any I'd ever had. I didn't know what to say to him. I suggested we go outside for a cigarette.

The day was cold and overcast. We huddled next to the wall, smoking, and a couple of other inmates came up to join us. A.J. introduced Doyle Williams. I knew about him from Paul Delo, as Doyle is the most litigious inmate at Potosi. A southerner, Doyle speaks in a fast, high-pitched voice. He was wearing a brightly colored sweat suit and a knitted red cap on his head. He carried a leather briefcase in his hand, and a box of legal papers under one arm. Another inmate, thin, with tattooed arms, introduced himself as Eric Schneider. He said he was part of a band called The Greystones. He introduced another member of the band, a young boy who didn't say much.

Normally, when A.J. and I talked, or went out into the yard together, we stood almost shoulder to shoulder. But now, as the group of inmates grew around me, it widened out into a very loose circle, so that each man was at least two arm lengths away from the other. We were a circle of five people, the diameter of which was nearly twelve feet. I didn't know then that A.J. and Doyle were close friends, nor that he and the other men were not particularly friendly; but I realized that the protocol for this type of encounter was to give the other man room. I understood that I had bridged some distance with A.J. faster than he might have been used to, living in prison.

Eric Schneider told me about his band, and showed me some lyric sheets. One of the songs was an anti-drug number, and the other, called "Twelve-O-One," was about the death penalty. "They tell you about some of the stuff they do to us here?" he asked. "They tell you about the cocoon? It's a form of punishment. They put you between two stretchers, and they strap those together. Just your head and your feet are sticking out. They'll beat you in there, drop you on your head, or just stand you up against a wall all day."

A.J. gave me a little nod to say, "Yeah, there's a thing called the cocoon." And then another look that said, "Sure, but so what?"

We talked for a while, and when only A.J. and Doyle and I remained, A.J. told me a little about Doyle's case. He said that Doyle had been on deathwatch earlier in the year, and had received a stay three hours prior to his execution.

Doyle asked me about the film I was making, and we agreed to meet the next day.

When we resumed our conversation in the interview room, A.J. said he thought I would learn a lot from Doyle, particularly since he had been so close to being executed earlier in the year.

"One thing that struck me about his almost being executed," said A.J., "is that he was allowed to have a visit from his girlfriend in the deathwatch cell. And it made me aware of something, and it's real sad to say this, but I have one more chance to get a piece of ass. And it'll be right before I die."

But when we resumed the interview, the banter of the past half hour faded and was replaced by the hard reality of A.J.'s forthcoming execution.

He told me: "When a crime is committed, that person does not have the thought of getting caught. I didn't even know that Missouri *had* the death penalty when I came here. It wasn't even a remote thought. I had revenge on my mind, and that was what was motivating me, and nothing else. The consequences of getting caught, I didn't give it a second thought."

I asked A.J. how time passed for him while under sentence of death.

"The actual act of execution I don't think is cruel and unusual. It's what leads up to it. Those last few days or hours . . . what . . . what a man has to go through knowing that it's going to happen and that's . . . there's not . . . there's nothing you can do about it. And being forced to think how it's going to affect my mother, how it's going to affect my brothers and sisters. What's this person going to think? What's the news media going to say about me afterwards when I cannot defend myself? And the regrets and remorse for things that I do have . . . Not having the chance to maybe tell this one person that you cared about them, that something in the past . . ."

A.J. hung his head.

"All the things you think about in those last hours. I haven't been down to my last hour, but I've been within a couple of days. That was in 1985. I think that's the worst part of the execution, the years and years prior to it, leading up. All the hopes and expectations that get built up, and dashed down every time you're turned down by another court."

After a while, we decided to call it a day with the formal part of the interview and go outside to talk and smoke. A.J. asked what I was going to do over Thanksgiving, a few days away. I said I didn't know. He told me he was looking forward to next week, when he'd be receiving a visit from his mother and his sister. He told me that his sister was doing a degree in criminal justice. It brought a smile to his face, and mine.

"Mostly though, people don't look forward to holidays here," he said.

I said I could understand that.

A.J. looked at me as if to say, "I'm not sure you do."

"I lose track of weeks. Months. All because there is something at the end that I don't want. I don't want that time to come. And it seems like I make the comparison to Christmas when I was a child. It seems when the first of December got there, the days dragged by. It's just the opposite here. Time goes by, I don't want to see holidays. Because as they progress, they just go as quickly in between, because at the end of the rainbow there is no pot of gold for me. And then there are other times when I do have something to look forward to, like a visit from my mother, or my sisters, or some friends of mine. When I know they're coming a week or two weeks in advance, the time drags by for me, and I become much more aware of each hour of each day. Because I am looking forward to something. But for the most part, it goes by too quickly. Not enough hours in the day to do all the things I would like to do."

I told A.J. I wanted to get in touch with Tiny Mercer's wife, Christy.

He thought for a minute. "I don't know exactly where she is. Somewhere in Jefferson City. I know she works as a waitress in one of the cocktail lounges there."

"Sounds like a tough job of investigative journalism," I said.

"Oh, I think you'll bear up," A.J. told me.

He gave me the telephone number of a woman in Jefferson City who would know where to find Christy Mercer. "She's a friend of hers," said A.J. "A Christian. Christy's kind of crazy sometimes. But she's a good gal."

I wrote down the number and put it in my pocket. My Thanksgiving plans had just been finalized.

I asked A.J. if he'd received my last letter.

"Ages ago," he told me. "Didn't you get mine?"

"No."

"I sent it, oh, a couple of weeks ago."

I knew instinctively that he had. But I hadn't received it.

"Perhaps the letter and I crossed in the air," I said with a laugh.

"Maybe," said A.J.

He asked when I was coming back.

"For the next execution, I guess."

A.J. nodded. "Well, you probably won't have too long to wait. Take care."

DOYLE WILLIAMS stepped into the interview room and took off his red knitted cap to reveal a shaved head. He thrust out his hand and said, "Man, it's cold out there."

Doyle is from North Carolina, and unlike many southerners, his speech is rapid, so quick that his voice raises in pitch from the speed of his delivery. Not one to mince words or evade issues, Doyle jumped right in with a comment about James Schnick's recent reversal, and what Schnick's case symbolized for him.

"Mr. Schnick had a successful military career," Doyle told me. "He fought for his country in Vietnam. And when a man like Mr. Schnick, who's never got a parking ticket, never a speeding ticket—an absolute law-abiding citizen all his life, a farmer, I tell you, what we would consider one of the pillars of the community, just an average, just a very dependable . . . Now, one morning, when that man gets up and kills half his family, *something happened*. There's something wrong. This was not a crime that was to collect insurance money. There was no insurance money. *Some-*

thing happened. A rubber band snapped in that man's mind. That was the act of someone with a mental problem."

As we began to discuss executions, Doyle, like Paul Delo and other members of the execution team, used a military metaphor to describe the way the death penalty currently functions in the United States. Doyle views it almost as a "secret war."

"As long as they're killing people—whether it's me or anybody else," said Doyle "—and they're doing it a hundred miles from any city of any size, and they do it in the middle of the night, it might as well be the boat people in Cambodia, or the Vietnamese. They get rid of us. Out of sight, out of mind. If they'd executed me that night, or whomever, it would simply have no effect whatsoever on the average workingman in St. Louis. Or Des Moines, Iowa. Or anywhere else. If you're ever going to change that perception, then the execution should be at least televised. Maybe, done at high noon, on Sunday, in downtown St. Louis in the square. I mean, if the public wants to kill them, then the public should be involved in the killing. At least get involved in it, at least watch it on television. At least do something. Because you're taking part in it when you cast that ballot. If you vote for George Bush and declare a war, then you take part in that. You step up, and your sons and your daughters put on the uniforms, and you actually, physically participate in the killing of Iraqi soldiers. If you think it's a right and just cause, then vote for it and participate."

I asked Doyle what he thought of President Bush's anti-crime bill, which then seemed set to become law.

"Well, that's ironic, that Mr. Bush is now pushing a bill to impose the death penalty for a wide range of crimes not including murder." He smiled at the irony of it: "It seems to me that we're progressing in our evolution. A hundred years ago, we use to execute people for stealing horses. And then, there's been more people executed in America for the crime of rape than any other crime; but the Supreme Court, probably forty years ago, ruled that was unconstitutional, that was cruel and unusual, to execute someone for any crime except for the capital offense of taking another life. Now we seem to be reverting back to saying that 'if you do this, if you do that, even though you do not take a life, we can still execute you.' I think that's sad. Now they're going to start killing people who they claim sell drugs."

"Do you think the death penalty has any deterrent effect?" I asked.

Doyle smiled. "Mr. Delo has made this comment on two different occasions, when he's been interviewed after executions. He says, 'The death penalty *is* a deterrent. It absolutely prohibits that person from committing another murder.' "

"So what do you think is the real reason for having the death penalty?"

"It's society's revenge against killers."

Doyle and I discussed the practical alternatives to the death penalty. "What about the life and fifty sentence?" I asked.

"Life and fifty, that's called the slow death sentence. That means you have to serve a minimum of fifty years before you become eligible for parole—not before you make parole, but before you become *eligible* for parole. Of course, that's a sentence you can't possibly serve. Unless you happen to be sixteen when you started. I think it's ironic that the alternative to the death sentence was fifty years without any possibility of parole; and then the Missouri legislature felt that wasn't severe enough, because some people were coming in at sixteen and seventeen and could honestly serve fifty years. So they changed it to just straight life with no parole."

Knowing that Doyle had an extensive knowledge of death penalty law, I asked him what his main legal objection to capital punishment was.

"It's grossly unfair," he said, "because it depends on which county you happen to be arrested in. There are a number of factors that come into play long before you reach the jury: the county you happen to be arrested in, and the political ambitions of the prosecutor—whether or not he's up for reelection any time soon, or whether he's just been reelected. If he's just coming into office, he probably won't be seeking the death penalty, because it's a lot more work and a lot more expensive for the county. However, if he's about to go out of office, and trying to secure reelection, nothing brings the headlines like notoriety. Like the death sentence. And, people are beginning to think that the only way to deal with violence is with violence. That's why I think this death penalty is still so popular."

Doyle was convicted in 1980 and is CP#14. He had spent nine years on old death row at MSP, and I asked him how he found the new prison at Potosi.

"Well," he said, "this is a very rural area. And I suppose it's true anywhere in America, when you have rural areas like this, you have two kinds of people: people that are agriculturally oriented, or very, very small-business oriented, such as shoe manufacturing or hats. I think there is a hat factory here locally. But predominately, you have people that are farming. In fact, one of the first conversations that I had with Mr. Delo, he told me, 'Doyle, this is going to take awhile.' He said, 'Six months ago my caseworkers were working in a shoe factory, they have absolutely no idea of, or, shall I say, no experience of, running a penitentiary or dealing with people.' We have a prison here that's about half black, and I think we have one black corrections officer. And for reasons not known to me, they keep him on the midnight shift. That causes some friction between the white officers and the black inmates."

"What is it like here on execution night?"

"Up at Jefferson City, every time they thought there might be an execution, they would play four or five videotapes that were very sexually explicit. Obviously, they played these videotapes to take people's minds off what was happening, and have them focus on the tapes. Here, while the tapes are not as sexually explicit, they do show at least four or five movies."

Doyle's anger at this custom was unbridled. He saw it as an attempt on the part of the administration to counter any solidarity there might be among condemned inmates, or even among the life and fifties and the condemned men. Doyle and A.J. and some other death row inmates boycotted the movies, and they developed their own ritual of flicking their light switches on and off at 12:01, when executions take place.

But while Doyle's concern for the plight of other death row inmates means that he spends much of his time patiently going through their appeals, and helping them with their legal work, he maintains a certain distance from the execution procedure.

"You just pure and simply can't let the fact that the guy you was playing cards with yesterday, or playing basketball with yesterday or whatever, and you know they're fixing to kill him tonight—you have to keep that at a distance. There is no other way to deal with it. You have to keep in mind, yes, they are killing him tonight, and probably in a few nights they'll kill me. So it's a little hard to sit around and feel sorry for yourself, which is self-defeating. And how can you feel sorry for somebody else when you know the same thing is happening to you? You empathize with them. But it's a war, and there are casualties. I don't know how else to describe it."

Doyle's attitude toward living with the killing is, in an odd way, not very different from that of the execution team. He accepts the inevitability of it, and also views it in terms of a war. The only difference is that the execution team knows they will kill him, and he knows he will be killed by them. There is none of the randomness or chance that attaches to killing or being killed in a war. Only the certainty of who the condemned are, and who the executioners are.

"How do you deal with it?" I asked.

"I don't know. *You* say how do you do it," he challenged. "You just get up each and every day, deal with it on a day-to-day basis. You try not to think too far into the future. By that I mean, you might want to think about what visits you may or may not get this coming weekend; but beyond that, you don't want to plan, or think. No one sits around thinking, 'We'll do this a year from now, or two years from now.' I mean, where you're accustomed to saying, 'I'll buy a car and I'll have it paid for in such and such a period of time,' or 'I'll buy this house,' or 'I'll work at this job and in two years I'll try and get a promotion'—no one even tries to entertain thoughts like that. You just force those out of your mind."

I knew that Doyle had spent some time working as a clerk for the chaplain, Gary Tune—a piece of information I had found surprising. I didn't think that Doyle was a particularly religious man, so I asked him how that had come about.

Doyle's expression was a mixture of cynical humor and disgust. "Let's talk about Reverend Tune," he said. "The reverend is a very unique man. Let me put this into perspective by telling you that working with the law day in and day out, year in year out, becomes a very heavy burden for me. So, a year and a half ago, I decided to give myself a break. I thought, I'm going to quit messing with this law as much as possible, and I'm going to take a job working for Reverend Tune as his clerk. The more I got to know Reverend Tune, the more impossible that was. I think I can sum it up from one little conversation we had. We are sitting at a table, and there was about three or four inmates, all death row inmates, and there was a Catholic priest and there was Reverend Tune. And just three or four days before that, they had executed George Gilmore. One of the men asked the priest, 'How do you feel about that? Was that a good thing? Did they do the right thing?' And the priest said, 'Certainly not. That is a ridiculous question.'

The same question was posed to Chaplain Tune. He said, 'Yes, they did the right thing. They should kill him. They should kill all of you. You have been tried and convicted, and that's the law, so you should be put to death.' "

Doyle shook his head at the absurdity of it.

"How does the chaplain square executions with Christian belief?" I asked.

"Well," Doyle said, "you can rationalize anything. You can take the Bible, and take one verse out of it, direct it. You can read the parts that say 'An eye for an eye, a tooth for a tooth.' So, okay, that means you took a life, you deserve to be executed. Of course, if you try to take into account the New Testament, and you say, 'what about this thing, "Thou shalt not kill"'? *How much more of a premeditated murder can this be? You plan it for years in advance.*' And he has no comment. He just says that he thinks it's God's will. The man is an absolute hypocrite. I'm telling you the man is everything that you would think that a priest is not, or that a man of the cloth is not. He is very hypocritical, very judgmental. An ass."

I was anxious to hear of Doyle's experience of deathwatch a few months previously. He agreed to tell me the story, but he wanted to know if I was aware of the case which had brought him the death penalty.

I knew the outline of the state's case. The prosecutor alleged that Doyle had killed Kerry Brummett, who knew that Doyle had burglarized a doctor's office in Auxvasse, Missouri. The state alleged that Doyle handcuffed, beat, and pistol-whipped Brummett. While trying to flee, Brummett ran into the Missouri River and drowned.

"Okay," Doyle began. "If you believe everything the state says happened in my case—and I vehemently deny it—but if you believe everything the state's witnesses testified to, and there's only one . . . The witness says that I and another man took a man out of the trunk of a car, and this man broke away from me and took off running. They said I was two or three steps behind him, reaching out like I was trying to grab him. The man outran me, and jumped in the Missouri River. I ran to the edge of the river and stopped. Waited a minute, then jumped into the river and tried to find him. The state's evidence is I pushed the man into the river. The man could have run in any direction he wanted to run. The cause of death was drowning. That's the story."

"Were his hands free?" I asked.

"No, his hands were handcuffed."

Doyle looked at me. "I'm responsible for the man's death. But I didn't knowingly and deliberately and with premeditation kill him."

With that preface, Doyle told me the story of how he came within three hours of being executed in March 1991.

He had secured a reversal of his death sentence, but this had been taken away. Once that happened, Doyle told me, "I knew in advance, with a reasonable degree of certainty, what was going to happen. I knew that when the Eighth Circuit Court of Appeals denied my petition, I knew they'd ask the Supreme Court to refuse to hear it, and thirty days after that they would set an execution date. And I firmly believed—and that's what I told my family—there was an eighty percent chance they was going to kill me. I fully expected to die on March the twentieth, 1991."

What I wanted from Doyle was another perspective on the Missouri Protocol. I had read the eleventh revision in Mark Schreiber's office, and had discussed it in detail with each member of the execution team. Doyle was unusual in that he had experienced being the subject of the Missouri Protocol, right up to the last-minute preparations for an execution. He had lived to tell the story of what actually happens.

"I was put in the holding cell three days before. They were going to execute me on Tuesday, and they put me in there on Friday. And they *told* me they wouldn't do that."

I wasn't sure what Doyle meant. "They told you they wouldn't do what?"

"Paul Delo called me up to his office on that Friday and said, 'When do you want to go over there?' And I said, 'Why don't we just go over on Sunday?' And he said, 'Okay, fine.' And that's when I come back down, and was going about my regular routine—in fact, I was intending to play some basketball, and spend some time with my friends, say good-bye to them—and the guards come up and handcuffed me behind my back and started packing up my bunk. See, he just lied to me. He didn't want me knowing when they was going to take me over. We call it kidnapping."

Doyle offered no criticism, no commentary on what had happened to him. He simply described it to me.

"What happened next?"

"They took me over that Friday. My mother lives in Jefferson City, Missouri, and my sister come in from Nashville, Tennessee, and my niece came. And they would come during the day. He'd allow me to have visits starting at one o'clock. My family could come inside the little cage with me. My family would stay with me from one o'clock until about five-thirty or six. Sitting around, eating popcorn and drinking a Pepsi with your family, assuming that they're going to kill you Monday night, is much harder on me, because they were there. I could have dealt with it much better by myself."

A.J. had told me his worry about having his mother and the rest of his family present for his execution. It was difficult enough to prepare to die; to have to console others seemed an almost impossible task.

"I at first thought that having family would make this time pass easier. But, because I believed this was going to be the execution, I found that it made it quite a bit more difficult. I found that having my mother sitting around, seeing her doing all she could do to keep from breaking down and crying, and my sister the same way, I found that, if you know you're going to die, sitting around with your friends, it seems like you just impose your suffering on them. They don't relieve yours; you *impose yours* upon them. But what are you going to do? You can't tell your family they can't come. You can't tell them, 'No, I'm not going to spend my last hour or so with you.' So I guess you just deal with it the best you can."

I asked Doyle how he spent most of his time in the deathwatch cell. He told me that he watched a lot of videotapes.

"Then my girlfriend would come in about five-thirty or so. You see, I was engaged at the time. She would get there about five-thirty or six o'clock, when she got off work. And she'd stay until about nine-thirty or ten o'clock at night. And so at ten o'clock I'd probably watch one more movie with the guard, whichever one he wanted to watch, usually."

"How did you sleep?" I asked.

"It really surprised me," Doyle replied. "I slept real well. In fact, I usually have a lot of problems sleeping. I have a lot of trouble *going* to sleep, switching my mind off. But during that period, I slept like a baby."

I asked Doyle if he thought the deathwatch procedure was necessary.

"You could get enough heroin to give yourself an overdose. Three hundred dollars would do it. If you put the word out, in a few days you could get enough."

"What about the officers who work in the deathwatch cell? How do they behave while they're waiting for you to be taken away to be executed?"

"I think they're very detached from it. Of course, I don't see how they could be any other way. If they're going to get emotionally involved in it, they'd have to get out of it. Unless—and I don't know how they feel personally about me—but let's assume that they did not like me. And that would be the only other alternative, that they're getting some kind of satisfaction out of this thing—'This is the right thing, it should be done, I'm going to help do it.' Like fighting Germany in the war. If they do, they don't express it to me. They're very careful not to show any emotion towards you. I would say they were all courteous to my family."

"What happened on the day they were going to execute you?"

"Paul Delo came down, and he asked me what I wanted for my last meal. He wanted to know what I wanted done with my property and stuff. He asked questions like, 'Do you know at this point who'll be claiming your body? Do you want it turned over to your mother, or do you not want it turned over?' Things like that. He said, 'We will bring the gurney down *to* the room.' And he suggested, 'Before it reaches this point, I want to strongly suggest that you take the sedative.' He said, 'I don't want you to have a sedative for *you*.' "

"Meaning?"

"They want you to be virtually incapacitated so that you can't possibly offer any resistance. The sedative is so that the thing will go smoothly. Not for the psychological effect it will have on *you,* but so there's no resistance. And if they give you a real heavy dose of liquid Valium, then you're going to be pretty docile. Although he said it's not mandatory."

"What happened about the other medical procedures?"

"Calling them medical procedures is a little bit of a joke. They give you a pre-execution physical. They take your temperature and weigh you, and the doctor hits you on the knee to see if you have some reflexes. And if I remember right, he got his stethoscope out and listened to my heart. I thought it was kind of silly. I said, 'What are you going to do if I'm sick?' You know? And he didn't answer. So that was a three-minute ordeal. They asked what I wanted for my last meal, and I ordered that and they brought it.

"I found out about eight o'clock at night that they weren't going to execute me. I got a call from my lawyer telling me that the United States Supreme Court had given a stay. After I got the call from my lawyer, and I didn't let on to the staff what my conversation was, that doctor came in. Dr. Cayabyab. He come in and said, "It's time for your shot.' I said, 'I don't want no shot.' "

Doyle's voice became hard and cold as he recalled Dr. Cayabyab's visit.

" 'It's time for your shot,' he said. 'So it'll make you more relaxed.' And he's got another man with him. I said, 'No.' I said, 'I don't want no shot. I don't need to relax. I just need you to leave me alone, so I can spend some time with my girlfriend.' And he stood there a minute. You see, we believe that they had forced them shots on other people. I told him, 'If you force that shot upon me, and you don't execute me, we'll get plenty of money out of this lawsuit." And they stepped over in the corner and had a little discussion, and they left. They decided against forcing it upon me."

We discussed how the Missouri Protocol stated that the pre-execution sedatives were optional.

Doyle laughed. "How would you know? They killed the only witness."

"So, after the doctor left, what happened next?"

"My attorney called. His exact words were 'It's all over.' "

Doyle told me his first reaction was panic. He said to his attorney: "What do you mean?" Doyle's attorney told him the Supreme Court had given him a stay of execution.

"I can't imagine what that would be like," I said. "How did you feel at that time?"

"I was prepared to die. And I wanted to live. *Desperately*. At the same time, I didn't want to put my family through that same ordeal again ninety days down the road. I don't know what the words are to say. Relieved is obviously what would normally come to your mind. But I don't know if that's a fair characterization. I do remember sitting around thinking, that afternoon, there were so many things that I wanted to do over. . . . "

"When you were in the deathwatch cell, what did they tell you about the procedure? About how they would actually kill you?"

"They put you on this thing about thirty minutes before they do it. Thirty, forty-five minutes before they get around to killing you. They would put me on the gurney around eleven, or eleven-thirty."

"And what was running through your mind then, when you were focused on being put to death?"

"I just assumed it would be very similar to major surgery or something, and you just wouldn't wake up."

"Do you think it's 'humane,' as they say?"

"That's really not the issue, is it? Really and truly, the issue is, what difference does it make if they walk up behind you and put a pistol to the back of your head and pull the trigger? Nobody knows what the sensations are that are going through your brain while this poison's going in your veins. There is no such way as a humane way to kill people. It's wrong."

"How did the various members of the execution team behave that night? What did you observe?"

"I don't even know how to express what people do, but when they are about to kill you, they just seem very, very nervous. They seem like they can't stand still. They make idle conversation; you know, 'How's the weather?' would be complex conversation for them. They seem very, very uncomfortable about what they're fixing to do. But, at the same time, they seem anxious to do it. I can't quite understand why these particular individuals seemed to take some satisfaction in thinking, 'We are about to kill you.' I don't know."

Doyle told me that nearly an hour passed before news of the stay was made official within the prison, and that he continued to be held in the deathwatch cell.

"How did they announce it?" I asked.

"I heard it over a guard's radio," he told me.

"What did they say?"

Doyle's answer confirmed the military or warfare metaphor for executions at Potosi.

"They said, '*Stand down from the exercise. Stand down from the exercise.*' That's how they referred to it, as an exercise. When they said stand down from it, that meant go back to normal status. It took almost an hour after my lawyer told me there was a stay for them to make that announcement. And there was obvious disappointment on their faces."

"After the order went out to stand down from the exercise, did anyone come to talk with you?"

"Probably twenty minutes after that, Paul Delo come down here and stuck his hand through the door and shook hands, and was telling me how glad he was it worked out for me. He's a lying son of a bitch. He would much prefer to kill me. The fact that Mr. Delo is the warden of a prison that does conduct the execution gives him a pension and a stature that he would never have anywhere else. And he enjoys that stature, and that pension. I believe Mr. Delo was looking forward to killing me.''

"What happened after that?"

"They leave you right there. You see, my visitor was still there. Paul Delo come in, shook hands, said he was glad it worked out for me like that. And he turned to my girlfriend, and he looked up at the clock—it was ten after nine—and he said, 'Miss————can stay till nine-thirty. Mr. Williams, we'll return you to your housing unit tomorrow,' and left. Next day, they rolled two laundry carts in there, plastic carts, and said, 'Pack your stuff up.' So you put all your stuff back in. Your television, your rug, your sheets, your blankets, and put it all back in those two laundry carts. And you push them, one at a time, back to your housing unit.''

"What was it like, returning to the housing unit after everyone expected you to be executed?"

"My friends came over and shook hands with me. Some hugged me. It's like somebody who'd come back from a battle.''

"And how did you feel," I asked, "when you came out of the hospital? Never expecting to come out of it alive?"

Doyle shifted in his chair, and his voice broke slightly.

"I came out on the twenty-first of March. I remember having . . . I don't know why this particular phrase kept coming to my mind, but it did: 'The sun is shining, and I see it.' And it made me cry. Because I sure didn't expect to see it. It's a frightening experience. One I hope you never share.''

*   *   *

After I said good-bye to Doyle, one of the caseworkers was sitting in the waiting area. As Doyle was walking out the door, the caseworker said to me in a loud voice: "So, Steve, you gonna come and watch us kill Doyle?"

PHIL BANKS is Paul Delo's second assistant superintendent and was the only other key member of the execution team I had yet to interview. Phil came to Potosi after working for eight years in probation and parole, as opposed to corrections. He is a tall, soft-spoken man from northern Missouri and is the newest member of the execution team. He has participated in two executions, and he first performed the role of operations officer during the execution of Maurice Byrd. He is an easygoing person, but somewhat enigmatic. He has unusually eclectic musical tastes, from new country to Chicago blues and R&B. He looks more like a businessman than a corrections official. He jokes about giving up his job to go and sell BMWs.

I remarked that he was the only member of the execution team whose previous experience had been in probation and parole rather than corrections. Phil told me that, in his opinion, his work in probation and parole had made him particularly suited to his role as assistant superintendent. I asked how he found prison life at Potosi.

"It's remarkable, the feeling of danger you get when you're walking in the yard. But that's true of our minimum- and medium-security prisons too." Then he laughed. "It crosses over into post offices and the streets."

"What about being the newest member of the execution team?" I wanted to know. "Was it difficult to fit in?"

"It wasn't a problem," Phil said, leaning back in his chair and crossing his ankles on his desk. "It was pretty easy to fit in because of the camaraderie, from department level down to the staff."

Phil appeared to be a more mild-mannered man than some of the other members of the execution team. He certainly looked less the part than the others.

"How do executions affect you personally?" I asked.

"It becomes kind of task oriented," he said.

I looked at him and waited for further elaboration; but there wasn't going to be any.

Phil was gregarious on the surface, but he was not prepared to say very much about his role in executions. It appeared that, for him, the Missouri Protocol worked. By spreading the responsibility, by breaking the execution process down into a series of key tasks, each member of the team is able to focus on his or her part of the process, rather than on the whole process and its result.

"What about when there's a stay?" I asked Phil. "How are you affected by that?"

"Personally, it's just like anything else that's planned that doesn't go off. There isn't a down or anything. We begin to stand down."

We talked for a while, and during future visits to Potosi we would have lunch, or go for a beer after work. But Phil always kept his private feelings about participating in executions to himself.

I WAS IN Paul Delo's office having coffee one morning when two visitors from the Illinois Department of Corrections arrived. Gary Sutterfield was there, and Phil Banks. The men from Illinois, one black, one white, both in their early forties, were senior corrections staff, and were visiting to see how things were done at Potosi. They were uncomfortable with my presence in the room, and it seemed as though Paul Delo took a certain pleasure in their mild discomfort—as if to say to them, "We don't have anything to hide, and this proves it."

Illinois had been the second state to use Fred Leuchter's lethal injection machine, and they had, at that time, 139 people on death row. The Illinois Department of Corrections had expressed its appreciation to Paul for allowing Gary Sutterfield to travel there and assist with its first execution by sending him a nameplate for his desk that read "Paul K. Delo."

Paul told me with a smile, "It was made by the guys who make the gravestones over there."

I was invited along for lunch that afternoon with the men from Illinois.

It turned out that both were Vietnam veterans, and they said which units they'd fought with. The conversation turned to deer hunting, and then to the real business at hand.

"You know we've got a problem in Illinois," the white one began, "because the American Medical Association kicked up a fuss about doctors being involved in executions."

Paul nodded.

Gary Sutterfield looked at me. From his point of view, doctors were a problem, too. But only because, at the execution of Charles Walker, three of them hadn't the experience to put the IV in correctly. They had inserted it so that it was flowing in the wrong direction, away from Walker's heart.

"Here," Paul explained, "we have a nurse on contract who comes in and actually sets the IV. It's kind of a specialized thing."

The black corrections official held his chin in his hand and nodded.

"Of course," Paul continued, "down here, the law doesn't require that we have a doctor to pronounce death. The coroner can do that. But you don't even need the coroner, really, because a sheriff's deputy can pronounce death. I've done it a number of times, when I was with the sheriff or the highway patrol. So, I'm a deputy, Greg Wilson here's a deputy, and theoretically we don't need a doctor to do that."

"But you still use the doctor?" the white one asked.

"Yes. Our doctor monitors the EKG and pronounces death," Paul said.

The men from Illinois chewed over the problem for a while, ignoring the obvious solution of getting rid of the doctors. When that was suggested, they seemed uncomfortable with the idea. Perhaps because lethal injection has the outward appearance of a medical procedure, I thought, people involved in executions by that method feel the need to have a doctor present to lend confirmation to the view that it is a "humane" procedure. The Missouri Protocol had a certain ritualistic aspect, and this seemed an important part of it.

Before I left for Jefferson City, two days before Thanksgiving, Paul and I were alone in his office. He said: "You know, we really haven't had any problems with executions. I haven't. You wonder, before you've done one, what it's going to be like. But it just doesn't seem to have had any adverse psychological effect. Perhaps it will later on, I don't know."

"What if it did?" I asked.

"I'd find another job."

We said good-bye, and as I started the drive up Highway 8 to Jefferson City, I thought of the executioners who had written their memoirs. Albert Pierrepoint, Britain's hangman for decades, came down against the death penalty in his autobiography. So had Clinton Duffy, the warden of San Quentin, who conducted ninety executions by gas; and so had Robert Elliott, New York's executioner.

ON THANKSGIVING eve, I met with Bill Armontrout at the Department of Corrections in Jefferson City. My Missouri odyssey had started in his office three months earlier, and I filled him in on what I had learned during that time.

Bill told me some stories of his time at MSP—of murder, revenge, and sexual jealousy among inmates.

"Of the ones on death row," he said, "there's about ten of them that are mine, that I sent there for murder of an inmate, or murder of an officer. A good part of these guys on the row are my own cases."

He told me the story of Frankie Guinan and Richard Zeitvogel, who had become lovers at MSP. Frankie Guinan ended up on death row after killing two fellow inmates. He and Zeitvogel stabbed John McBroom to death in 1981; then, in 1985, Guinan and Gerald Smith murdered Robert Baker. After Guinan was sent to death row, Zeitvogel committed another prison murder, strangling his cellmate, Gary Dew, with a piece of wire. Bill told me Zeitvogel had done it in order to be reunited with Guinan on death row.

Bill said he thought of Frankie Guinan almost as a son. "I feel like I raised him, and I failed. And I think it will be hard doing Frankie."

I asked Bill if he thought the penitentiary was a school for crime; whether it was the case that young men with first offenses left the penitentiary ready to embark on a life of violent crime.

"You see, the thing that sometimes happens is, they'll come in on a small charge. And they end up killing somebody. And then they're setting there with the death penalty. Years ago, if they killed an inmate, they wouldn't get time. Years ago, they didn't even prosecute them for it. In the last twenty years, we've prosecuted every crime that's committed in the institution. It makes you feel bad, in a way, when you see these young ones come in there, and then they end up on death row. It makes you feel in a way like you're a failure. That you should have protected them better."

I wanted to know more about Bill's experience in the execution of Edward Earl Johnson in Mississippi. He told me how a BBC film crew had been there, and that he had been amused to see how they "just took off out of there at two o'clock in the morning, in the middle of nowhere. They just couldn't get away fast enough."

"Did you meet the inmate before you executed him?" I asked.

Bill said that he hadn't had much conversation with him, except toward the end.

"What did you say?"

"In talking with the youngster, he did just exactly what I told him to do, you know. I said, 'When you hear that lever rack, and you see the fumes start up in there, you take a couple of deep breaths.' And he did that. And once I heard the lever rack, I started counting. And I counted to fifty-eight. And by the time I hit fifty-eight, the kid was gone by that time, I'm sure."

Bill and I had spoken before, on my first visit to Jefferson City, about the gruesome nature of executions by gas. I asked him whether, if Missouri were still required to carry out gas executions, he would be able to put together a team who would carry out the executions with as much dedication as the lethal injection team had demonstrated.

"It takes really dedicated staff to do a gas execution," Bill said. "Especially with the washing down of the body. But we were practicing on the gas chamber for a year before the lethal injection bill was passed. I was prepared for over a year to do one with gas."

The question made Bill think of a story that he wanted to tell me.

"In order to buy my cyanide pellets, I had to buy four hundred pounds of them. I couldn't buy like a quart, or whatever. So I had four hundred pounds of pellets. It only takes me thirty-seven to do it. So I had enough pellets to kill everybody in Missouri."

"What do you think's going to happen in other states," I asked, "where they still have the gas chamber, or where they have electric chairs that are always going wrong?"

"I think eventually you'll see lethal injection be the most common way. For some time. Until some other, more humane method is found."

We ended up talking about Dr. Jack Kevorkian, who had recently been in the news after two women had lethally injected themselves with his euthanasia machine. Bill commented that there was some similarity between Kevorkian's machine and the one Missouri had bought from Fred Leuchter. I told Bill that Dr. Kevorkian had published a number of papers in medical journals advocating lethal injection as a method of execution.

I wanted to know more about Tiny Mercer before I tried to get in touch with his wife, Christy. I asked Bill about his relationship with Tiny.

"This is kind of a funny thing for a warden to say, I guess, but Tiny and I were friends. If I had any kind of a problem coming up on death row, I would say, 'Tiny, quiet these guys down. Find out what it is they're bitching about, and let's see if we can do something about it. If it's something I can do without jeopardizing security, I'll do it, you know.' Because we're all just human. And Tiny was that sort of a guy. And his wife, who lives in town—she and I are friends."

That surprised me. I asked Bill how he came to meet Tiny.

Bill first met Tiny when he was deputy warden at MSP. "I knew Tiny from before, when he came and did a short sentence. And when he came with the death penalty, he got to lifting weights and working out, and he started reading the Bible. Of all the inmates I've seen that profess to have found the Lord in prison, I'd never seen one I believed. But I do believe Tiny. Tiny actually found the Lord. And he was at peace with himself. Even at the last minute, he wanted to hold my hand. And I said, 'Tiny, I can't because I've got things I have to do.' And he said, 'Can I hold my Bible?' And I said, 'Certainly you can hold your Bible.' My wife escorted his wife as a witness. And like I say, we're friends today. Not social friends, but we know each other real well. And I have no fear of her at all. I just saw her the other day."

I found it extraordinary that, having executed Christy Mercer's husband, Bill claimed that they were friends.

"What do you talk about when you meet?" I asked.

"She's kind of funny in a way. Every time I see her, she'll say, 'Bill, why did you kill Tiny? God loves you, but why did you kill Tiny?' Stuff like that. Or if she's waiting in one of the restaurants in town, and she serves me, she'll always come up and say, 'Bill, God loves you, but why did you kill Tiny?' Very strange gal."

I asked Bill about how Tiny and Christy met, and what their relationship was like.

"They married after he was on death row," Bill said. "The day that they got married—I was deputy warden then, and my office faced the street over the penitentiary—and after the marriage ceremony was over, and of course we allowed them no time together, she had two bridesmaids with her. And they all walked across the street from my office and took off all their clothes. Stripped down buck-ass naked. I'm looking, I'm eyeballing them, and my secretary come in, and I said, 'Carol, call the police—in about thirty minutes.' Anyway, that was some sort of a ritual that they were going through."

Bill wanted to tell me about Tiny's crime.

"Tiny was a motorcycle gang leader out of Kansas City. The girl that he killed, a couple of gang members brought her to Tiny as his birthday present. It was Tiny's birthday. So they go out and abduct her and bring her in and say, 'Tiny, here's your birthday present.' Tiny maintained all along to me that he didn't actually kill the girl, that it was one of the other people that did that. But he was convicted. And just like I told him, I said, 'Tiny, you've had a number of appeals, and courts say you're the one that did it, and of course I have no recourse but to do what the court tells me to do.' And he understood that. But I could always count on Tiny to help me in any way, if he could. And right up to the last minute, he wanted to hold my hand. He wanted a cigarette, and we gave him a cigarette. It was hard. It was hard doing him."

There was no doubting Bill's sincerity in regard to Tiny Mercer; and for a tourist in the strange world of capital punishment practice, it was perhaps the hardest thing to comprehend. I took some comfort in the fact that no one else I knew could understand it—neither the execution team, nor inmates who had been close to Tiny Mercer.

Talking with A. J. Bannister about the Mercer execution, he confirmed what Bill had told me about Tiny.

"He had a reputation that he brought with him, and whenever there were problems, he would try and sort them out with our unit sergeant," said A.J. "He and Armontrout got along real well. In fact, I think Bill had mentioned that he regretted to have to be the one to execute Tiny, because they had known each other all these years. But he did it nonetheless. It's his job as warden, I suppose."

Gary Sutterfield, who had worked closely with Fred Leuchter to set up the lethal injection machine in the gas chamber where Tiny Mercer was executed, remembered that night.

"When we executed Tiny Mercer, I did find out at the time that Mr. Armontrout and Tiny were pretty close during Tiny's incarceration in the Missouri State Penitentiary. And I did notice a very sober attitude with Bill. Bill's a very outgoing person who jokes a lot, likes to fish, and everything else, but I did notice that evening after the execution that he was very quiet. Very withdrawn from the crowd around him."

At the end of the day, the thing that allowed Bill to execute Tiny Mercer, apart, perhaps, from a belief in his guilt, was Fred Leuchter's machine, and the Missouri Protocol. But, while the protocol gave him a certain amount of security, there was a worry about the machine. It had never been used, and no one knew for sure that it would work.

"We really didn't know whether it would work," Bill told me. "We had tested and tested, and we had trained and trained and trained, and everybody was just at the point where they were fine-honed. And even the press were very complimentary on my staff, about how serious they took the job —they didn't see any horseplay around—and how dignified things were. But we had trained so goddamn much for it, they were at the peak of perfection, that's what they were. And the only letdown that we had was when we would have a stay of execution at around ten o'clock at night. And that's as big a letdown as actually doing it, you know."

"Why is that?" I asked.

"Standing down is very difficult mentally. Because you're so prepped for this thing, you see. I've found that when we go ahead and do the chore that we have to do, that you're not as depressed as you are when you stand down. That standing down just tears you up. You're so keyed to it. You're so tired."

Bill told me stories about the other executions he had performed at Potosi, where one or two moments stood out in his mind. He said that, sometimes, inmates who had previously professed their innocence would confess just prior to their execution. That was the case with Gerald Smith.

"When we executed Gerald, Gerald kept telling me, all along, he was not guilty of killing this girl. At the very last minute, he told me, 'Bill, I did what they said I did. But I didn't do it the way they said I did it.' So, in essence, Gerald Smith was telling me, 'Yes, I'm good for it.' But all those years, he kept telling me, 'No.' "

In the case of Leonard Laws, Bill told me, "We got him within two hours of an execution one time, and when we got the stay, he was really hostile about it. He didn't want the stay. He was like us, you know. It was a hell of a letdown for him. He wanted to go ahead and get this thing over with. So the next time we got him up there, he was ready to go without any problem. He was all hyped up and ready for it."

"But," said Bill, "of all of them, the one that took it very manly was Tiny. About being a man about it. And Leonard Laws, of all things. But none of them gave us any problems."

Bill said he had to go, as he was driving to Oklahoma to spend Thanksgiving with his mother. We smoked a cigarette in front of the Department of Corrections building, and Bill asked me how I'd enjoyed my time in Missouri.

"It's a beautiful place," I said.

T

HAT NIGHT, I called the number that A.J. had given me in an effort to track Christy Mercer down. Her friend answered the phone and listened to my story about why I was searching for Christy. She said she didn't have Christy's home number, but that she worked as a cocktail waitress in Jefferson City, and she gave me the address. She also said that Christy had changed her name. She told me what it was, and then she asked what I was doing on Sunday, and if I'd like to go to church with her. I thanked her for the invitation, but said I would probably have left town by then.

I had no idea what hours Christy worked, or what days. At six that evening, I went to the lounge, which was in one of the hotels just off the highway into town, and took a seat at the bar. A.J. and Christy's friend in Jefferson City had described her to me: tall, slim, long black hair, very attractive. The woman who took my order was certainly not Christy. Nor were any of the waitresses who came in from the restaurant for bar service in the lounge.

I waited for a while, then asked the college student who was serving me if—and I used Christy's new name—she was working that evening. The student said no, but thought that she would be in sometime the next day, Thanksgiving.

On Thanksgiving, I woke up to discover that the restaurant in my hotel was closed all day. I grumbled at the woman who was sitting at the front desk, knitting. When I went out into the parking lot, there were only two cars—mine and hers. After finding breakfast in another hotel, I spent the morning piecing together what I knew of Tiny Mercer's execution from the execution team, from inmates, and from newspaper accounts.

Tiny had been scheduled to die on October 20, 1988, but the three-judge panel of the Eighth U.S. Circuit Court of Appeals gave a stay on October 19. Then, on January 3, 1990, the same three judges ordered that the execution proceed on January 6. Tiny's lawyers appealed to the U.S. Supreme Court on January 4. The appeal was turned down by the Supreme Court on the day before the execution; and, on the same day, Missouri governor John Ashcroft refused to grant a pardon.

There was a cold rain on the night of Tiny's execution at MSP. While Bill Armontrout told me that Tiny had been "ready to meet his maker," I had heard from other prison officials that he had been distraught at the news that the U.S. Supreme Court had refused his final appeal. He ordered his last meal—barbecued steak and ribs, tacos, burritos, and a salad with oil and vinegar dressing. He offered Bill Armontrout a burrito that he couldn't finish.

At 11:00 P.M., reporters were loaded into vans and driven into the penitentiary, where they waited in the rain near the death chamber for the execution to begin. At 11:09 P.M., the doctor who would perform the IV cutdown on Mercer, inserting the IV into his groin, and would then pronounce death arrived at the prison in a car bearing vanity plates which read ICEMAN. At 11:42 P.M., the journalists' van wound its way through the roads behind the death house and the reporters were led into the building.

Outside the penitentiary, along with the television trucks and the dozens of reporters who had not secured a place inside the death house, a hundred or so protesters stood silently in the rain, holding candles to mark their opposition to the execution. One of them carried a sign that read: "Why do we kill people to show that killing people is wrong?"

Inside the death house, Christy Mercer and an old friend of Tiny's from his motorcycle club were allowed to stay with him after he had been strapped to the gurney inside the gas chamber. While Bill Armontrout denied Tiny's request to wear his motorcycle club colors at his execution, Tiny was allowed to wear a black headband. He had grown a beard again during the final months of his life.

After the witnesses had taken their places in the bleacherlike seating around the old gas chamber, the director of the Department of Corrections, Dick Moore, read a statement from Governor Ashcroft, which said: "This painful event is necessary to reaffirm the value the state of Missouri places on innocent human life."

When the blinds went up to reveal Tiny, his head jerked off the edge of the gurney as he looked around to find Christy. Doug Waggoner, who witnessed the execution for the now defunct *Jefferson City Post-Tribune,* wrote that Tiny's eyes were "slightly disoriented," and that his "expression appeared to be one of anger or agitation at not seeing his wife immediately or at the spectacle around him." When he saw Christy and his friend, Tiny began trying to speak.

"It was impossible to tell what Mercer was saying," Waggoner reported, "but his dark-haired wife could be seen smiling down and nodding. Her look was one of sad resignation as she tried to respond to him.

" 'Hi. I love you,' he appeared to say. Seconds later she shook her head and mouthed, 'I can't understand you.' After a few moments of silent communication, she raised two fingers in the peace-victory sign, then nodded and pointed heavenward.' "

All the time Tiny was trying to talk to Christy through the thick glass, Bill Armontrout was reading the death warrant.

Contrary to Bill Armontrout's recollection that "there was no coughing or gagging," Waggoner reported that "the effects of the drugs were immediately apparent. A brief coughing-gagging spell brought Mercer's head off the gurney twice before dropping backward a final time. His head didn't move again, but his eyes remained open and fixed on the ceiling as he drifted in a sleep-like state. By 12:05 A.M. he lost consciousness and soon there was no discernible breathing."

For Christy Mercer, the execution was an ordeal. "As the drugs took effect, Mrs. Mercer watched for half a minute before moving away from the window overlooking her husband. She came back to the window to gaze, blurry-eyed, at Mercer for several moments before walking away again, this time accompanied by Mercer's other witness. She returned one last time for a few seconds before the shades were pulled at 12:09 A.M. and Mercer was declared dead.''

I remembered what Fred Leuchter had told me just after Labor Day: "The first time my lethal injection machine was used was on Tiny Mercer, in the state of Missouri. It was an interesting first, not only for myself and the machine, but also for the state of Missouri, it being the first execution conducted there in many years, it being in Middle America, and it being in the middle of the Bible Belt.

When I asked Fred if he had been present at the Mercer execution, he told me that he had never witnessed an execution, that "it's not necessary for what I do." But Gary Sutterfield contradicted the statement Fred had made to me. He told me: "We had gone through I can't tell you how many practices with the machine, to ensure that it functioned. We had gone through a lot of training with it, to hopefully have no problems. The manufacturer of the machine stayed with us during this whole time and was with us the evening of the execution. It performed just as he said it would perform. I think it met his expectation and ours."

I tried to imagine what that night was like, from all points of view. From the point of view of A.J., Tiny's next-door neighbor on death row, and other men locked in the basement of MSP; from the point of view of Bill Armontrout, who had a genuine liking for Tiny; and from the point of view of Christy Mercer, who, in all the years she was married to Tiny, had only briefly felt the touch of his hand on her. She had spent more time in physical contact with him as Missouri prepared to execute him than she had on their wedding day.

At noon, I drove out to the lounge where Christy worked. The restaurant was full of family groups enjoying Thanksgiving dinner. The parking lot was full with out-of-state cars, of people who had driven across three or four states to be with their families on America's least commercialized holiday.

Christy was nowhere to be seen. Nor was the bartender who had served me the evening before. I had a drink and watched football on TV, not wanting to draw attention to Christy by asking too many questions about her. I struck up a conversation with a waitress who was rushed off her feet, taking drinks back and forth to the dining room. She persuaded me to take a table in the dining room, and I had a solitary Thanksgiving dinner surrounded by groups of six, ten, twelve people.

After eating, I returned to the bar and finally asked one of the bartenders when Christy would be in. She told me that Christy had changed her work schedule with another bartender, and wouldn't be in for a few days. Disappointed, I wrote Christy a note and asked her friend to give it to her when she returned.

The next day, I flew to New York and visited with friends.

"When is the execution?" was almost the first thing everyone said to me. Nervous television executives and publishers called with tedious regularity to ask the same question. Bill Armontrout had said the day before Thanksgiving that he was surprised they hadn't had one since Maurice Byrd the previous August. He said he would be very surprised if they didn't have at least one before Christmas. I got tired of answering the question by explaining that I did not set execution dates. The Missouri Supreme Court and the U.S. Supreme Court had already demonstrated, time and again, that they had no compunction about ordering executions.

When the time came, it would be soon enough.

PART THREE/NEW YEAR

I RETURNED to New York City during the week before Christmas to begin preparations for shooting "The Execution Protocol." On the twenty-third, I drove to Ballston Spa, in upstate New York, and spent my first Christmas in fifteen years with my family.

My mother was glad to see me, but my work made her anxious. "It can't be doing you any good spending so much time with those people," she said.

"Which people?" I asked. "The inmates or the execution team?"

"Both," she said.

"Most of them are fairly regular guys," I said. "Some aren't so different from me."

My mother frowned.

It snowed on Christmas Day, and as the family sat down to a two-hour-long feast, I thought about what A.J. had told me: that he no longer looked forward to Christmas, because it marked the passing of another year and reminded everyone facing execution that their time was that much shorter.

On the second of January, shooting of "The Execution Protocol" began in Malden, Massachusetts, at Fred Leuchter's house.

After the shoot, I went back to New York to view the dailies, and to prepare for filming in Missouri. My life had become a permanent death-watch. I was on twenty-four-hour standby to receive the fax from Potosi that would tell me who was next to be executed, and when.

One night while eating in a restaurant, I picked up a *New York Post* that another customer had left behind. I came across the headline: "Eichmann's 'Diary' Sparks Israel Furor." There was a photograph of the Nazi war criminal Adolf Eichmann in Israel, listening to the death sentence being read to him before he was taken away and hanged. But what caught my eye was the name of David Irving, the British Holocaust revisionist who had been instrumental in bringing Fred Leuchter to the Zundel trial, and who had published *The Leuchter Report* in Britain. The story concerned a newly discovered 1,000-page diary, which Irving said he had obtained from a contact in Buenos Aires. Irving was reported as saying in a television interview that the diary, the authenticity of which had not been independently verified, proved that Eichmann did participate in the Holocaust. As a result, Irving had done a total about-face and now believed that the Holocaust had indeed taken place. I wondered what Fred would make of that news, and if he would continue to stand by *The Leuchter Report*.

I returned to London, and after a few weeks of waiting, there was an anxious moment when the director of Missouri's Department of Corrections, Dick Moore, expressed some reservations about the film I was planning to make at Potosi. It was potentially a major stumbling block, and required delicate handling. All of the members of the Missouri execution team I had interviewed were happy to explain their point of view, and were keen to participate in the film because of the ground rules that I had set. The only people interviewed in the film would be those involved in the execution process: Fred Leuchter, the Missouri executioners, and condemned inmates. I explained that there would be no external voice-over narrator, no written script. No editorializing would take place. The only words in the film would be those of the executioners and the condemned.

All of the members of the execution team had an abiding distrust of the media, particularly television news. All too often, they complained, they would give a lengthy interview, only to have a ten-second sound bite aired out of context. I promised that the interviews would be lengthy—in fact, they would take weeks to complete—and that everyone would be allowed to have a full say about their role in executions.

Finally, I offered to travel to Missouri to speak with officials from the Department of Corrections to negotiate access to shoot the film. At the end of January, I flew directly from London to St. Louis, then drove to Jefferson City. I arrived at about eight in the evening so that I could get a night's sleep before my 10 A.M. meeting the following day. When I arrived at my hotel, the receptionist greeted me warmly and said, "Welcome home." And then she said: "Your friends are waiting for you in the bar."

I put down my suitcase and went into the bar, and found Bill Armontrout, Paul Delo, and Phil Banks. I hadn't expected to see them. They had driven up from Potosi so that we could have a pre-meeting before the next day's crucial one. They had a bourbon and a beer chaser lined up for me. It was a genuine surprise, and despite my fatigue—it was now two o'clock in the morning for me—I sat down and had a drink with them.

"You missed happy hour," Paul told me. "We saved some toasted raviolis for you, but then we ate them."

Bill Armontrout sat with us for an hour or so, then said he had to get home. Phil Banks went off to bed an hour after that. Paul and I sat up till around midnight, drinking and talking. They had all discussed the problem of access to film among themselves. It was clear that the department director, Dick Moore, was uncomfortable with his role in executions. He had religious feelings about them that conflicted with his responsibility as head of the department. It was also clear that he was close to Governor Ashcroft, and that he had reservations about any discussion of capital punishment procedure in Missouri. Paul and his colleagues had come to the conclusion that "The Execution Protocol" was a good thing. In my conversations with them, they had always maintained: "We have nothing to hide."

Early on in my research, I had some misgivings about their position. In my experience, I had never found such an unaffected openness among state officials. Already, Paul had given me free access anywhere and to anyone in the prison. He had not refused to answer a single question I had put to him. I couldn't help but respect the open approach that he and Bill Armontrout had taken after my first request to speak with them.

Five hours later, at 6 A.M., I met Paul and Phil in the lobby and we drove over to a restaurant near the Department of Corrections. Bill Armontrout was waiting for us. We had a final discussion of how the argument for the film would be presented, and I returned to my hotel to wait for our 10 A.M. meeting.

When I got to the Department of Corrections, Mark Schreiber greeted me, and we joined the others in George Lombardi's office. Mr. Moore had delegated the task of negotiating film access to Mr. Lombardi, who, as director of Adult Institutions, was Bill Armontrout's boss. The meeting took an hour, and all of the issues were resolved by negotiation. Mr. Lombardi made it clear that there would be no chance of filming an execution. I made it clear that that had never been our intention, and that I felt that even if we did have access to an execution, the film would not be strengthened by it.

That evening, I planned to track down Christy Mercer at the lounge where she worked. I lay down for a nap around 6 P.M., and woke up at 4 A.M., cursing myself for missing the opportunity.

Fifteen hours later, I resumed my search for Christy Mercer. I took a seat at the bar, and she came up to serve me. She was unmistakable. I ordered a drink and she served it, giving me a nice smile.

Even dressed in her bartender's uniform—white blouse and black skirt, with black pumps—she was extremely attractive. She is tall, statuesque, and moves with subtle grace. As I watched her, she began to cash up. She told the other bartender what I was drinking, and it was obvious she was about to leave. When she turned around from the cash register, I smiled at her and said, "You're . . ."

"Yes," she said pleasantly.

I told her who I was.

"Oh, hi. I got your note at Thanksgiving. How long are you here for?"

Her voice was gentle. Her expression was open, without guard or guile. I told her that I had to go to Potosi the next day. She explained that she was doing a college degree at night, and had an exam in an hour's time, so she couldn't stop to talk. We made a date for the following Sunday.

I asked her what she was studying.

"Criminal justice," she told me. "I've only got a few more credits to go before I get my bachelor's degree. How is A.J.?" she asked.

I told her he was doing fine. I meant, as well as could be expected under the circumstances.

She understood well enough. "Tell him hi from me."

T HE NEXT day, I set out for Potosi at 6 A.M. It was a sunny morning, and the drive from Jefferson City, which had become familiar by now, was pleasant.

The only key persons involved in the execution process whom I had yet to meet were the doctor and Gary Tune, the chaplain at Potosi. After drinking a cup of coffee with Paul Delo, he arranged for Gary Tune to come up and see me. We met in Phil Banks's office.

Gary Tune is a slightly odd-looking man. Unkempt, and with a fat, flesh-colored hearing aid in one ear, he didn't give the impression of one best suited to a pastoral role. While he agreed to be interviewed, he seemed rather uncomfortable at the prospect.

Before coming to Potosi, Gary Tune had spent five years as the pastor of a Baptist church in Fredericktown, forty-two miles south of the prison. I was interested to know why he had left a comfortable position to work at Potosi.

"I felt God leading me into another area," he told me in his broad country accent. "I started out in prison ministry as a volunteer. I used that as a testing ground to prove this particular direction,'' he explained. After six months of volunteer work, he applied for the job at Potosi and was selected from a shortlist of seven interviewees.

"Why did you choose to work in a prison?"

"Why? I've been pretty much a fighter for the underdog much of my life, and most of my ministry. I wanted to get out and minister with the nitty-gritty. Some of the church members, the ones with the suits and ties, didn't like that.''

"But why choose death row?" I asked. "Why choose Potosi as opposed to some other situation?''

He told me, "The Bible says that the healthy don't need a doctor. Those that are sick need a doctor. And that's my attitude on salvation and Christianity.''

"What was your previous prison experience like?" I asked.

He told me that he'd been at Farmington. "There you're dealing with Level Three and Level Four inmates. Then, coming over here, you're looking at guys who are in for nothing less than fifty years. That kind of overwhelms you, the thought of that. And death row was overwhelming.''

"Why?"

"At first, there was a sense of intimidation. And then, as time goes on, you find out that they're just people. That in here, in this institution, it's a society all of its own. It's a different breed than what you're used to on the street. You tend to play by a little different rule book. They run games on you. But people on the street run games on you. It's just a different level.''

I asked Chaplain Tune whether he found many believers among the inmates at Potosi. He told me that when inmates are received into the prison, they complete a questionnaire that asks what religion they are. It also includes a category of "no known religion.''

"The computer says there are one hundred seventeen Baptists, one hundred sixty other Protestants, and ninety Catholics. That's maybe what they had a connection with, but it doesn't mean they're firm in that belief,'' he told me.

"Since there is an option to mark 'no religion,' '' I asked, "do you find it interesting that they elect to call themselves Baptists or Protestants or Catholics?''

"By and large,'' said the chaplain, "most of them are not practicing.''

I learned from my conversations with inmates that the chaplain was one of the least popular staff members at Potosi. Betty Weber had mentioned that of the five men executed at Potosi, only one had requested to see Tune prior to being put to death.

"How do you find your role here? Was it difficult to establish relationships with inmates when they arrived three years ago?"

"It is a job to establish credibility," he replied. "It's tough. You're staff, therefore you're a cop. Because you're part of the administration, you make decisions. And you make decisions they don't like."

"Such as?"

"You've got a policy and procedure you go by; you've got rules you've got to go by. From time to time, an inmate does something he's not supposed to. And if you witness it, you end up having to write him a ticket. So you lose that credibility with them."

"Does the cop function compromise your ministry?"

"There's no way around it. What would be neat is if I had no authority. Then I could walk out and talk with the inmates, and they'd say, 'This guy has nothing to do with where I am or what's going on in here.' In here, they're real quick to say, 'It's us against them.' And they say, 'Which side are you on, Chaplain?' But the very nature of the job demands that you've got to abide by the policy."

In many respects, I found it much easier to understand how Bill Armontrout, Paul Delo, and the other members of the execution team rationalized their roles. It seemed to me that Gary Tune's position would be difficult to square with the role of Christian minister, just as the doctor's role in executions might be difficult to square with the Hippocratic oath, or the American Medical Association sanction against doctors participating in executions. Before asking Chaplain Tune about how he reconciled executions with Christian belief, I wanted to know how participating in them had affected him personally.

He took his time considering my question. He warmed to his answer by telling me about Gerald Smith, the first man to be executed at Potosi.

"I had developed a little bit of a relationship with Gerald. He and I had talked a time or two. These guys—and I think I'm giving a fair description of Gerald—Gerald was hollow. There was nothing there. There was just an empty shell of a man. Spiritually. In that aspect, I felt pity for him. As far as the execution, the fact that his life is taken, let me *separate* just a little bit. I look on the spiritual side of things, as a man who believes there is an eternity, who believes that there is a life after death. Our actions and decisions in this world are going to make the determination as to where our boat is in the next world. And I look at a man such as him, and I see that he is stripped of all spirituality. He is practically a man who has no soul."

I looked at the chaplain. I didn't understand what he meant.

"I don't say it judgmentally. I say it as I can see him. I feel sorry for him. The fact that he's entering into eternity with nothing. Ill prepared. Not prepared. I look at it, and I see the greater question should be eternity, and not the matter of this physical life. A man lives—Gerald was thirty-five— so you say, 'What's he got left, another thirty-five, forty-five years of earthly life?' You *could* say, 'Oh, let's let him live.' Or you could also consider eternity. And I'm more concerned about his preparation for eternity than whether or not he gets another thirty-five or forty-five years of physical life. And with Gerald, there was nothing there."

"Let's say that Gerald Smith had received life and fifty rather than the death sentence," I proposed. "Do you think there was any chance that his spiritual side might have developed?"

"That's a judgment call. From what I could see, I don't think so. Now, I believe in miracles. We've got some individuals down there who were not any less cruel, or any less of a hard person than what he was, and yet I have seen a change in their life. Coming to a point of repentance."

Yet the chaplain still felt that executing Gerald Smith was the correct solution.

"Of the five executions," he continued, "my perception has been that they have been hollow. Void of spirituality. Like Mr. Delo says, we've had a run of atheists and Muslims. There was one, he was a nice guy and easy to get along with. I had enjoyed a relationship with him. But he was a man who could put up a front. He could smile and be friendly to you, but inside he was empty. Stokes was one that had two sides to him; he could be smiling at you while he was stealing from you."

I repeated my original question about what effect executions had on him personally. "What about the first one," I asked. "You'd had no experience of executions. How did you find it?"

"Exhausting. You're running on adrenaline. You're stressed out. And when it's all said and done, because you're running on the adrenaline of stress, it's anticlimactic. And I've talked to some others. I've talked to Mr. Roper. He and I are pretty close in our spiritual connections. I said, 'How do you feel?' And he said, 'Blank.' I said, 'Blank? That's it?' And he said, *'That's all I'm feeling. Blank.'* There's nothing there. You keep thinking there's going to be some emotion. You're searching for something. *How do I feel?* It's just a blank. And we feel like we've determined that you're running at such a high level of stress that it just takes it all out of you."

I listened in silence.

The chaplain continued, interviewing himself: "Reflection? I don't know. Stress takes the reflection out of it."

"If the level of stress meant you couldn't feel anything on the day of the execution, or just after, how did you feel when you were building up to the first one?" I asked. "You couldn't be running at such a high level of stress all the time."

"Yeah," he said. "I wondered, 'How is this going to affect me?' You're concerned about that. And you don't know. And, at the same time, I'm concerned about the inmate. And you do what you can."

Which, I knew, was nothing, at least to date.

"The first time we had a—I don't want to say a dry run, it was an aborted attempt, Leonard or George, one of them—anyway, we got within six hours of the execution, then we stood down. During that time I was very restricted in my access to the inmate. The security around here was just overwhelming. I could not go to the inmate unless that inmate requested me. There had been some lawsuits up in Jefferson City," he explained, "by inmates not wanting to be bothered by any spiritual individual, any religious individual. Some grievances had been filed saying, 'Get that preacher man out of here,' and I don't know what caused it."

The chaplain explained how he pleaded with Paul Delo to be allowed to at least ask whether Gerald Smith would see him. Paul agreed that he could visit him in the holding cell.

"I went in to Gerald. I visited with him. I asked him if he was at peace with God. Of course, he tells you one thing, but you can see in his eyes something else. And he said, 'Yes.' I came back the next day and saw him. And then I received a message saying, 'Gerald's complaining, saying you woke him up.' I didn't think I woke him up. I may have, but I didn't think so. So Mr. Delo says, 'Don't come back.' Since then, the procedure has been, I'll call on the phone, down to the holding cell, and I'll say, 'Officer, I'd like to see the inmate if he'll receive me.' And if that inmate says yes, then I go on. If he says no, I don't."

I mentioned that, as far as I knew, there hadn't been much call for him in the holding cell.

"At first," he explained, "I had no relationship with any inmates. As time goes on, I began to develop relationships with the inmates, realizing that some of those relationships are negative and some are positive. As time goes on, whether I'm received is going to depend on that relationship."

"So what is your involvement in the Missouri Protocol? What's your role, and what procedure do you follow in the execution plan?"

"The procedure on the day in question? I'll come in on that day and check on the inmate. And then, too, I'll look at staff. We will have, after our briefing meeting around six o'clock, a devotional time set aside for the staff who want to stay. We do it in the training room, in the assembly room. Of course, most of the staff don't stay. Only a handful will stay. And it's something I sometimes wonder: Am I being effective, or is there some other way I could deal with staff? After the devotional time, usually the inmate is visiting with his family. So usually the psychologist and I will just kind of roam around, from the housing units. We visit in the bubbles with the officers. We're looking at the stress level of the officers coming in. I asked one officer, 'I don't feel like I'm doing anything.' And he said, 'You don't realize what your presence means.' And I said, 'What do you mean?' He says, 'You walked by the office where I was with several other people, and just your presence seems to bring a sense of peace.' Sometimes, some of the inmates themselves will be stressed out. And we have a couple that, at least every other time, they flip out. So we'll go visiting. We'll go out into the wings and visit with the inmates. Those that want to talk. And some of them do. They're mellow. They're depressed. Hey, some of them have been together for a long time. The older hands, they've been around for ten or twelve years, and they've developed relationships themselves. And so they realize, this is a friend of theirs that's being executed. And there's an emotional impact on them. So we're out there trying to deal with them, minister to them."

"When it gets close to midnight, what do you and Betty do then?"

"Usually, around the time of the execution, as it gets close, both of us are back in the hospital area. As much as anything else, just on standby. Because that's when the element of the highest stress comes in, the highest emotions. To be there not only for staff, but you're looking to be there for family. Maybe the family may need some help in some way. Part of the reason that Betty and I run together is that sometimes people say, 'I'd like to talk to somebody, but I don't want to talk to that preacher.' The other individual may take it the opposite, and say, 'I want to talk to somebody that is a minister.' "

Gary told me that he sometimes has to work late on execution nights.

"A couple of times, during the time of the execution, a call would come in that inmates were upset over in the housing units. We'd go back to housing units at twelve-thirty or one, and there's times I haven't got out of here until two or two-thirty, 'cause we go back and deal with the inmates then. And just try and talk with them, talk them down. And, occasionally, you might have a staff person that might want to talk at that point. So, sometimes the night doesn't end at midnight. It ends later on."

"What's your impression of the process? Of executing people by lethal injection?"

"It's extremely sanitary. And I think that's part of why I feel it's anticlimactic. If you see a guy in a chair, and you see him jerk, and go through all the gyrations they do, or even if you watch the movies about when they hung people, it would seem to have an impact on you. But this is so sanitary. The guy just goes to sleep. That's all there is to it. All of a sudden. And when it's said and done, he breathes a sigh, and he's gone."

I asked: "Do you think that the feeling of blankness you experience might be different if they still used the old gas chamber, or the electric chair? Would that have more impact on people watching?"

The chaplain answered indirectly, giving his view of lethal injection. "It's remote. I think that would be a good word, remote. Just distant. We pick up a newspaper and read about something happening clean across on the other side of the nation, and now we're having something that's happening right here just in the next room to you, but because it is so sanitary, it just seems completely remote."

I nodded.

"The older I get," he continued, "it seems the things that impacted me in my younger days don't bother me as much. You look at death from a different perspective. I have some of my kinfolks that have died, and it doesn't have the same impact on me as it used to."

"Have you ever discussed lethal injection with any of the inmates?" I asked.

"I've never got into any discussion with any of them on that."

Gary did tell me that he'd had conversations on the morality of the death penalty, and that he was surprised to find that some of the inmates were pro–capital punishment. But he also found it disturbing.

"For you and I to discuss the right or wrong of an execution is one issue," he said. "But to me, for an inmate to say it—he didn't feel any compunction about going out and committing his crime. And so I don't know that he's got a right to discuss the subject."

Chaplain Tune, not surprisingly, perhaps, took the view that "there can be no acceptance of death unless you believe in eternity. How can you come to a point of acceptance if that acceptance means 'That's it, it's over'? You've earned a nonexistence. So, that individual, I don't know whether he ever works past denial. Maybe that's why they're so hollow."

My last question to Chaplain Tune was so obvious that I nearly forgot to ask it. "How do you square executions with Christianity?"

"Difficult. My personal belief is this. If you want to take the Old Testament, you can build a solid case for the death penalty. In the Old Testament it says, 'Thou shalt not kill, but if you shed the blood of an innocent person your life shall be taken.' So there is a good argument for it. You come to the New Testament, and the New Testament speaks of grace and forgiveness and whether we shall forgive an individual for whatever he has committed. And so there is another side to it. And, of course, you can become very liberal on that and say, 'We should give him just a very light sentence'; or you can say, 'Well, they should do something, but it should not be the death penalty.' My personal belief is, and I base this biblically, the Scribes and Pharisees came to Jesus and they said, 'Is it lawful to pay taxes?' And rather than answer their question directly, Jesus asked for a coin. They gave Him one, and He said, 'Whose inscription is on it?' And they said, 'Caesar's.' And He said, 'Render unto Caesar that which is Caesar's, render unto God that which is God's.' So I've come to the conclusion that the death penalty is not a spiritual issue. It's not a Christian issue. This is our government, it's what our government has said we will do, and we will abide by that. And so from that basis, I come over to Romans, where it tells us that we should render unto the higher authorities and higher powers over us. And if our government says it will go with a life sentence, I'll agree with that. If our government says, 'Go with the death penalty,' I must accept that.''

DURING THAT week, Walter Blair received a death warrant, which was stayed twenty-four hours after it was issued.

It was the end of February, but the weather at Potosi was springlike, and over a week-long period, the temperature got up to eighty degrees. I met A. J. Bannister again on one of those warm days, and we were allowed to sit and talk in private for half a day. We alternated between sitting in the interview room and strolling out in the yard for a cigarette.

A.J. offered his commentary on a number of recent court cases, including the William Kennedy Smith rape trial, the Tyson rape trial, and the Dahmer conviction. It seemed to him grossly unfair that in one state, a murderer could cannibalize his victims and receive a life sentence, while in another state, a homicide like the one he had committed—which, with a different attorney, could have resulted in a conviction for second-degree murder or manslaughter—ends in a death sentence.

I speculated that Mike Tyson might have a difficult time in prison.

"Oh, I don't think so," said A.J. "He'll fit right in. He'll be Mike Tyson the boxer—for a while. Then he's just going to be Tyson, with a number behind his name."

I asked A.J. whether there had been any progress with his appeals.

"I still haven't heard anything. But I've been doing some things since then. In early December, we had a man die over in Illinois. Richard Speck. He died of a heart attack. He was notorious throughout the Midwest. He killed nine nurses in Chicago in the mid-sixties, and he's the one they pinpoint as the beginning of serial killing. I heard about his death, and the local radio station up in St. Louis picked it up, and made a big farce out of the fact that no one came forward to claim his body. He was that much of a monstrosity. And they were making jokes about it. And I got to thinking, if my appeal gets turned down, I know that they set the execution date about ten days off. Like Walter Blair, who heard last Monday that his appeal had been turned down. On Tuesday, he knew the execution date, which was March fifth—until it got stayed. There's not much time in between to make any preparations. So I got to thinking about what the policy is after an execution here. And it's sort of sad, because these people are given a pauper's burial. And because I'm not from this state, the last place I want to rest in peace"—A.J. laughed—"or whatever, is in the state of Missouri. And I've come to find out that you've got to make your own preparations—a will, and everything else—to get out of state. And they wouldn't have told me this."

"How did you find out?"

"I had to circumvent these people to get it. Delo's response was, 'You'll find out at the appropriate time.' And with ten days left, what am I going to do, beg money from everybody to take care of costs? So what I did is, I wrote to family and friends, close friends, and basically spelled it out to them. That I needed this to get this done, and this is why."

A.J. explained that he wrote the letter on an electronic typewriter, then printed off copies and personalized them by hand. He said he felt bad about doing it that way, but that dwelling on such an unpleasant subject by writing it down over and over again was too much.

"It was sort of stressful, because with each letter, it just sort of hit home, the fact that I'm getting into dire straits here. And it's not a musical group."

He calculated that if he asked each of his family and close friends for fifty dollars, it would raise enough money to take care of transporting his body from Missouri to Illinois for burial. He told me he was very anxious that the financial burden not fall to his mother. He was more concerned that she shouldn't dwell on the problem until it arose, and so he asked everyone not to discuss it with her.

"I didn't want to give the impression to these people that I'd given up hope," he said. "And some of them got that impression. But I just wanted to get it taken care of now, so it's not a financial burden on my family at the end. Because they're going to have other things to worry about at that time. And so am I. I pretty much explained to them that this is why I'm doing this now, when I have some time to think it out and look at it objectively. But I just *do not* want to stay here in Missouri. Once I've done my time here, I want to go anywhere else."

A.J. showed me a copy of the letter. It summarized where he was with his appeals. That his writ of habeas corpus had been denied in the Western District Court on August 23, 1991. He then filed a Motion to Recall the Mandate in the Missouri Supreme Court on September 16, which was denied on September 20. On September 23 he filed a Motion to Reconsider. After that is ruled on, A.J. will have to file his last appeal to the Eighth Circuit Court. He told his friends: "If I'm turned down there, the Missouri Supreme Court will set an execution date about 10 days off. My lawyers will then file a number of appeals into various courts trying to get me a stay of execution, because I've already been forced to use my rule 60b, which is routinely saved till the last to circumvent what's known as 'successive habeas petitions.' I will not be allowed to use it a second time, and in all likelihood will be put to death."

In the letter, A.J. explained that he'd looked into funeral costs back in 1988, when prices for cremation ranged from $875 to $1,000. He'd checked again recently, to find out that they'd risen to between $1,000 and $1,400.

"It is sort of stressful to have to start thinking about things like that. For years and years, I've always felt that I was aware that I was in pretty serious shit here. And I wasn't of the mind-set that, *This isn't going to happen to me*. I just pretty much held on to the hope that things would change. But I've got ten years in now, and it's not going at all well. I've got to think realistically about what will probably happen, and that's sort of rough. More and more I'm finding myself sitting late at night, thinking about . . ."

A.J.'s voice drops to a whisper.

". . . how am I going to act on that night? Am I going to punch that son of a bitch on the nose?"

For the first time since I'd know him, A.J.'s voice broke for a moment.

"And it's a real rough thing, like that."

He recovered and said: "It's not something I want to think about, but it's something that common sense tells me I ought to start thinking about, just to be mentally prepared a little bit for it. I don't know if anyone can psych themselves to it all beforehand."

"I suppose one thing to be optimistic about is that the Eighth Circuit does seem to be sitting on things, and not charging ahead with executions at the moment," I said.

"It depends on which judge you get out of the Western or Eastern District Court. And on what day of the week, it seems like. But this is an election year here in the United States, so I think that is going to speed up how the courts rule, and how quickly they rule. It's not going to surprise me if there's three, possibly four, executions between now and the end of the year. Blair will be one of them. Martsay Bolder will be another. Bobby Shaw could be one. Of course, Shaw might get out on this new House bill they have on mental competency. And there's a few others that are right at the end. Larry Griffin, Doyle Williams. There's a lot of them. In Walter's case, we know that he doesn't have much longer. The stage he's at now, nothing good is going to come out of it. It's just a stalling technique. I think Walter knows that too. I talked to him Wednesday morning, and I've known Walter since I arrived on death row. And I could see that keeping his composure was a real task for him. I think he's realizing that the end is coming."

A.J. told me that he'd gone to the gym the night before to play basketball, and that afterward he'd gone to the chapel to rest, because it's the coolest place in the building.

"I went in to cool off, and there were some ministers in there. I stood at the door, and I saw Walter there, right in the middle of the crowd. He's the most nonreligious person I know of. But there he was, right in the middle, and I thought, he's giving this serious consideration—getting right with God *now*. There's little things that you notice like that."

I also told A.J. that I'd finally tracked Christy Mercer down, and gave him her new name.

"I think she's been lost ever since Tiny was executed," he said.

I told A.J. that I'd met Chaplain Tune.

"What a joy that must've been," he laughed.

He said that the chaplain was bound to be disappointed at Potosi, since many of the black inmates belong to the black prison gang, the Moors, and some were serious in their Muslim belief. "He's not going to have much luck there," A.J. predicted. "I don't think he's all that holy at heart himself. I think he's found himself a permanent job here with a few benefits, and authority."

A.J. wanted to tell me some stories from the deathwatch cell that he thought wouldn't make it into the film for television. He pointed out that one of the ironies of being on deathwatch is that, just as you're about to lose your life, you can have pretty much what you want in the holding cell. He mentioned that the administration, apart from supplying a VCR and videos, also supplies items like Nintendo to distract the inmate.

"And one of the things," he began. ". . . I've not been with a woman in ten years. Well, seven, because I screwed one in my lap on a contact visit over at MSP. And they actually just let me get away with it. But the thing about here is, most of us know that we can have visitors during the day, and the guards aren't going to say anything. For years, we visited behind a screen. Here, with the contact visits, at the end of the visit, you get to kiss your visitor once and hug them, and that's your only human contact. And if you start squeezing on a boob or anything else, that visit is *over*. Right then and there. And they suspend visits for six months or a year, put you behind the glass to visit. I was told I was going to have a visit terminated because I kissed this girl in the *middle* of the visit. The guard took me into the hall and said, 'One more time, and your visit's over.' They always push you right to the edge to see how far they can take you."

Talking about the possibilities for sex in the deathwatch cell, A.J. joked: "I'm going to screw a bunch of them. If I have five or six of them visit me when I'm over there, I'll never make it to the chamber because they'll probably all get jealous and kill me, right then and there. I can see the obituary. 'Killed by six jealous women.' All three hundred pounds or better. But you know that your last chance to share any intimacy is going to be followed very closely by your death. I have actually sat here and thought, wishing I could do like Doyle—go over there, have an execution date, get some pussy, and then get a stay. But I don't want to push it. It's rather like playing Russian roulette with a loaded gun."

Because I wanted more privacy than the caseworkers' offices afforded, I had been talking to A.J. in the attorney room of the administrative segregation wing—the hole. The door, which had a window, was closed. A.J. said: "Look, there goes Walter."

I stuck my head out the door and saw him from behind, being taken to the hole in handcuffs by two officers. He was wearing loose clothes, but it was easy to see what a well-developed physique he had—particularly his shoulder and neck muscles. Walter had received a stay of execution a few days before. I wondered if it had been lifted.

A.J. said he doubted that was why they'd come for Walter. "Maybe he got into a skirmish," he speculated.

After we heard the heavy steel door slam behind Walter Blair, we were allowed to go outside for a cigarette. The temperature had climbed up to around eighty degrees. Shadows fell across the stone walls of the prison at a forty-five-degree angle. A.J. put on a pair of round sunglasses with pink lenses.

"They'll get you a spell in the hole," I said. I had been studying the inmates' rule book, and had discovered that sunglasses were prohibited.

A.J. smiled. "I've got a medical dispensation. My cataract."

Although we'd enjoyed some light banter during our meeting that day, I had noticed a change in A.J. since we'd last met. He was more reflective, somewhat subdued. The death of Richard Speck had been one more event that caused A.J. to focus even harder on his situation. He still had hope; but what set him apart from most people on the outside, and a majority of people on the inside, was the way in which he forced his hope to collide with reality. A.J. expected the worst, but he was doing his best to help himself. He was pursuing his appeals, thinking out strategies. He was measuring a political climate in which the public was determined to support tough measures against crime but was not always willing to bear the tax burden. He was noting the fact that Missouri's prisons were already overcrowded with death sentence and life without parole inmates, and that the state could not possibly continue to hand down those sentences without a financial commitment that was not only unpopular with voters, but impossible: The state did not have unlimited funds for the elimination or indefinite warehousing of criminals. There was speculation that the Missouri legislature might commute the life without parole and life and fifty sentences to life. If that were to happen, and if A.J. could get his death sentence reduced to life, then it was conceivable he would be free again one day.

The trick was to entertain that hope while preparing for the more likely prospect of being executed in less than a year.

AFTER A.J. returned to his cell for a count, I went into the officers bubble in the administrative segregation unit, or the hole. Betty Weber was there, and we said hello. I could see that she was distracted, and I followed her eyeline to see what was going on in the unit. One of the female lieutenants was reading from a clipboard, flanked by a number of burly CO Is and CO IIs. Another officer was videotaping her statement.

"What's going on?" I asked.

"One of the inmates is refusing to take a TB test. He's been asked a number of times, and refuses to come out."

"So, what's the video for?"

"We're going to send a movement team in. Before we do that, we record what has happened, and then we record the movement team."

A.J. had told me about the movement team, or E-Squad. He referred to them as the goon squad. From his cell window he could watch them at their monthly training sessions, scaling the water tower near the prison, and going through their paramilitary-style exercises.

When the administration feels that an inmate needs to be subdued, they send in a team of six officers who are dressed in full riot gear, including padded black suits and black helmets with face masks. The first officer through the door wields a large Plexiglas shield, which backs the inmate up against the wall. The other officers secure his hands and feet.

I returned to the office just outside the ad seg unit and sat down to write up some notes. The officer there was rounding up people for the movement team. It took about half an hour to gather them all together. As they arrived, they pulled their riot gear from lockers; it was difficult for six burly men to suit up in the small room. After they put on their helmets and the point man picked up the riot shield, they marched down the corridor and pressed the buzzer that would admit them into the ad seg unit. The six men waited in a straight line for the officer inside to admit them. The door popped, and the black-suited men filed in. The door banged shut behind them. A few minutes later, I could hear the sounds of the movement team going into the cell, and the response of the other ad seg inmates as they beat on their doors and shouted at the top of their voices.

WOULD YOU like to go fishing this weekend?" Paul Delo asked before we went to lunch.

I hadn't been fishing for more than twenty years. I jumped at the prospect.

"This time of year we usually go to Clearwater, which is about an hour south of here," he said. "I can't guarantee that the fish'll bite, but the weather looks pretty good."

He told me that there would be five in our fishing party. Paul's wife, Sharon, and another couple, Kyle and Patti would be coming. We would be staying in a cabin in Piedmont, a couple of miles from the reservoir. He told me where to get a Missouri fishing license, and said he had spare fishing tackle I could use.

"Oh, and I hope you don't mind dogs. Mine will be coming," Paul said.

"What kind of dog is it?"

"A Pekinese," he said. "His name is Chi."

The thought of a large man like Paul with a little dog struck me as amusing. It suggested another side of him. It reminded me that he was a complex character, and not someone to be pigeonholed in any convenient way.

Paul and I picked up Greg Wilson, the investigator, and drove over to lunch at a Chinese restaurant in Flat River, halfway between Potosi and Farmington. Greg told me that his old truck had died temporarily since we last met. He was thinking about buying a late-model used car, but was hesitating committing to a loan because of his impending divorce. Greg was still hurting from his wife's departure at the end of the previous summer; and now the divorce proceedings were turning acrimonious.

When we were driving back to the prison, I asked Paul why Walter Blair had been sent to the hole.

"Oh, Walter made some threats against one of the staff," he said.

"What kind of threat?"

"Well, he said that before he goes, he's going to fuck the librarian."

I was disappointed, because I wanted to meet Walter. When an inmate is in the hole, he's not allowed any visits, except by his lawyer.

"How long will he be in for?" I asked.

"Walter's time is getting short," Paul said. "I may leave him in there right up to the end."

"I did want to talk to him," I said, disappointed.

"I guess we can let you," Paul told me. "But he'll have to be handcuffed. You can use the attorney interview room over in ad seg."

I thanked Paul for bending the rules so much. "Would it be all right if I'm alone with him? I think it would be difficult to talk if there was an officer in the room."

Paul thought it over and said: "Okay. But I'll have to keep an officer posted outside the door, where they can see in."

"Thanks," I said.

"Hey, Steve," Greg called out.

"What?"

"Go easy on Walter."

O N SATURDAY, I woke up at 5:00 A.M. and packed warm clothes for the weekend's fishing. At 6:00, Paul and his wife, Sharon, pulled up to my motel in a red pickup with white trim and a sixteen-foot bass boat hitched to the rear. His Pekinese, Chi, sat on the front seat between him and Sharon.

Even at that early hour, it promised to be a magnificent day. It was hard to believe that it was the first weekend in March, and the forecast was for temperatures in the nineties. Sharon and I had a hearty breakfast of biscuits, gravy, sausages, and potatoes in the motel restaurant. Paul ordered an omelet, and we all drank plenty of coffee.

Paul's truck was a little crowded with Chi in the front, so I followed in my car. We took Highway 67 south, past Fredericktown, where Gary Tune had been minister of a Baptist church, and on to Silva, where we turned left onto 34 and crossed the St. Francis River. We drove through small towns with tiny, run-down houses, and shortly we passed through Piedmont. We found our cabin, which was situated near the junction of the road that led to Clearwater.

Paul's friends Kyle and Patti had arrived before us and opened up the cabin. It was one of four situated on one side of Highway 34, on a little bluff overlooking a creek. Across the road was a pine wood. Our cabin had a screen porch, and inside was a large living room with television, sofa, chairs, and a double bed. There was a decent kitchen off to the left, and there were two bedrooms at the back.

When we arrived, Kyle was checking his boat. He wore a plaid hunting jacket, and a baseball cap the wrong way around, with the brim pulled down hard against the collar of his jacket. He and Paul were old friends and had known each other since Kyle had been in corrections, and then probation. Patti also worked in the system. Kyle came up to shake hands.

"So, this is the Englishman, huh?"

"Yeah, sort of. He's American, really."

Kyle assumed a humorous manner, casting himself as a yokel. He asked me how I liked Missouri.

"I certainly have met a lot of interesting people," I said.

I went inside and met Patti, an attractive woman with a practical, commonsense air about her.

"What do you think about baloney sandwiches for lunch?" she asked.

"Great," I said.

Kyle came in and said: "Do you want to see *my* baloney sandwich?"

I didn't really know what to say. I looked at Paul, who had just come in carrying the two cases of beer we'd brought. He just smiled.

"Let me show you my baloney sandwich," Kyle said.

He pulled out an object which looked like a couple of sandwiches wrapped in tinfoil.

"Now, if I'm out in the woods, and somebody tries to start something, what I do is say: 'Would you like some of my baloney sandwich?' "

I was still perplexed.

"It kind of wrong foots them, you see. Now, if they still want to mess with me, I'll let him have some of my baloney sandwich."

Kyle unwrapped the foil, to reveal a .45-caliber pistol.

"Hey, Steve, you like to read, right?" Kyle continued.

"Sure."

"Here's something you might like."

Kyle pulled a book off one of the kitchen shelves. It was an old hardback copy of a book by Jessica Mitford called *The American Way of Death*.

Kyle handed it to me. "Go on, open it up."

I took the book and opened it. The pages had been cut neatly to make a secret compartment. Inside was a .25-caliber pistol.

Kyle took it back from me. "Can't be too careful," he said.

*   *   *

We spent a pleasant couple of hours getting our gear ready and loading the boats with the day's supplies. I asked about the fish we were after.

"Croppies," said Paul. "They're a little like a bass. They don't grow too large. A twelve-inch croppie is a good fish."

"Someone said the bass were running," Kyle added.

"We'll see," said Paul.

We had a discussion of what bait to use. Kyle had brought minnows. Sharon said she thought worms would be best. I asked if lures worked, and Kyle said that a spoon or a jig sometimes did the trick.

"Really," said Sharon, "I've had just as much luck with a piece of tinfoil or a hunk of baloney."

"Whatever it takes," said Paul.

While it was warm in the sun, there would be a wind on the reservoir. We all erred on the side of prudence in dressing warmly for the day.

Clearwater is formed by a dam at one end of an abandoned mining site. It's a good three miles long and a mile and a half wide, and is surrounded by state and national parkland. When we got to Clearwater it was midmorning, and the parking lot was half-full of pickup trucks and boat trailers. Sharon expertly backed Paul's truck up to the water's edge. Paul started the outboard and eased the boat off the trailer and out onto the water. Paul drove off in a large circle around the front of the dock, warming the engine, while Sharon parked the truck.

I knelt on the dock, holding the boat, while Chi and Sharon climbed in. I got in and we set off for the far end of the reservoir, with the sun beating down and the wind in our faces. Kyle and Patti caught up with us a few minutes later, and we settled down to fish with our boats fifty feet apart.

Both our boats had fish finders—electronic devices which identified the location and depth of our prey. The fish finder told us that the fish were on the bottom, so we baited our hooks and fished deep for the first two hours. For the first hour, no one had a bite.

Paul asked: "You about ready for a beer?"

I said I was, and reached back into the ice-filled cooler we'd brought with us.

"Going fishing isn't necessarily about catching fish," he observed.

"You don't have to be hungry to eat doughnuts," I replied, reciting my brother-in-law's favorite truism.

As we fished, Kyle struck up conversations with other fishermen as they passed by. The one party that had been catching fish was using bobbers, fishing at a depth of about three feet. Kyle announced this news, and we all promptly reeled in and set our bobbers.

Within minutes, Kyle and Patti were rewarded with fish. Sharon got one, then Paul. From then on, Kyle didn't go more than an hour without catching a fish.

At lunchtime, we drew our boats together and anchored near the far shore. We ate our sandwiches with potato chips and beer and hot cheese.

The afternoon's fishing finally brought success for me, and we went home that evening with about fifteen croppies. We went out behind the cabins and filleted them on an old table the owner had set up for the purpose. Kyle gave me expert instruction, and after an hour we had a couple of pounds of fillets ready for the deep freeze.

After going out for dinner in Piedmont, we watched television and drank beer in the cabin. Everyone had caught the sun, and we were all ready for bed by eleven. Paul warned me that he was a light sleeper and that, being a military man, he always got up early. I said I was an early riser by nature. He smiled skeptically.

I woke up around four-thirty, and could hear Paul moving about in the kitchen. I climbed out of bed and had the coffee going by quarter to five. Kyle was up next, and we prepared breakfast while Sharon and Patti slept. Paul addressed breakfast duty as a military exercise, and produced biscuits, gravy, bacon, and eggs that were as good as I'd had in Missouri.

It had turned cold overnight, and there was frost on the trucks and boats. We tuned into the Weather Channel, and passed the time in a lengthy speculation about what the day would bring. It had dropped to near freezing in St. Louis. And in Cape Girardeau, less than fifty miles east of where we were, the temperature was well below freezing.

It had warmed considerably by the time we got to Clearwater for our second day's fishing. By lunchtime we had stripped off our warm clothes, and I was comfortable in a T-shirt. There were a lot of people on the water, but it was an excellent morning of fishing nonetheless. Paul, Sharon, and I had hauled in ten fish by lunchtime. Paul lost the biggest fish of the trip—a fourteen-inch croppie—bringing it into the boat. Kyle didn't believe it, since he had caught a twelve-inch fish the day before.

After lunch, the fish stopped biting. Paul and I had a long talk about the film I was proposing to make, and we agreed on a schedule. The film would be shot in two parts. The bulk of the shooting would commence in two weeks' time. The rest would be done around the time of an execution. When that would occur was anyone's guess, and could never be the subject of a schedule made in advance.

It was about five o'clock by the time we got the boats back onto the trailers. Paul suggested that, in a week's time, we all meet at his house for a fish fry. We set the date, and said our good-byes until Tuesday. I had an appointment to meet Christy Mercer that night in Jefferson City.

I DROVE along the dam at the western shore of Clearwater and headed toward Ellington. I turned onto Highway 72 into Salem and on up to Rolla, where I picked up 63 to Jefferson City. The drive took me through some of the most beautiful countryside in Missouri, and I arrived at my hotel feeling tired, with my face and neck red from the sun and wind, but refreshed by a weekend in the open air.

I had arranged to meet Christy in the lounge of one of the hotels in town at 11 P.M. She was on her way to Memphis that night, but agreed to spend an hour with me between finishing work and setting off on the drive to Tennessee.

She found me in the lounge, and I stood up and took her hand. I offered her a drink, but she told me she didn't touch alcohol. She ordered a tonic water, and showed me some newspaper clippings about Tiny.

It was a difficult interview to start. But I didn't need to. Christy had things she wanted to tell me.

"It's wrong," she said. "It's killing. No matter what these men have done, it isn't right to kill them because they killed someone else."

Christy smiled, but her eyes gave away her sadness when she told me about Tiny.

"He was a beautiful man. He was so close to God. And he was always good to me. Right up to the end."

Christy said it had been difficult sometimes, working two jobs to make ends meet, and only being able to see her husband for an hour at a time.

"Sometimes, you know, I'd be feeling low because of this problem or that. And he was always understanding. He'd talk to me about it. And he had more problems than I did. He was on death row."

I told Christy all of the things that other death row inmates had said about Tiny. It pleased her to hear my secondhand knowledge of him. I think it made her feel that, at least in memory, he continued to live, and that the memories were good ones.

I told her that I had met with Bill Armontrout a couple of times. I told her how he had explained that he was friends with Tiny, and that he found it a difficult task to have to execute him.

"Bill is not a bad man," Christy said. "I see him from time to time. I don't blame him. But he will have to answer to God."

I wanted to ask Christy about the story A.J. had told me in his letter—about how he came to discover that an unwritten part of the Missouri Protocol was to insert a rectal plug and catheter into the person about to be executed. Christy had found out when she had dug up her husband's body.

"I understand that Tiny's last request was denied," I said.

"Yes. They wouldn't let him wear his jacket."

But Christy understood the real purpose of my question, and she told me the story.

"You know, when they killed him, it was really difficult for me. It was hard that night. Everything went so quickly. They killed him, and then the funeral home. I needed to say good-bye to him. So, with a friend, I went to the graveyard and dug up his body. I just wanted to see him again."

The waitress came by to ask if we wanted another drink. When she left, Christy resumed the story.

"It was terrible. I opened the coffin. His face was all . . ."

Christy told me about the experience in detail. She was very open and direct. She knew that, in her mind, she had done something that made sense. Another person might find it incomprehensible. It made no difference to her. She told her story, and left it to me to make what I would of it.

Christy simply couldn't bear the fact that she would never see her husband again. The circumstances under which he was put to death were horrible for her—to see him laid out on a hospital gurney, covered with a sheet, surrounded by strangers who stared from behind a thick glass window at him to watch him die. The events had been so traumatic that she could hardly take them in. After that terrible night, she wanted to see her husband one more time.

She lent me some newspaper clippings, and said she had to go. She would be away for a week, but looked forward to meeting again.

I asked Christy if she had any photographs of Tiny. She promised to bring them next time we met.

DURING THE first week in March, A.J. introduced me to another of his friends at Potosi. Joe Amrine is thirty-six years old, black, and has been on death row since September 1986 for the murder of another inmate at MSP. Joe carries himself elegantly, with an economy of movement. His voice is soft but deep. He immediately struck me as articulate—a serious man.

Joe looked at me carefully rather than suspiciously as I explained about the film I was making. As with A.J. when I first met him, I could see him sizing me up, making a decision about me. I started by asking him how he compared Potosi with MSP.

"When we was at MSP, in some ways it was better, and some ways it wasn't. We was locked down more when we was up there. But there was more unity. And as far as conditions wise, the conditions up there was a lot worse than they are down here. But being transferred has its bad points and its good points."

"How do you find the officers here at Potosi compared to MSP?" I asked.

"Most of the guards I run into here are . . . I would want to call them hillbillies."

"A.J. did time in the hole for calling one of them a 'hillbilly fuck,' " I said.

"Yeah," Joe laughed. "See, most of them are new. They ain't never worked in a penal institution before. So they come in with an attitude. Then the fact we're death row inmates—I guess they don't want to show signs of being intimidated by us, but at the same time they try to be hard, you know. Put up a front."

"What about the administration? What's your experience?"

"Naturally, I have a lot of animosity towards them. And I try to understand the executions, the court's point of view and everything. But I can't relate to that. Actually, I can't relate to the administration, period. Just two different types of people. We're the captives. They the keepers. And to me, they're the enemy. Because they trying to kill us. They're trying to kill us because we killed somebody; or allegedly killed somebody. It don't add up."

"What about racial discrimination here?"

"For me, it's something I've been used to. I've been locked up for fifteen years, so I'm basically used to that. But here at Potosi, it's even worse than at MSP."

"Why is that?"

"Because here, most of these guys, most of the white officers, I don't think they've *ever* been around any blacks before. And their mentality is just all messed up. Because they treat whites and blacks different here. They feel that blacks are supposed to be the more dominant group, the more aggressive. And there's just a big difference between their attitudes towards the blacks—from the CO Ones all the way up to Mr. Delo. It creates problems with the administration and the blacks; and it also creates problems between the black inmates and the white inmates."

"Is there a lot of racial tension between inmates here?"

"Well, I'm the type of person, I've been locked up so long around the whites and blacks, I'm like this here: If you dislike me because I'm black, naturally I'm going to dislike you. Unless you do something wrong to me, then I have no reason to dislike you. I'm willing to accept people as they are. Because in my opinion, we're all here in this together. Whether you have a death sentence or a life and fifty years without parole, the results are going to be the same. They're here to kill us. So we are first convicts, and then we are white, and then we are black. We got to stick together."

"How do you spend your time here? How do you deal with the waiting?"

"I might go out and play baseball, basketball. Mainly basketball. Walk around. Just hanging out. Waiting on the mailman, hoping I get some mail. Going to the law library. There is not much to do *for real,* you know. Especially when you know you're just waiting here, idly sitting here, waiting to be executed."

"How do you deal with facing the possibility of being executed?"

"By accepting the fact that I'm either going to be executed or I'm going to get out. And if I accept the fact that I'm going to be executed, well, then you leave it at that. Because to dwell on it serves no purpose. And so the only thing to do is to accept that, and try to deal with that, and try to focus in on *right now.* Because these days—whether three years or four years from now—these may very well be my last days. I try to do what I can in them days. Try and keep that off my mind."

"When your fellow death row inmates are executed, what effect does that have on you? What about the execution of Winford Stokes, the first black man to be executed by lethal injection?"

"Stokes' execution? The only effect it actually had on me was the fact that he was the first black to be executed. As far as me and him being close, we wasn't. But the fact that he was executed made me sympathize with him, *because he was executed.* I don't think anyone should be executed. Period. Whether I like them or dislike them. As far as it having an effect on me? Tiny Mercer's execution probably had the most effect on me, because he was well liked and he was the first."

Joe had been on death row with Tiny Mercer for three years. Every inmate I had asked about Tiny added some new aspect to his character, making him a modern Missouri legend. It wasn't that anyone suggested Tiny had been a candidate for sainthood. It was simply that no one—staff or inmate—had anything other than admiration for him.

I asked Joe what his memories of Tiny were.

"Tiny? The part of Tiny which I knew was pure to me. He was a born-again Christian, no problems with anyone, everybody's friend. He just didn't have a care in the world. As long as he had his Bible, he knew he was at peace within his self and with the Lord. He was all right. He was nothing like the Tiny which caught that case. That was not the same one. No."

"After they executed him, how did you feel?"

"Everybody acted like they had been hit in the face. They woke up to reality. Nobody had been executed yet. When he was executed, I guess a lot of guys realized this wasn't no game, you know. Everybody stood a chance of being executed. I guess it affected everybody in certain ways."

"Did Tiny's execution make you think more about the possibility that you would be executed?"

"Well, I hadn't really thought about mine much. After Tiny was executed, basically all I thought about was the fact of him being executed and there probably would be some more executions. As far as my own execution, I try not to even think about it."

"But when you do?"

"When I do think about being executed, it's basically like anger. Probably a lot of fear, because nobody likes to be executed. I mean, just the thought of being executed is enough in its own to make me scared. But if that's what it's going to be, that's what it's going to be. Everybody likes to live, but if that's the way it's going to be, I like to think I'm ready when that time comes."

None of the death row inmates I spoke to had much affection for Winford Stokes. But A.J., Doyle, and Joe were all united in the view that the administration had acted callously in letting inmates off lock-down minutes after Stokes had been executed.

"Apart from that," I asked Joe, "did the Stokes execution cause you to feel anything else?"

"Well, the thing that was upsetting about Stokes's execution was the fact that it was an on-again, off-again execution. They set an execution date, then they gave him a stay two days later. A day after that, they issued another death warrant. You know, it's on and off. And the only thing I was thinking about was, if that was me over there—you know, the on and the off—I don't know what I would have did. I thought, that was real. That was a traumatic experience. It had to be. It just had to be."

I had heard that when Stokes was executed, some of his fellow inmates had cheered. I asked Joe if that had happened in his housing unit.

"Yeah," he said. "That really made me mad. Because I can understand not liking him; but to cheer on an execution when you're in the same predicament, it just don't make no sense. A lot of them just have their priorities mixed up. Because he was one of them, actually. What he did in the past, or anything else, shouldn't even have mattered other than the fact that he was being executed. And not only that, they cheered in front of the officers. And that really made me mad. I didn't appreciate that, and I hollered out my door and I said, 'The same one of y'all just laughing, when you go down there, somebody might laugh at y'all or cheer at y'all.' "

I discussed with Joe the conversation that A.J. had with Tiny Mercer prior to Mercer's execution, regarding the gas chamber versus lethal injection as a method of carrying out the death sentence. I asked Joe how he regarded lethal injection.

"I feel like this here: This is just the administration trying to make it seem as clean as possible. But to me, it don't matter how they do it. The bottom line is, you're executing them. You know, you cannot commit a clean murder. It's impossible."

"What about the fact that the prison doctor is involved in executions; does that bother you?"

Joe groaned. "The doctor." He laughed in disgust. "We got a doctor here, where you don't understand nothing he says. He don't want to listen to you, and I don't understand. He's just here. That's it, he's just here."

"What about the chaplain?" I asked.

"Reverend Tune." Joe spoke his name with derision. "I don't know if he's a *reverend* or not. But here in Potosi, we don't see him as a reverend. We consider him as a *officer,* as a guard. Because he do more of the officers' duties than he does of a reverend. He don't have no concerns for execution, or he don't have a sympathetic ear. He's primarily here when they search your cell, or put on the goon squad gear. He's one of them, barking orders and carrying his nightstick just like the other officers. So it's hard to relate to him in any fashion, like when you have a death in the family. It's like, you might as well go and talk to the guard rather than talk to him."

"What do you know about the execution process? The procedures they go through?"

"They never told me anything about the execution process. Basically, from reading the paper. Or you might pick up a few things from the officers, or guys who came over here from deathwatch. But they haven't told us anything about how it happens."

I asked Joe again: "What do you think about, when you consider your own situation? The fact that you might be executed?"

"I can't imagine what that would be like. I try not to think about it, even though I know I do. The only thing I think about, if I come down to that, is I hope and pray that I be strong enough, and I don't break down or I don't scream or I don't holler. Hopefully, I'll be able to take it like a man. I'm not saying that I would holler and scream out of fear—basically, out of anger. The majority would be out of anger. I can't imagine sitting in there in that room and seeing my family, my mother, and wanting to talk to her; but at the same time, I can't imagine hurting her by not talking to her, you know, saying, 'I don't want to see you.' I can't imagine any of that. That's going to be hard. No matter how it happens, it's going to really be hard."

"Do you think there's any point to the death penalty? Do you think it has any effect?"

"In my opinion, it doesn't do anything as far as the murder rate. But I actually believe people support the death penalty because the crime rate is so far out of hand. And I can understand that. But I don't think starting to kill people is going to solve their problem. I believe the problem stems way farther back than that, and that's not going to be the solution. You just can't keep killing people for killing other people."

"Being condemned to death, how do you feel that people outside view you? What sense do you get of how the public regards death row inmates?"

"I feel that the public views death row inmates as being animals. And I believe they get this conception from the media and the administration. Because the only thing you ever hear about death row on the news is when something bad happens, or when they have an execution date set. You don't hear anything about the good things about the death row inmates; you don't hear about the death row inmates that win reversals. So I think it's just a lot of propaganda which makes the public think that the death penalty is working, and that executions is good."

"Do you find an unfairness in the way the death penalty is handed out?"

"I believe there you come back to the racial thing. Discrimination. It depends on if you white, if you black, if you have money, if you don't have money. Basically, here in this society, there is a difference between whites and blacks, whether you in prison or on the streets, whether you in a courtroom or on the jobsite. There's a difference. They're treated different. And it's more pronounced in the courtrooms because the blacks don't have any money to afford attorneys, and the state takes advantage of that."

"What are the other factors that you see, that determine whether a man gets a death sentence as opposed to a life sentence?"

"The victim. Whether he's white or black. What county you come out of. Where you catch your case at. What prosecutor you have. There's a lot of things that play a role in whether you get the death sentence or life without parole. Maybe you might get lucky and have one black on your jury who might refuse, just flat out refuse, to give you a death sentence. And, naturally, you get life without parole. But nine times out of ten, if you get a jury, it's going to be all white, especially if you're black. And if you're black and you've got a white victim, then you're almost ninety-nine percent certain to get a death sentence. Whereas, if you're black and the victim was black, you stand a fifty-fifty chance.'

What was evident about A.J. and Doyle was that each of them had found a way to do their time, a way of facing the reality of their situation, while at the same time maintaining hope. Doyle spent most of his time at legal work, while A.J. was constantly writing, and communicated as much as he could with the outside world.

"How do you handle time?" I asked Joe.

"I try to keep busy all day long. I get up at eight-thirty, I go to the gym. Whether I just sit out on the bleachers, or walk the track, or play basketball, I'm not going to return to my cell until lock-down time, because there is nothing to do. I just try to keep active. It's bad enough sitting here idly waiting for them to kill me; I'm not going to go brain-dead just by sitting around doing nothing. I just try to keep busy."

I'd seen Joe playing basketball. He's an excellent player. I told him I thought so and he said, "Nah, I'm getting old." The truth is, he's better than a lot of college players half his age.

I said to Joe how unusual I found Potosi, compared to other prisons. I asked him how he found it, having come from one of the most notorious death rows to what is probably the most progressive capital punishment facility in the United States, where capital punishment inmates are integrated in general population.

"Death row inmates in this state have a lot of unity. That was one of the reasons why the administration here chose to mix death row with the general population inmates—because they had to find some way to try and shake that unity. So they figured if they put us out here with these guys, we would kind of branch out and that unity would not be as strong. And, you know, to a certain extent it has worked. It has worked."

During the months that I had been coming to Potosi, I had seen various tour groups being escorted around, and chaplain's volunteers coming in to talk with the inmates. Many of them seemed to take the view that the inmates had it better than they deserved.

"The appearance of this institution—it would appear to someone who didn't know any better, that we had it made. But actually, to me, this is like a tomb. Just a bunch of walking dead men. There is nothing to do. There is no way out. You go through the same thing every day, and you all waiting for the same thing. You waiting on tomorrow to do the same thing you did yesterday. You just basically on your own. You got to make do with whatever you can do in a day's time. If you get caught up doing nothing, then that's what your life going to be about. Nothing."

There had been considerable speculation that Bobby Shaw would be the next man to be executed in Missouri. Joe and he had been together at MSP, and I asked what his view of Bobby's situation was.

"Bobby Shaw? I guess you know the type of case he had, for killing an officer. He's been through hell and back with the prison guards, and I believe they are determined to execute him. If they don't execute nobody else, they going to make *sure* they execute him. I believe his situation is more like a political thing for the administration and the attorney general's office, because they feel he killed one of theirs. And they make you pay for that."

"Were you there when he killed the officer?"

"I was there. I didn't actually see the murder, but I seen when they was chasing him, and they was shooting at him, and telling him to drop the knife. And they attacked him right there on the spot. At MSP we was in the basement together, where he was being held at one time, and I was being held down there. And for them to go in his cell and just whup him at will, five or six times a week, was nothing. If they wasn't whupping him, they was keeping him full of some type of drug. Constantly harassing him. He just opened up a little bit more since we been here at Potosi, because he's coming into more contact with other inmates. And, like I said, we always had a lot of unity, and we try to help him as much as we can. Not so much giving him things, but trying to bring him back. Talk to him. Offering to play Ping-Pong with him, cards, or whatever, trying to save him. Because I can't imagine nobody being locked up all this time and not talking, not doing nothing. And that was the type of state he was in when we was at MSP, because he's in a one-man cell. No TV, no radio, no nothing. The administration there, they liked that. They liked that."

I told Joe that I'd got permission to talk to Walter Blair later that day. He was surprised to hear it.

"Like I said, this institution here—they are scared, simply because we are death row and we are life without parole. It seems to me like, by Blair being a big guy, and he's on death row, he intimidates them. And because of that, every chance they get, they want to lock him down. Because they are scared of him. He's not the only one; but he's primarily the one who they constantly harasses, because he speak up for what he believe in, and he's a good convict. And they don't appreciate that. He tries to instill unity among the inmates, and they don't appreciate that either. So every chance they get, they lock him down, or harass him. They going to take that opportunity. And you can believe they are hoping that he *do* be executed in the real very near future."

WALTER JUNIOR BLAIR'S reputation as the most dangerous inmate at Potosi Correctional Center is one that elicits a slight smile from some fellow inmates; but staff take it seriously. They are frightened of him, and that was evident in the way officers handled him as he was brought to see me, hands cuffed behind his back.

Walter Blair is CP#8. The only men on death row with numbers lower than his are Martsay Bolder and Bobby Shaw. Now thirty-one, Walter was sent to death row in 1981. He was convicted of the murder-for-hire shooting of a woman who had been scheduled to testify in a rape trial against a cellmate of his from a previous incarceration in a county jail. The state alleged he was paid $6,000 for the killing.

Walter Blair has striking, sculpted features. He speaks very slowly, in a deep voice which, for the most part, betrays little emotion. He had received a death warrant in the last week of February which had been stayed on February 25. I spoke to him a few days later, on March 3. Walter continued to be held in administrative segregation, and I suspected, from his speech, that he had been sedated.

Walter was led into the room. His presence was imposing. I waited silently, watching the officer hesitate before withdrawing to leave us alone. Walter had kept his eyes wide open and fixed on the ceiling while I waited for the officer to leave. When the door closed, he turned his gaze to me. I said hello and reached behind his back to shake one of his cuffed hands. It was an awkward maneuver, but it eased the situation. I found something a little embarrassing about the extraordinary precautions taken with Walter. It was like having a chained beast brought in for me to look at. I pulled up a chair for him to sit on. It was impossible for him to sit comfortably on his hands, but he ignored that and focused on me.

I began by congratulating Walter on having got a stay of execution.

He said: "These people don't seem to realize that."

He was referring to the fact that, having got a stay, he still remained locked up in the hole.

"So why are they keeping you here?" I asked.

"Well they said, prior to the day they locked me up, I was under investigation for possibly being intoxicated. I said I wanted a urine test, and I wanted to be examined by the nurse or the doctor."

"So you asked for a urine test."

"I *demanded* a urine test, and to be examined by the nurse or the doctor at the time they called this so-called investigation, so I could prove that I wasn't on any type of drugs or alcohol or whatever on the twenty-eighth. They refused to give me that because they want to keep me locked down, under investigation, for as long as possible, in case my stay is lifted."

"Why do they want to do that?"

"The administration here is scared of me. And they are scared of me more than any other death row inmate in this penitentiary."

"Why's that?"

"They feel that I'm going to kill them. And they talk about it all the time. Every time there's a ruling on my case, they put me under investigation. And every time I receive a stay, or my appeal is granted, then my investigation is 'resolved,' and they release me back to population."

We talked about Walter's appeals. When he received his death warrant on a Monday, he and his lawyer decided to wait until Tuesday to see what the courts would do before deciding which motions to file. Walter received a stay on Tuesday. He told me he read in the newspaper that he had thirty days to file his next motion to the Eighth Circuit. "And if the Eighth Circuit turned it down, I would be executed in thirty days. But this is something I'm used to. I've been going through it since I've been here. It's not strange. What do bothers me is the fact that every time the court rules on my case, they lock me up and take away my legal papers, preventing me from working on my case."

"You don't have your papers?"

"I do not have my papers at all. I cannot work on my case at all. And even if I was to be executed, it wouldn't be because I failed to fight, to keep it from happening. But these people are so scared, they're keeping me away from my legal papers to prevent me from putting up a fight."

"Did you think that the death warrant you received this time was a real one?"

"This time? No."

"So it didn't make you very worried?"

"No. Maybe next time. But, even so, it *was* real. I will fight my appeals until I can't fight them no more. Even if it is serious, I have no problem with that. I'd rather be dead than have to spend the rest of my life in this prison. I'd rather be executed than have to live around these, uh, people. Rednecks, hillbillies, honkies, whatever. They are straight-up racists. They don't treat none of the whites like this, and they are feared to death of me. No matter what I do. I can walk and just look at them, and they think that I'm going to do something to them. And they panic, and they run for cover. And I ain't never seen an institution like this. I ain't never seen an administration like this. I'd rather be at MSP. I wish we never came here. If you speak up, they think you're crazy. If they raise their voices to you, and you raise your voice back, they feel that you're a madman. I feel like I'm human, I'm a man. I've got the right, if you disrespect me, I'll disrespect you. But they lock you up, tell you you can't have no toilet paper, put you in a strip cell, and just aggravate you. And hope like that they can break you. And then, when you get out, they say, 'How you doing?' They smile in your face. Like you ain't supposed to have an attitude, the way they treat you. I've never seen anywhere like this."

"When did you arrive at MSP?"

"I went to MSP January fifteenth, 1981."

"On the case you've got now?"

"Murder."

"But a lot of people talk about how horrible it was at MSP, compared with here."

"MSP was horrible in a way. No recreation. You had recreation, but it was caged down there in the cellar. But in spite of all that, the officers down there treated you like humans. They didn't come in there and try to torture you, they didn't mess with you. They knew that you had a problem, they knew that a problem can come from family, or working on your case, or being stressed out about being locked up. And they came up to you and dealt with it. They talked to you. The officers down there, they was trained to treat you more like a person. You had one or two officers down there who messed with people, but not like here. These people here don't have no type of understanding whatsoever. They talk real nice when there's visitors, and they clean the place up. And as soon as they're gone, you're back to Cambodia, or someplace. You'd think you was in a Vietnam prison camp. That's the way it is."

"Did you know Tiny Mercer well?"

"I knew Tiny Mercer real well. In fact, I loved Tiny Mercer. He was like a brother to me. I know his wife very well. She still writes to me, sends me Christmas cards, birthday cards every year. She was like family to me, and to other guys on death row."

"Before they executed Tiny, did people on death row think they weren't going to have any executions?"

"When Tiny was first taken to the holding cell, everybody thought it was going to happen. But then Tiny Mercer came back to death row. Then back to the holding cell. And everybody thought it was going to happen. Then Tiny Mercer came back to death row. Four or five months later he went back over to the holding cell with another execution date. Everybody thought it wasn't going to happen. He'd be back. And then he came back, and then he went again. Four times. Everybody thought he wasn't going to be executed. Even Tiny Mercer thought he wasn't going to get executed. The officers down there took me and another inmate out there to talk to Tiny Mercer before they took him down there that last time. And Tiny Mercer said, 'I'll be back.' He said, 'Don't even worry about it man, I'll be back.' And I said, 'Are you all right?' And he said, 'Yeah, I'm all right. I'll be back. I don't think they're going to kill me.' They took him, and the next day, they said it was real. They definitely were going to execute him that night. So Tiny Mercer sent word down, and he said to 'Keep your head together,' and 'I love you, brother,' and 'No matter what you do, don't let them get to you.' And they executed him that night. And a lot of people on death row knew that night, about ten o'clock, that he was definitely going to be executed. But I can honestly say that a lot of people didn't care. And you can tell that by the response you got that night, from the other inmates on death row. See, one of the things I disrespect the administration for is the way they play with people's minds. On death row that night, there was about three or four people who were keeping up with what was going on with Tiny Mercer. Watching the news on TV. The administration showed a movie that night. An X-rated movie. And most of the guys on death row was busy watching this movie at the same time this execution was going on. The administration are real smart. They felt that if they didn't do something that would take their minds off what was going on, there was going to be a riot. And while I was down there watching the news, they was driving Tiny Mercer's body out in a hearse. And you could hear guys hollering, 'Look at the tits on that bitch,' look at this and the other. And everybody was off into this movie. And it hurt. It hurt. And at the same time, it made me realize that these guys, they don't really realize where they're at. Or they don't care. And a couple of days later, after Tiny Mercer was executed, the guys start to rise and say, 'What's going on? What happened? I can feel the pain.' *You feel the pain two days later, you late.* You have to realize what's going on, you have to keep up with what's going on. To keep it from happening to yourself or whatever. I believe I learned a lot that night."

"In some way, did it make it any easier for you to accept the fact that you will probably be executed?"

"Me and Tiny Mercer had talked before his execution. And we thought that death would be a blessing. If it comes, there's nothing you can do about it. You have to accept it. And a lot of people try to fight it. But if it's your time to go, it's your time to go. No matter how much crying, or fighting, or struggling you do, it's just your time to go. I've always been the type of person who thought, when it comes to me dying, no matter how it is, I will handle it. So, I didn't have no problem with it then, and I don't have no problem with it now. I'm not saying that if I was in a gunfight I would leave my gun in my holster and let the other man draw, but I can accept it."

"But would you rather be out of here?"

"I'd rather be out of here, and I feel that I should've been out of here. Based on my case, I feel I should be out of here. But, for some reason or another, they keep on turning me down. No matter how good my points are, they ignore them. And there's other cases that've been reversed for the same issues. Since I've been in federal court, my lawyer and I have been fighting each other for the points I wanted him to raise, and he refuses to raise them. And I continue to argue with him, telling him that these are good points. And he says no, he's not going to put them in there. Okay. And now the courts are saying I'm responsible for that. For not putting them in there. And I'm saying, I cannot be responsible when I have letters here requesting that he puts them in here and he refuses to do so. The state, of course, was the one who appointed him as my attorney. And I've requested several times that he be taken off my case because he wouldn't raise none of the issues that I thought would get me a new trial."

"How do you feel about your chances on your next appeal? Do you have confidence about it?"

"Nope. I feel that I have confidence in the work that me and my lawyer is capable of putting in it. Then again, I have to see my lawyer, because it don't look like they're going to allow me to do any work on it. I have confidence in what he's capable of doing. And I feel that, just like always, no matter how good it looks, anything's capable of happening. Also I feel like they would refuse it."

"What do you think about the possibility of being executed by lethal injection, as opposed to some other method?"

"Tiny and I spoke about that before. I'm glad that they have the lethal injection. Me and Tiny Mercer spoke, and we decided that either one is bad. But at the same time, the gas chamber is a lot worse than lethal injection. So, if it's got to be one or the other, then why not lethal injection?"

"You know that they do it over here in the hospital?"

"Right."

"If I were here, knowing that, it would bother me every time I had to go to the hospital, because I was sick, or got hurt."

"Right."

"I'd have a funny feeling about being there."

"I've been over to the hospital many times. And I've seen the room—

the holding room and the area where they put the individual. A funny feeling? I think about it. But it don't bother me to the point where I be sick and I wouldn't want to go back to the hospital just because of that. As I've said, I have no problem with walking that walk. If I have to walk that walk, I have no problem with it. The only problem I do have is the way I've been treated. The way these people interfere with me working on my case. The chances that I could've had was taken from me by these people. The only thing I do have is the satisfaction that these people, the administration, these hillbillies, they fear me. So, the only anger I have is, them getting any type of satisfaction out of it. But I don't have a problem with death. If I was told I had to spend the rest of my life here in this prison, I'd rather be dead. If I can't get a reversal, and get an opportunity to take this back to trial, then I'd rather be dead. I don't want to grow old, or spend the rest of my life here being told what to do by people who are getting a thrill out of it. I don't like to be told what to do, period. I don't like being cuffed, I don't like sitting in here, or anywhere, all day, being cuffed, while they sit around and drink coffee and laugh. They get a big bang out of the authority, and they treat you like a kid or an animal. And if you say anything back to them, you're wrong. I cannot be wrong. I'm a grown man, I've got the death sentence, and they're talking about killing me. And then you going to tell me I can't speak up for what I think is right? And I do speak my mind. And most people here don't want to do that. Most death row inmates feel that they'd rather be out there watching TV than to be locked up for speaking their mind. And that's what I have to go through in order to let them know I feel they're wrong."

We talked about the fact that Walter had thirty days to file his next motion. I asked him what he thought the prospects were.

"If I'm to be executed, it won't be until August or September. They don't know that. They think it'll be the end of this month. But they're mistaken. It will be August or September. Or maybe July."

An officer knocked on the door to say our time was up. I shook hands good-bye with Walter, in the same awkward way we had when we met. Just before he returned to his solitary cell, I asked him how much of his time since arriving at Potosi three years previously had been spent locked down. He thought back and calculated for me. The answer was, the whole of his first year. After that, he was locked up three further times, with intervals of freedom adding up to four weeks. Then another year on lock-down. He had spent 80 percent of his time in the hole; and in all likelihood, he would be executed in the next few months.

*   *   *

Walter, along with all of the other inmates I had spoken with, was candid in his view of the administration. On the whole, Paul Delo and his senior staff refrained from offering opinions about individual inmates. One after-noon, I asked Paul how he regarded some of the death sentence inmates I'd been speaking with. He prefaced his remarks by telling me: "I try to get out and talk to the inmates as much as I possibly can. But of course, the higher you go in this system, the less time that you have for that. But I try to get out as much as I possibly can, and I do see all of the inmates fairly frequently."

Paul had already mentioned Doyle Williams a number of times, since Paul was the subject of a number of Doyle's lawsuits. I wondered what impression he had of Joe Amrine.

"Joe is . . . we can't say carefree, because obviously he has got a death sentence over his head. But Joe at least maintains the outward appearance of being fairly well adjusted. He does a lot of sports, he's in the gym almost constantly, and is a fairly congenial fellow. Joe seems to be a pretty well adjusted fellow."

"What about A. J. Bannister?"

"Bannister is somewhere in between. He is a very intelligent individual, as you have probably noticed when interviewing him. He's a loner to the point where he keeps most of his ideas to himself unless asked. He doesn't get into trouble, or doesn't have problems obeying the rules. I would have to classify him as a good inmate. Not a model inmate, but a good inmate."

"And Walter Blair?"

"Walter is pretty much a loner. I probably have not had ten minutes of conversation with Walter since he's been down here, which is a little over three years now. He does articulate well when you do talk to him. He's got some fairly violent—no, not violent, he has some fairly *extreme* mood swings. One day he will be congenial, and the next day he won't speak to you at all. I would classify Mr. Blair as probably a dangerous inmate, because of the mood swings. It would depend on which day he was approached, how he's going to react."

Later I asked Don Roper about Walter Blair, and why he was almost constantly in the hole.

"In my opinion," he told me, "Mr. Walter Blair is a dangerous inmate. We have allowed him some open free movement within general population, but recently have had to put him in lock-down because of his assaultive, aggressive behavior and his threats against staff."

"What kind of threats?" I asked.

Don told me: "The death warrants over the last few months or so on Walter Blair have been stayed for one reason or another. Walter Blair is probably getting real close to being executed; and Walter, out of his own mouth, has said that he is going to take someone with him before he goes. So we are very cautious of Mr. Walter Blair. But I hasten to add that all of these individuals that you've brought to our attention are dangerous individuals. They killed people, many of them multi people, and I'll assure you that if they had the opportunity, they would probably kill you or I. Especially if they thought it would get them freedom. They would kill you or me in a minute. Any one of them."

N O ONE among the inmates I had spoken to could pronounce the name of the prison doctor. Over the weeks, I had been making phonetic spellings in my notebook. Finally I got Paul Delo to spell it for me and coach me in the pronunciation. Dr. Cayabyab. Dr. Kie-yob-yob.

The doctor was difficult to pin down. He worked three days a week at Potosi, and two days at another prison. After numerous attempts, I managed to get an appointment with him. The administration seemed generally to like him, but to consider him somewhat unusual. Dr. Pedro Cayabyab is Filipino by birth, and I was warned that I might have some difficulty understanding his accent.

"I *can* understand him," said Paul Delo. "But then, I've had a lot of practice."

The officer who took me down to the hospital wing to see Dr. Cayabyab asked, incredulously, "You're going to *interview* him?"

"Yes," I replied.

"Good luck," she said. Then she rocked on her heels for a bit and said, "Strange guy."

"What do you mean?"

"Well, I went into his office a few weeks ago, and he was holding a raw pork steak. When I came in, he put it in his pocket."

"What was that about?" I asked.

The officer shook her head as if to say, That's the kind of stuff that goes on around here. Nothing's surprising after a while.

"Do you think it was his lunch?" I asked.

"Beats me," she said.

I was shown into Dr. Cayabyab's office, which is a few feet away from the execution chamber.

A short man of unusual appearance, Dr. Cayabyab sat behind a desk with a nameplate, and he appeared to be looking through some patient notes. One of the inmates had prepared me for my interview with the doctor by saying: "He looks like an experiment in which a frog and a human mated successfully."

Dr. Cayabyab stood up and extended his hand. He was wearing a rumpled blue pinstripe suit and a stained tie.

"You from BBC," he told me.

"No, I'm an independent filmmaker," I explained.

"What is that?" he asked suspiciously.

I told him, and said I would like to talk about execution procedures in Missouri from a medical standpoint.

"What do you want to know?" he demanded.

"My interest is in procedure and protocol. So I would like to know all of the things you do on execution night. And how lethal injection works, from a medical standpoint."

"The inmate walks from the holding cell to the gurney, accompanied by the guards. And he is placed in a supine position on the gurney and he is strapped. Legs, abdomen, chest. Strapped to that gurney. The arm that takes the IV is exposed. We have an armrest. What do you call it? An elbow splint. Elbow splint. So it will be full extension."

The doctor was difficult to understand, but not totally incomprehensible.

"The nurse-anesthetist," he continued, "who acts like a nurse consultant, starts the IV. Using a number-sixteen-gauge needle, and a plastic catheter about this long." The doctor stretched out his arms to show how long a catheter was required to connect the inmate to the delivery module of the lethal injection machine. "Then he connects it to the tubing, to the saline solution. And after that is secured, we tape it. We tape it to the elbow so it sticks. So the thing don't fall out of the vein. Then we connect it to the black box on the wall. And there's a clamp between the tubing from the wall and IV to the patient."

"So you unclamp that when it's time to start the execution?"

"Yes. At one minute past midnight, the superintendent of PCC, Potosi Correctional Center, Mr. Paul Delo, comes in, and reads him the death penalty order from the Missouri Supreme Court, in conjunction with the United States Supreme Court. He reads this. 'Mr. John Doe, um, according to the . . . '—this is like an example."

"I've seen the death warrant," I told the doctor. But he wanted to go through the whole procedure.

". . . according to the decision of Missouri Supreme Court, dated so and so, you are to be given a death penalty by lethal injection for the killing of so and so. He's awake and listening. And there are about twelve witnesses. And he says, 'Mr. Doe, do you have anything to say?' And he says, 'No, sir.' And then Mr. Delo holds him on his shoulder and says, 'God bless you.' Gets out. Goes to the back. That's how it is. And then they say, 'Green light.' And it means warm up the machine, or something. And then, after one minute, they say, 'Foxfire one!' They press the button. You can see the patient—I can't see the patient, because I am behind a screen looking at the EKG. The first solution, sodium pentothal, goes into the person. He's awake, and then he goes to sleep. And then, after one minute, the event coordinator says, 'Foxfire two!' But there's no need for that, because the machine does that, really. It's just a signal. The Pavulon, or pancuronium bromide, is injected, and it arrests the respiratory muscles. Paralyze the lungs and depress the respiratory center. And this is how you will see it. You see the patient doing an agonal, or terminal, breathing."

At that moment, the doctor's face became a death mask. He took a deep breath, imitating terminal breathing, let it out, and closed his eyes and remained motionless. It was a weird and chilling performance.

"And, after one minute, 'Foxfire three!' During foxfire one and foxfire two, the monitor on the EKG is still normal. Normal sinus rhythm, and the heart rate is normal. It may go up, when he takes his agonal breathing, from one hundred to one-thirty, one-forty. After one minute, 'Foxfire three!' and the potassium chloride is given. And it's three times the lethal dose. Then there are changes in the EKG, from normal sinus rhythm to idioventricular, or dying heart rhythm, and then straight line. And then the heart is zero. It is none. And my part then, as the medical consultant, is to say 'Number eight!' meaning no more QRS complexes in the EKG. And so the event coordinator says, 'Checkmate!' "

"Checkmate?"

"It's a password to the officers guarding the windows outside to close the shade so the observers cannot see. They say, 'Doctor, examine the patient.' And then I go there. I check with my penlight, I check the pupils. They're dilated. And then I listen to the heart. Heart sound's absent. Lung sound's not there. And I say, 'Inmate Jones is dead. What time?' And then I sign the chronology of events. I sign that, and then I sign the death certificate for the institution, and for his body for burial."

"After the inmate is dead, what happens to his body?"

"The nurse-anesthetist removes the IV. Then the mortician comes in and removes him from the gurney to his table, and takes him to the funeral parlor. With the death certificate."

"What do you think about lethal injection as a method of execution? As opposed to gas or electrocution?"

"I would think it's the most humane way. Sometimes I have an old dog, an old cat, and I bring it to the humane society and they put it to sleep. It's the same thing. Like the vet. Five minutes. In the Philippines, where I came from eight years ago, we give electric shock. And sometimes after they've given so many volts, he's still alive. They have to repeat two or three times. It's very inhuman and cruel way of doing it."

"What about the American Medical Association's view of doctors participating in executions?" I asked.

"What I'm worried about is this. The AMA, they wanted in their 1990 meeting in Florida, they want to keep out physicians in the execution process. That's what I'm just worried about. I don't want any flak from them. I got enough trouble of my own."

"But what is their view of the physician's role in executions?"

"They want completely the physician to be out of the execution process. But what I do is, I just pronounce the patient dead. That's all."

"What about the medical duties you have in preparing the inmate for the execution?"

"In the morning, I examine the patient. I do a pre-execution physical. Vital signs and everything. Blood pressure, pulse, respiration, temperature, and all that."

"Why is that necessary? What's the point of it?"

"We have to determine if he's alive, very much alive. Not dead. It's just a legal way of showing that he was alive, and then he's dead now. You have to have it in writing that he was once upon a time alive in the morning, during the day and everything. I'm a licensed physician in Missouri. And I put the time and the date that I examined him. You can't execute someone if they're dead."

"No," I agreed.

The doctor smiled.

"Are there any other medical procedures?" I asked. "What about the pre-execution sedative?"

"At seven-thirty, we give 2.5 milligrams of Versed, intramuscular."

"What's Versed?" I asked.

"Versed is a tranquilizer, like Valium, but about five times as strong."

"Five times as strong?"

"Yes. And then we give a second injection, 2.5 milligrams of Versed, one hour later, at eight-thirty. And then, around eleven, we give one to two milligrams of Versed intravenously."

"That seems a lot," I remarked.

"It is so the patient has an anxiety-free state of mind," said Dr. Cayabyab.

I told the doctor I had no further questions, and thanked him for his time.

"Anytime," he said.

I RETURNED to Jefferson City to talk with Christy Mercer. We spent a long evening drinking coffee. She showed me some photographs of her and her husband.

"You have to guard these with your life," she said, handing me a manila envelope. Inside were snapshots of Tiny, from the time of his arrest, and at various intervals over his years on death row prior to his execution. He had arrived at MSP a burly, bearded figure with long, straight black hair. He was, as A. J. Bannister put it, "a menacing figure to look at." But on the other hand, "he was a real soft-spoken man. And a real smart man."

Looking through the photos, I saw the last ten years of Tiny Mercer's life laid out in front of me. As time went on, he cut his hair shorter, and perfected his physique through weight lifting. The photographs showed him to be an uncommonly attractive man. He had transformed himself from a staring figure with piercing blue eyes into a reflective man whose humanity had only increased under sentence of death. There were some photos of

Tiny and Christy taken in the visitor's area at MSP. Her suntanned face is smiling, framed by her beautiful dark hair.

"You look really happy," I said.

"I was," Christy told me. "Happier than I'd ever been."

As I looked through the photographs, I was moved by the transformation of Tiny Mercer. Having shed excess weight, his body was finely tuned; and by all accounts, his mind was active and focused on the spiritual path he'd chosen. But toward the end, he became ill with kidney disease. He shrank to half his physical size. He grew skinny, and his eyes were sunken, his cheeks hollow. He was treated by dialysis. But, as A.J. observed, "They kept him alive so they could kill him."

All of Tiny's friends had presented a positive image of him. I wondered, from time to time, what a fuller picture of him was. One afternoon, when I was sitting around talking with A.J., Doyle Williams, and Joe Amrine, they made a sad observation. Toward the end, Tiny began to repeat himself in conversation. He began to lose some of his focus. All of his friends agreed that the pressure of facing death, of being taken to the holding cell and back again so many times, coupled with his serious illness, had taken its toll on Tiny. Death row had broken him.

These observations were at the back of my mind when I said to Christy: "It must have been very difficult sometimes."

Her eyes filled slowly with tears, but her voice did not crack or give away the powerful emotions she contained inside. Tears flowed slowly down her face. She didn't wipe them away, but looked directly into my eyes and said: "Nobody knows this. But, towards the end, it was terrible sometimes. We'd argue. We were irritable. It was just awful."

I tried to imagine how that would be. The intolerable pressures of a life shared in letters and fleeting visits behind glass, but lived apart, knowing that your husband's life would eventually be taken by the state. Knowing that there must have been tension, some of it caused by petty things, and that the burden of guilt and frustration that caused was incalculable.

I asked Christy how she had found the Lord. She told me that she herself had been in prison when it happened. I knew from other sources that she had spent a year in the county jail for stabbing a man. While she was in prison, the authorities wanted her to implicate a man in another crime. They threatened to bring further charges against her if she refused. She prayed for help and said she had told the Lord that if this situation could be resolved, she would turn her life over to Him. What happened next, Christy described as a miracle. The threat dissolved. She kept her promise. She did her time in prison, and since then has changed her life.

She told me how she had been brought up in a strict, God-fearing home, but had rebelled against her parents from an early age. She started using drugs and running with a motorcycle gang. She found herself living a life of excitement—but also one of crime, and danger.

I admired Christy for her honesty, and for her courage in facing her life and taking control of it. She had endured a great deal, and in finding the Lord, she had not become preachy or sanctimonious. She made constant reference to the Lord, but largely by way of taking any credit for the changes in her life. When I congratulated her on doing well in her criminal justice exams, she said: "I have the Lord to thank for that."

As she prepared to leave, Christy told me: "And the Lord has chosen you. He may have saved you from the same fate that these men on death row are suffering, so that you can help them."

"Maybe," I said. We embraced, and I kissed her on the cheek.

And thought, not for the first time, there but for the grace of God . . .

O N FRIDAY, March 6, I had arranged to travel from St. Louis to Los Angeles. Paul Delo and I met for lunch before I left, and he had something to tell me.

"We have had a death warrant this morning," he said.

"Is it Walter Blair?" I asked.

"No. Lloyd Schlup."

I hadn't met Lloyd Schlup, and was not familiar with his case. "What number is he?" I asked.

"Forty-two," Paul replied.

A.J. was number twenty-four. It showed how the appeals system is something of a lottery, and how easy it is to be sent to the head of the line.

"Is it a serious death warrant?" I asked. I was aware, as I spoke the words, of the absurdity of a system which causes death warrants to be referred to as "serious" or "nonserious."

"I really don't think so," Paul told me. "But there's no way of knowing."

"What's going to happen next?" I asked.

"Nothing. It'll be a normal weekend here. I don't expect anything out of the ordinary to happen."

"When have they set the execution date for?" I asked.

"The twelfth."

"That's six days from now," I said. "And it's Friday. That only really gives him four days to fight his appeal next week."

"You can never tell when a death warrant's going to come," Paul observed.

Paul explained again that nothing would happen over the weekend, and that there would be no news until Monday.

* * *

When I returned to Potosi from Los Angeles, Lloyd Schlup was on death-watch and the institution was gearing up for an execution. What was remarkable about it was that the ordinary routine of the prison did not change.

Lloyd Schlup is thirty-one years old and had been on death row since 1985. He was convicted, along with Robert O'Neal, Jr., in the stabbing of a black inmate, Arthur Dade, at MSP in February 1984. The state alleged that O'Neal was a member of the Aryan Nation Church, that he stabbed Dade while Schlup held him. O'Neal had a previous first-degree murder conviction. Schlup had prior convictions for sodomy, assault, and escape from a lawful place of confinement.

Lloyd Schlup is a thin man with a mustache, piercing eyes, and prison tattoos on both arms. He is a man of intense appearance, and when I met him he was trying hard to control his emotions.

I had asked Paul Delo to describe him to me, and he had said: "Lloyd is a younger fellow, and he's been in prison many, many years, for his age. In my opinion, he is fairly easily led but doesn't get into a tremendous amount of trouble. Frankly, I expected some problems with Lloyd when he came here, but he's acclimated pretty well. Lloyd has a problem with abuse of drugs, and always has. He simply can't leave it alone. And his only resource is to put himself into a segregated status. He simply can't resist temptation." Paul also added, "He has some rather unusual views on race relations."

Lloyd was taken to the deathwatch cell on Monday, March ninth, with his execution still scheduled for the twelfth. When I arrived on Tuesday, he was still on deathwatch, and his family had traveled to Potosi and was with him almost constantly. Later that day, he received a stay.

However, the institution remained on standby for the execution. Talking with Paul Delo on Tuesday, he said he did not think there was a very good chance that the execution would proceed. However, when I arrived at the prison on Wednesday morning, and parked near the front entrance, I was told by an officer to move my car to the rear of the parking lot.

The Missouri Protocol was in operation: Parking arrangements had been made for Department of Corrections officials, witnesses, and the press.

Paul and the other members of the execution team were all dressed in suits and white shirts.

"The appeal's going back and forth," he explained. "Of course, the attorney general is trying to get the stay lifted. The judge said that Lloyd's appeal was a brick short of a load."

Lloyd's appeals were successful, and later that afternoon he was let off deathwatch, and the execution team stood down.

When I interviewed Lloyd, he had been returned to ad seg, at his own request. He was obliged to wear handcuffs throughout our conversation, and he looked pale and drawn. He told me that it had been a nerve-racking experience, and that they had given him Valium, at his request.

I asked him what had happened in the deathwatch cell.

"For a couple of days it was real hairy. The state was appealing the case pretty hard, and so for me and my family it was hard not knowing what was going to happen. As a matter of fact, on Tuesday I was getting pretty worried that it was going to go off as scheduled. Things wasn't going right. And then, by a miracle or whatever, I gained a stay on Tuesday, and then, of course, later on Tuesday, I got an indefinite stay—filed another habeas corpus. So I left the executions cell, the watch cell, on Wednesday afternoon."

"So where is your appeal now?" I asked.

"I'm back in the Eighth Circuit for a second habeas corpus. Some things have happened that I don't quite understand. I thought I was in the Federal Court in Kansas City, and I thought maybe some good things would come out of this. But I received a letter in the mail today, where the case was transferred back before the same judge in St. Louis, in the Eastern District. And that's not where I want to be at, you know, because I haven't had any luck there before in the past. Although it's an indefinite stay at this time, I feel like it's going to come off pretty fast, 'cause it all happened pretty fast when it come down within thirty days. So I feel like my second habeas will be turned down, be rubber-stamped, and go on through. And another execution date will be set. Originally they had set one for the twenty-third, a second execution date for the twenty-third. And that's when I got the indefinite stay. But I'm pretty worried right now. I'm just kind of hanging tough, seeing what my attorney is going to do."

"Why do you think they'll just rubber-stamp your appeal?" I asked.

"I feel that election year coming up, and as a matter of fact, the same person who's been on my case since my appeal started in eighty-six, the attorney general, is running for governor now, and I just feel that it makes good politics: Somebody's got to go."

"Do you want to tell me how you caught your case?"

"It was a prison murder in 1984. Up in the main prison in Jefferson City. My case, all along, since day one, has been a mistaken identity. My innocence and everything in this case surrounds around this evidence—videotapes, testimony by the officers and whatnot. Fifteen, sixteen different inmates that say I wasn't there. So that's where my case is before the courts right now. You know, you can't execute an innocent man. So that's where I'm trying to go with it. I don't know what's going to happen."

"Tell me what happened when the death warrant came down."

"They told me the execution had been set, and they come and got me and escorted me to the deathwatch cell. And about a half hour later, they brought my property over to me and gave me whatever I could have over there. Which is everything, pretty much. And there was some papers to sign for any witnesses that I might want at the execution. And last meal, request for a last meal. The superintendent, he come down that same morning, about an hour later, and we talked a little bit. And mainly, it's just sitting in the cell twenty-four hours a day with an officer in the cell with you, and they stay there round the shift. Three different officers. And they record everything you do. At night you can't sleep, because there is a lot of typing going on. It's all in a closed cell, so there is no sleep at night.

And then, during the day, it's all lawyers and family, and superintendent. I slept about five hours in three days."

"What did Paul Delo say to you while you were in the deathwatch cell?"

"Well, he just asked me if I was comfortable, if I needed anything. And he went out of his way to do what he could. He approved several special visits for me, from family coming in out of state, and people who were not on my regular visiting list. In my case—I guess it's kind of the conversation around here now—I had requested as a last meal things that aren't usually requested. I wanted some rabbit and some venison, and some things like this. Some catfish. And he said he would do what he could to get some things together. And, of course, after I got the stay, he still gave me the rabbit and the deer. So I thought that was pretty good of him. Even though I gained a stay."

"What did they tell you about the procedures they would be taking for the execution?"

"Nothing, because they didn't get down far enough into the evening for them to tell me anything about it. So, even now I have no idea about that. It is my understanding that at seven o'clock they start running through the procedures. But I'd done gained my stay by then, so didn't have to go through any of that."

"Do you think much about lethal injection as opposed to gas, or some other method of execution?"

"Yeah, I have. You know, I've had, over the last few years, different reactions to it. I mean, as far as family-wise, the easier the better. For them. But for myself, the more violent it could be, you know, that's the way I'd like it. And that may sound cruel, but that's what I'd want people to hear and see. Just the more violent the execution could be, that's the way I'd like for it to come off. Which I know it won't in Missouri."

"How do you think that the public perceives lethal injection?"

"I just think people have a different view. And if they don't now, in time they will. They keep hearing about this electric chair and that electric chair, not getting it on the first try, and breaking down. And the gas, you know. How you gasp for ten, fifteen minutes or whatever, and go through all this agonizing pain. And I just think that at some point in time, this might be part of the . . . you know, it's cruel and unusual. And the people in these other states that have to endure this pain, you *know* that's barbaric. That's like putting your head in a guillotine, you know, three hundred years ago or whatever. Putting a shot in your arm and just laying there, then a few minutes later, *that's it,* and supposedly no pain or suffering. That's how we do our dogs, you know. It's just too . . . it's just too easy."

"How do you deal with the thought of being executed?"

"I've prepared myself. I've done a lot more praying than I ever have. And I just hope that whatever is beyond is got to be better than what I've endured here. I just try to reflect like that, you know. And I just keep telling myself, which is true, *I have no control over the matter.* So I just focus on that. You know, it's just another thing in life. I have no control over this. They're going to do what they're going to do. It's out of my hands. I've sat back and said, 'Hey, there ain't no sense in crying about it, being mad about it. If it's going to happen, it's out of my hands. Just wait for the day.' "

"You were at MSP for a while. How did you find death row there, compared to here?"

"I was on death row at MSP from December eighty-five to eighty-nine, when we come to Potosi. I don't have a lot of memories about it. I mean, I have the memories, but there's nothing good about it."

"Why, in particular?"

"Because I had been beaten. I went through a lot of hard times. It was the administration who made a mistake and decided to cover their mistake up. And I rebelled against it and I suffered beatings; you know, a lot of beatings. And I was put in the psychiatric ward, and locked down. I went through . . . That whole time was just total madness for me. And so as far as the difference, here it's a lot more professional as far as the way the administration is set up. It's got its problems, but every place has got its problems. It's a new prison. It's clean, and all that. But I think, being honest about it, the staff here, they try pretty hard. And I haven't had a whole lot of problems out of them. I've never been beat. I've done my share of wrong—nothing serious—but I can't say it's all bad here."

"Did you know Tiny Mercer?"

"Yeah, I knew Tiny Mercer personally."

"For how long?"

"I've been knowing Tiny since 1980. Over the years, our relationship and friendship grew pretty strong. And leading up to his execution, I remember when it come down, I just said to myself, I couldn't believe it was going to happen, you know. Not to Tiny. I just couldn't believe it. Not to Tiny. It's not going to happen to Tiny. And I remember listening to the TV, because they had a lot of coverage on it, and when they said he was dead I just cried and cried. I prayed, and I just cried like a baby. I just couldn't believe that Tiny was actually gone, and that none of us was ever going to see him again."

"Tell me how it was on death row, the night they executed Tiny at MSP."

"Well, for me, I got beat that night. About eight guards come in, and they beat me down pretty good. As a matter of fact, they put cigarettes out on my stomach that night. I just couldn't handle it. I just lost it that night. And I was in Five-C, the lock-down unit, and I just lost it. I didn't want to deal with it, just thinking about it. And they finally had to rush in and subdue me. And, of course, they're pretty cruel back there. Instead of just coming in and subduing you—you don't have to be doing anything—you know, when they come in, they're going to knock heads."

"What had you done?"

"What had I done? I refused a count. I had refused a count. I had wanted to see the warden. I'd just wanted to talk to somebody, is what it was. They just refused to speak to me. The COs wouldn't call anybody. So I just figured, if I refuse a count, if they don't see me, then they'll have to call the shift commander or somebody. So they just took it into their own hands. They just popped the door and rushed in on me."

"And, at the end of the day, what effect did Tiny's execution have on you? Did it affect the way you viewed your own death sentence?"

"It brought the reality home. That even though it had been so many years, and everybody was saying it wasn't going to happen, it did happen. And it just brings you back to the reality that, regardless of the circumstances—everybody on death row—there's a good chance that you're going to be put to death, going to be executed. And for myself, all since then I just know that the chances, despite innocence or guilt, you know, they kill people. When they put you on death row, they kill you."

Epilogue

I N MARCH 1992, just after Walter Blair and Lloyd Schlup won stays of execution, filming of "The Execution Protocol" took place over ten days at Potosi Correctional Center and at the old Missouri State Penitentiary. During the week before filming, I held pre-production meetings with A.J., Joe Amrine, and Doyle Williams. They, like the staff, were concerned that they not be portrayed in a biased way by "the media." I assured them they would be allowed to speak freely, and at length, and that I would do nothing to interfere with the meaning of what they told the camera. As with the staff at Potosi, each of the inmates became more than just interviewees in a documentary—they became actors in a film which, at times, could be mistaken for fiction, if not for the fact that it was real in a way that Hollywood could never simulate.

When I returned to London, I had a hundred rolls of film which would take sixteen weeks to edit. Day after day, week after week, the images and words of the men I had spent time with since my work began the previous Labor Day passed before my eyes and echoed in my ears. On film as in life, both the execution team and the inmates possess a strange and powerful intensity; one group in a constant state of preparedness to execute the other; the other desperate to fight their appeals and keep faith with themselves in an otherwise hopeless situation. As A.J. put it, "It gets harder and harder, as the years go by, to manufacture hope on a day-to-day basis."

After returning to London, I regularly spoke on the phone with Paul Delo, and corresponded with A.J. and other inmates. After six weeks in Missouri, my return to London was nearly as strange as it had been after my first visit to Potosi. Events in the prison, related by Paul Delo or by A.J., cast their shadows over my office and cutting room.

On April 12, the prison was locked down at 5 P.M. and the E-Squad (Emergency Squad) entered the cells of eighty men serving life and fifty sentences and packed their belongings into boxes. The next morning, they were transferred back to the old Missouri State Penitentiary. The prison remained locked down throughout the next day as eighty of the most disruptive inmates from MSP were brought to Potosi, where they were incorporated into general population. The move alarmed many of the Potosi inmates because they saw it as a threat to their security. Potosi's previous policy of limiting its general population to inmates convicted of capital murder had resulted in a relatively calm environment in which, over three years, no murders had occurred, and only minor injuries had resulted from fights. The "carrot and stick" approach of free access to facilities as a reward for good behavior, and the constant threat of administrative segregation for violation of the rules, had worked. Most of the inmates pulled together to see that their privileges were not revoked, and worked constantly to have them extended. The arrival of men who faced parole in a relatively short term, and had records of violent behavior in other Missouri prisons, was seen by the Potosi inmates as a retrograde step.

Four days later, Potosi had its first serious hostage situation. The local newspaper reported that a death-sentenced inmate who was "depressed" at having his sentence reversed to life took the prison librarian hostage. The prison librarian is an attractive woman, popular with inmates. The inmates' version of the story is that the man who had won a reversal was overjoyed at his good fortune; however, while high on PCP, he was planning to deal with two fellow inmates in a long-standing argument over jobs in the library. As the librarian tried to talk him out of it, another staff member intervened, and the hostage situation developed. During the two-hour drama, Paul Delo and Don Roper negotiated with the inmate, and the librarian was released unharmed.

On May 9, one of Missouri's three women death row inmates committed suicide. Nila Wacaser had been convicted of murdering her eight-year-old son. Her attorney argued, unsuccessfully, for mitigating circumstances based on the fact that she was using the drug Halcion, which has been identified as a factor in a number of otherwise inexplicable homicides in the United States. Nila Wacaser had, after some time, won a retrial, and was being held in the Platte County Jail when she committed suicide, apparently by a drug overdose.

During my last visit to Potosi, A.J. told me that he had a ten-year-old-daughter. In April he learned that she would be visiting later in the summer, and he was overjoyed at the prospect. The prison basketball season came to an end, and the softball season started. A.J. hit home runs in the first two games.

Paul Delo injured a finger, which became seriously infected. He was ill for two weeks, and eventually, part of the finger was amputated.

Inmates and staff speculated endlessly about the next execution at Potosi. No one had been put to death in Missouri since August 1991, and both staff and inmates anticipated a deluge of executions in the coming months. As Arkansas governor Bill Clinton's presidential campaign geared up in the spring, the state conducted its first two executions by lethal injection. The execution warrants were handed down by the Eighth Circuit Court, the same court that hears death sentence appeals in neighboring Missouri.

On May 27, A.J., anxious at not having heard news of his appeals, telephoned his lawyer. He was astonished to hear that his Motion for Reconsideration had been turned down on April 30—nearly a full month previously. It was the first he had heard of it, and he bitterly regretted having lost a month in planning the next stage of his appeals since, by his own reckoning, he had only a year left to live.

On death row, life continues.

Acknowledgments

T HE PERSON most responsible for getting this project off the ground is my agent, Imogen Parker, and it is to her that my first and deepest thanks are due. Both of my editors—Oliver Johnson in London, and Erica Marcus in New York—have given support and critical advice for which I am grateful. Louise Rosen read the manuscript and made many valuable suggestions for improvement. Mitch Wood tracked down some useful documents, and Chris Caltabiano helped with library research. My partner at Worldview Pictures, Paul Baker, has been, as always, a sustaining force and a preserver of good spirits.

This book could not have been written without the cooperation of the Missouri Department of Corrections, and I am grateful to the assistance given by Dick Moore, George Lombardi, Bill Armontrout, and Mark Schreiber. Paul Delo allowed me virtually unrestricted access to staff and inmates at Potosi Correctional Center, and showed me every courtesy. Superintendent Mike Groose of Jefferson City Correctional Center allowed me access to Missouri's old death row.

Very special thanks are due to the inmates whose contributions are an essential part of this book. Throughout the research, A. J. Bannister has offered a constant stream of insights and has, more than anyone else, guided me through the strange territory of death row. I am also grateful to Joe Amrine, Walter Blair, Ray Copeland, Lloyd Schlup, Bobby Shaw, Heath Wilkins, Doyle Williams, and all of the other death row inmates at Potosi Correctional Center who took the time to talk with me.

Christy Mercer was generous with her time, and in lending personal photographs of her husband, the late George "Tiny" Mercer.

Fred Leuchter provided detailed explanations of the design and function of his equipment, and supplied copies of many useful documents.

Thanks are also due to Rob Beasley, Amnesty International (London); Dr. Edward Brunner, Northwestern University Medical School; Mike Dutton, superintendent, River Bend Maximum Security Institution, Nashville, Tennessee; David Irving; Ali Miller, Amnesty International (New York); and Larry Helm Spalding, director of the Office of Capital Collateral, Tallahassee, Florida.

A note of special thanks is due to Greg Moyer and Janet Carlsen at the Discovery Channel for their complete and unwavering support of an unusual and difficult project.

Index